Praise for Books by

Over the Mountain and Home Again:
Journeys of an Adirondack Naturalist

"Ed Kanze has emerged as a fresh and joyful voice of the Adirondacks, with a merry eye, a sharp mind, a deep heart."

— Bill McKibben, author of *Wandering Home*

"Kanze has a vast knowledge of the natural world, and he complements it with a fine writing style, a sense of humor, and a joyful exuberance. His essays sparkle while they inform . . . We are lucky to have Edward Kanze as a resident writer-naturalist in northern New York. His pedigree is long and his writing precise. But more than that, Kanze brings a tremendous enthusiasm and delight to his descriptions of everything he observes around him."

— Betsy Kepes, book reviewer, North Country Public Radio

"In sharing these Adirondack adventures Ed Kanze reminds us to cherish the natural world we have today, all around us. *Over the Mountain and Home Again* is a delight for those of us who also cherish time spent afield with a kindred spirit."

— Bill Thompson III, editor, *Bird Watcher's Digest*

Kangaroo Dreaming: An Australian Wildlife Odyssey

"This deliberate odyssey is a beautifully written narrative, rich in natural history observation, woven into a marvelous story fresh off Penelope's loom."

— Ann Zwinger

"Ed Kanze is the John Burroughs of the twenty-first century—except that Mr. Kanze is a better writer . . . What an amazing continent and what a grand book about it!"

— Jack Sanders, author of *Hedgemaids and Fairy Candles:*
The Lives and Lore of North American Wildflowers

"An extremely satisfying look at a land most of us know little about."

— *Booklist*

Wild Life: The Remarkable Lives of Ordinary Animals

"Kanze speaks with several voices: that of the professional naturalist full of accurate information and scientific observations; the skilled writer with a grand sense of humor; the storyteller with a sense of drama; and the adult who has the capacity to view the world through the eyes of a curious child."

— Charlotte Seidenberg, New Orleans *Times-Picayune*

"The material is offered in lighthearted fashion and should be especially appealing to young readers with an interest in wildlife."

— *Publishers Weekly*

The World of John Burroughs

"[A] richly illustrated biography . . . the real essence of [Kanze's] subject is captured in a wealth of marvelous photographs."

— *Publishers Weekly*

Notes from New Zealand: A Book of Travel and Natural History

"Kanze takes us on an entertaining, adventurous tour of New Zealand's forests, parks and beaches and on a grueling three-day hike on the famed Milford Track."

— *Publishers Weekly*

"[An] insightful commentary on the congenial inhabitants, both human and animal, which first lured the author to this magnificent land."

— *Booklist*

ADIRONDACK

ADIRONDACK

Life and Wildlife in the Wild, Wild East

Edward Kanze

excelsior editions

State University of New York Press
Albany, New York

Cover photo by Edward Kanze

Published by State University of New York Press, Albany

© 2014 Edward Kanze

Excelsior Editions is an imprint of State University of New York Press

For information, contact State University of New York Press, Albany, NY
www.sunypress.edu

Production by Diane Ganeles
Marketing by Anne M. Valentine

Library of Congress Cataloging-in-Publication Data

Kanze, Edward.
  Adirondack : life and wildlife in the wild, wild East / Edward Kanze.
      pages cm. — (Excelsior editions)
    ISBN 978-1-4384-5414-6 (paperback : alkaline paper)
    1. Kanze, Edward—Homes and haunts—New York (State)—Adirondack Mountains.
2. Kanze, Edward—Diaries. 3. Mountain life—New York (State)—Adirondack
Mountains. 4. Country life—New York (State)—Adirondack Mountains. 5. Natural
history—New York (State)—Adirondack Mountains. 6. Seasons—New York (State)—
Adirondack Mountains. 7. Naturalists—New York (State)—Adirondack Mountains—
Biography. 8. Adirondack Mountains (N.Y.)—Social life and customs. 9. Adirondack
Mountains (N.Y.)—Biography. 10. Adirondack Park (N.Y.)—Biography. I. Title.

  F127.A2K36 2014
  974.7'5—dc23   2014002382

10 9 8 7 6 5 4 3 2 1

For my family, friends, and neighbors,
human and otherwise, past, present, and future

It is through the power of observation, the gift of eye and ear, of tongue and nose and finger, that a place first rises up in our mind; afterward it is memory that carries the place, that allows it to grow in depth and complexity. For as long as our records go back, we have held these two things dear: landscape and memory.

— Barry Lopez, "About This Life"

Contents

Prologue

A thousand feet above the wooded and rocky summits of New York's Adirondack Mountains, a hermit thrush, a deep woods songbird, traces an arc across the sky. It's the middle of a frosty autumn night.

Silver stars glitter on universal black velvet. The thrush, its breast spotted, back olive, and rump and tail a dull rusty red, keeps watch. With sharp eyes and a brain not quite the size of a table grape, the bird, about five months old, likely reads cues such as the earth's magnetic field and star patterns to orient toward an ancestral wintering place it has never seen.

On this moonless night, the Adirondack Park, largest in the Lower 48, looms below like a sea of India ink. It's wild country down there. Six million acres of mountains, valleys, and forest in varying degrees of preservation, of broad lakes and winding rivers, of sodden bogs thick with wild orchids and carnivorous plants, sprawl over a dome of billion-year-old bedrock. Those acres represent one of the nation's finest sanctuaries for birds, beasts, and nature lovers. This is a state park, one with inholdings of private land. My wife and I are privileged to own such an inholding. The Adirondack Park covers more territory than Yellowstone, Glacier, Grand Canyon, and Yosemite National Parks combined. The woods here are paradise for a hermit thrush—except during the cold, hard winter.

Down near a river whose waters reflect starshine as fine as tree pollen, a solitary glow pierces the blackness. It's a lamp. The lamp shines in a house. The house crowns a hill of glacial sand. Inside, in pajamas, half asleep, I crouch over an aluminum container about the size of an old-fashioned pencil box. It's a Sherman trap. Shermans are favored the world over by scientists for livetrapping shrews, voles, and other tiny mammals. Inside the trap rattles a deer mouse.

Above, the thrush pumps southward. It utters an occasional short whistle, barely audible on the ground.

I growl. The trap's jarring snap has summoned me for the third time this night. All I can think of is getting back to bed. I work like a robot. Opening a plastic bag half filled with fluorescent yellow powder, I shake the mouse into it, zip the bag, then shake. Inside, the unhappy rodent tumbles like clothes in a dryer. With each revolution, it looks more and more like a lemon with a tail.

"What are you going to do with it?" says my wife, blinking as she pads from the bedroom.

"Let it go right here," I say.

"*Indoors?*" Debbie is aghast. I make the case that liberating Technicolor mice outside the house, letting them mark their trails back in, has only gotten us so far. It's time to get serious, to banish rodents from books and bedspreads once and for all. The way we're going to accomplish this is to find the very last entry hole. Debbie is concerned about yellow stains on furniture and carpets. Yet she lets herself be persuaded. This is war.

I place the bag on the floor and open it. The mouse pokes its nose out twice, then bolts. The brown-and-white rodent is now a dazzling yellow—whiskers, tail, dainty feet, and all. Traumatized, the animal races toward the nearest wall, a contrail of yellow dust lengthening behind it. I'd laugh if I weren't so tired. The mouse traces the room's perimeter, reaches a bathroom, darts over the threshold, and vanishes.

I follow. A naturalist and writer, I'm beginning to doubt that life in one of the world's great wild places is all it's cracked up to be. I sprawl on the ice-cold floor, scrutinizing baseboards and the bottoms of cabinets. I'm tempted to abandon the entire enterprise, convince Debbie to join me, and, like the hermit thrush, head for a warmer horizon.

Yet there are compelling reasons to stay. We love the life we're cobbling together here atop billion-year-old rock, a southern prong of a formation called the Canadian Shield. We inhabit a great forest in which my four-times-great-grandparents were pioneers and in which their descendants have been scratching out livings ever since. Nobody in my Adirondack lineage has achieved fame, and only one got seriously rich. Yet to endure, these forebears had to be hardy and brave and extraordinary. This is a place that takes new arrivals, chews them up, and spits them out. One has to be defiant to survive here. We are, or think we are.

As the story of two centuries of Adirondack family history becomes my story, too, I savor the mingling of the past with present and future. Yet questions circle like vultures. Can we survive it all? The mice? The bugs? The long, hard winters that can bring June snows and July frosts? A house bent on collapse? The challenges of scratching out livings far from cities and suburbs? Can we claw our way over these hurdles and not only stick it out, but enjoy ourselves?

At last, I spy a hole. It's hidden behind trim that frames a shower stall. A yellow smudge circles the opening like a bull's-eye.

Carpentry at 3:00 a.m.? I can't face the alternative, which is to let mice run amok one more night; let the little miscreants leave droppings on kitchen counters and nightstands; let them gnaw holes in favorite shirts, violate apples, and tear into the wallboard that keeps them out of the pantry. The last straw for me came when I opened a dresser drawer and in place of a perfectly good wool hiking sock found a ball of carefully sculpted fluff. In the middle, a wide-eyed mouse looked up as if I were intruding. She was suckling young, pink and wrinkled and about the size of honeybees.

We could kill the mice in our house. That's what most people do. But we have qualms, and Debbie has a cat allergy. We also recoil at the thought of snap-trapping mice into oblivion week after week, month after month, year after year. Handling all those dainty little corpses would cut fissures in our hearts. And hey, if you're going to fit in in the Adirondacks, you've got to achieve some sort of equilibrium with mice. Their ancestors go much, much further back here than mine do.

Debbie retreats to bed. I march out under blazing stars to the shed, returning with hammer, nails, scrap of wood, and an aerosol can of insulating foam. I blast an outrageous quantity of foam into the mouse hole, then tack wood over the opening. The battle is won, for a while. I stagger back to bed.

Welcome to my life. Maybe it's your life, too. Maybe you've marched boldly out of the straight and narrow and set off in the direction of your dreams—say, to a log cabin in a cold, windy valley in Wyoming, to a houseboat in Seattle, to an inherited cabin among bald cypresses and water tupelos in the Mississippi valley, to an old house you've purchased in a small country town in Maine or Iowa or Arkansas, where life seems sane. Or maybe you haven't, but you'd like to. You wonder what it might be like to invent a life to your specifications, then live it.

Whatever your story, here's ours: a tale of how a couple of nature lovers and people lovers went searching for a better life and a working philosophy in the storied, celebrated Adirondack Mountains, and what they found—in terms of history, natural history, and personal history—when they got there.

But first, before launching, there's an issue rattling around the back of my mind, and I want to address it.

In my view of the universe, as in Debbie's, everything is nature, and nature is everything. Humans are made of the same stardust as woodchucks and tomato plants. Yes, our species alters the world on a grand scale, but why does that set us apart?

Perhaps our neighbors, the beavers, have a lesson to teach us. By building dams and lodges, creating ponds, digging canals, and felling trees, the world's second largest rodent utterly redefines the places it inhabits. Environmental impacts spread out in all directions, impacts that bring pros and cons to other mammals, birds, reptiles, amphibians, insects, plants, fungi, algae, bacteria, and all the rest of the beaver's neighbors.

And beavers are not alone. A million bison thundering over the Great Plains, trampling everything in their path, wrought great changes, too.

We, it seems to me, are as much part of the whole cloth of nature as the bison and the beaver, the squirrel and the spruce. A house in the suburbs? Much like a beaver lodge. A modern city? It's a variation on the prairie dog colony, although less likely to shelter rattlesnakes.

Creeds and philosophies that pluck *Homo sapiens* out of nature and put us on pedestals, lords of all we survey, make no sense to me. Indeed, they seem dangerous. By conceiving of ourselves as apart from nature and superior to it, we encourage twisted relations with our fellow earthlings and justify all manner of ecologic misbehavior. View ourselves as citizens of a republic of species, on the other hand, each with inherent rights to life and liberty, and we can begin to dream of a healthier world.

Among the increasing number of us who take an active role in protecting the Earth, there are, if I may coin a pair of labels, Muir thinkers and Burroughs thinkers. Each group operates within paradigms (whether they know it or not) voiced a century and more ago by renowned American naturalists John Muir (1838–1914) and John Burroughs (1837–1921). Among the Muirs, the operative philosophy tends to be the same as that which led to the creation of national parks: to protect nature, humans have to be expelled from it. Our species has no home in the wilds.

In the Sierra Nevada of California, John Muir found the Indians "dirty," "deadly," and "lazy," as quoted in Mark David Spence's fascinating but dark history, *Dispossessing the Wilderness: Indian Removal and the Making of the National Parks* (1999). At Yosemite, Muir complained that the Indians interfered with his appreciation of the wilderness's finer virtues and in his thinking and words granted them "no right place in the landscape." The National Park Service agreed with him and got to work. It took decades to fully accomplish the expulsion, but by 1969, the last of Yosemite's Indians had been forced out of the park.

Muir's belief that nature is distinct from humans and humans from it is unfortunate. It's not hard to see where his notions come from. Muir was raised in a stable of conventional Christianity, and he never quite broke out of his stall. Or, as his friend and verbal sparring partner John Burroughs put it, "[Muir's] philosophy rarely rose above that of the Sunday school."

Burroughs, sometimes portrayed as meek and mild beside the manly, swashbuckling Muir, was actually the more radical of the "Two Johnnies," as the press called them. More visionary, he dreamed that we might one day outgrow our world-wrecking habits. He found this hope not in setting his species apart, as Muir advocated, but in doing just the opposite. In essay after essay and book after book, Burroughs proposed that humans embrace their oneness with the world and all the life in it. He argued that mankind should abandon old and outdated creeds and adopt in their place a frank, passionate reverence for nature itself. He makes his case eloquently in the essay "The Faith of a Naturalist," first published in 1919:

> Every walk to the woods is a religious rite, every bath in the stream is a saving ordinance. Communion service is at all hours, and the bread and wine are from the heart of Mother Earth. . . . The beauty of natural religion is that you have it all the time; you do not have to seek it afar off in myths and legends, in catacombs, in garbled texts, in miracles of dead saints or wine-bibbing friars. It is of to-day; it is now and here; it is everywhere. The crickets chirp it, the birds sing it, the breezes chant it, the thunder proclaims it, the streams murmur it, the unaffected man lives it. Its incense rises from the plowed fields, it is on the morning breeze, it is in the forest breath and the spray of the wave. The frosts write it in exquisite characters, the dews impearl it, and the rainbow paints it on the cloud. It is not an insurance policy underwritten by a bishop or a priest; it is not even a faith; it is a love, an enthusiasm, a consecration to the natural truth.

A Muir thinker might argue that Burroughs's worldview holds greater menace for nature than the Judeo-Christian. It could be used to justify any horror. Up to a point, this makes sense. Global climate change, viewed through the Burroughs lens, is a natural phenomenon. And so, ultimately, it is. Yet must we see everything natural as good? Just ask a farmer whose crops have been ruined by a frost or hailstorm. What is "good"? It's half, of course, of another specious dichotomy, that between good and bad.

The essential facts, I'm convinced, are on Burroughs's side. We are *of* nature, not apart from it. Look closely at your hands and face and look closely at the hands and face of a chimpanzee. Reason demands that you accept the chimpanzee as your cousin. In fact, we are different fruits of the same family tree and share about 96 percent of our DNA.

What we should concern ourselves with, we Muir thinkers and Burroughs thinkers and all the rest of our kind, is the nature of the world we want to live in. Will it be one that includes free-roaming elephants, polar bears, blue whales, and magnificent places such as the Adirondacks, where myriad life-forms abound from horizon to horizon, or will it be entirely humanized? The landscape of urban sprawl, lorded over by a sometimes despotic species with inflated notions of itself, is natural, yes, but most of us reject it. The landscapes we embrace most passionately tend to be the ones we seek out for our vacations and retirements: the mountains, the seashores, the prairies, the deserts, the islands.

As thinkers of the Burroughs school, Debbie and I came to the Adirondacks not to live in one of Muir's vaunted wilderness cathedrals, leaving no trace of ourselves, remaining apart. No. Unlike the national parks, so influenced in their evolution by Muir, the Adirondack Park was built along Burroughs lines. The people remained. Here the human and the other-than-human intertwine. Here Debbie and I aimed to fit in, as best we could, to marvel, to learn, to participate at every opportunity, to gather wild fruits and plant an orchard and have a garden, and to revel in our citizenship in a vast and diverse community of species.

1

Why

The morning sun warmed my back as the cool, sweet exhalations of balsam fir trees bathed my face. Moose Mountain, an Adirondack peak deep in remote woods and rarely climbed, loomed over my right shoulder, several miles away but seeming much closer. I felt my life affirmed on all sides. Was this bliss? Maybe.

I didn't stay there long. Sitting on cold, waterlogged ground in our new front yard, I had a practical task to complete. A few inches at a time, I lowered a string into a rusty iron pipe sticking out of the ground. It was a well casing. We were preparing to do away with an old jet pump that broke down every day or two, which, in its little house of concrete blocks, would not stand up to Adirondack winters. Ours had been a summer place only. In order to make it habitable year-round, we needed to install a submersible pump. It would operate deep down in the water column, well beyond the reach of frost. My job was to determine how deep the well was, which in turn would tell me how much water pipe and electrical cable we'd need to buy.

I had tied a heavy iron washer to the string's lower end. The cord looked like it had been made by Dr. Frankenstein. Just for fun, as part of an exercise in Thoreauvian economy, I had saved tea bag strings, a few inches here, a few inches there. Tying each to the next, I created enough line to fill a spool. It had taken several hundred cups of tea to show me the well's depth was 117 feet.

Practicalities aside, I gave thought for a golden moment to the balsam firs that sent joyous news across a meadow and into my nostrils. They told me I was home, home in the North Woods, home in the woods my grandfather had known so well, home in one of those rare places on earth where humans are dwarfed by a large and thinly populated landscape. A black bear might saunter by at any moment. So might a moose. I might look up to see a bald eagle soaring. The thoughts filled me with a kind of idiotic rapture.

It all meant so much because place has always been vital to me. As a child, I came to realize that certain landscapes cheered or excited me while others made me sad or anxious. My spirits soared while I walked in woods, for example, yet plummeted during a run by bike or automobile through a gantlet of suburban sprawl. I seemed to be more sensitive to place than anyone I knew, or at least more than anyone talked about. Was something wrong with me? I loved woods and lakes, meadows and thickets. I grieved over neighborhoods filled with identical houses and felt threatened by roads crowded with automobiles, parking lots, and retail stores. I found it alarming that wild places were disappearing and sprawl was on the march.

Growing up in a suburb north of New York City, I saw a great many high school classmates gravitate to Manhattan for entertainment and illumination. Not me. I sought novelty and knowledge beyond the "No Trespassing" signs of a nearby watershed. There, as far from the synthetic world as I could get, I immersed myself in flora and fauna. Among the trees and wild animals, I felt a sense, rare at home and almost nonexistent at school, of belonging.

Looking back, I realize something I couldn't see at the time. I was lucky. I had the watershed and the good sense to seek solace in it. I grew up and kept on going. But a shocking number of the boys I knew in high school never reached middle age. Their stories are too important to be treated here in passing, but it's instructive to contemplate the causes of death: self-inflicted gunshot wound, self-inflicted hanging, death by falling, alcoholism, heart attack related to injuries sustained during a suicide attempt, automobile accident as a result of extreme speed, death by choking, and murder by gunshot wound. At times I fear I'm overly critical of the suburban culture in which I grew up. Then I remind myself of the bright young nonconformists who have fallen. Admittedly, they died directly or indirectly as a result of choices they made. Still, the control-obsessed culture that tormented and alienated them deserves some of the blame.

My boyhood cohorts were strong of will and difficult to tame. Of course! They were the descendants of explorers and pioneers. Yet society locked them up in classrooms on gorgeous sunny days when anyone in his right mind would have been better off playing hooky, which some of us did. In school and at home, boys such as these (and girls, too) were punished for perfectly sane acts of rebellion. Defiance of the established order often expressed greater reason than the order itself, while the alternative, conforming to the order, required a certain madness. What's more, as if five days of school each week weren't strict adult control enough, most of these young men were coerced, as I was, to attend church on Sundays. Yet their souls were not so easily bound to dogma. Each in his own way chose rebellion over surrender to higher powers of all sorts, and it cost him.

Somehow, I muddled through. After high school, I carried on my education at Middlebury College, in bovine Vermont. Amid pastures scented with manure, flanked by the Green Mountains to the East and the Adirondack Mountains to the West, life took a happier, more constructive turn. I majored in geography, the study of place, but only after a year of floundering.

First, as a freshman, I tried biology and English on for size and found each, as taught in that place at that time, narrow and cramped. I hungered to swallow the world whole, not nibble at the narrowly defined parts of it. The biologists I studied under, and all but one of the scholars of literature, suffered from myopia. They functioned efficiently and often brilliantly within narrow specialties, yet their work seemed scarcely related, or not related at all, to the vibrant rural landscape amid which we lived and learned. Beyond classroom walls, real life surged, brimming over with blood and chlorophyll. It was almost entirely ignored.

English professors, for example, talked about Wordsworth's Lake District, but not much about Lake Champlain, just down the road. We picked apart Frost while failing to witness the frost browning leaves just beyond the windowpanes. Botany started off right, commencing with a field trip up Snake Mountain. For a day, we looked at actual plants. But that was it. The professor locked us indoors for the rest of the semester. In a poetry course, verse was cut open and autopsied, also indoors, in bloodless discussions during which the teacher and half the class chainsmoked. I gagged, desperate for fresh air. Oh, the faculty did its best. There were bright spots and big hearts. Still, the landscape of learning had all the texture and appeal for me of a concrete wall.

Except in geography. Here professors regaled students with tales of adventures around the globe and showed slides that opened windows into the world. When we weren't camped in chairs contemplating Bavaria and Botswana, we were out in the Vermont countryside, expelling vapor from our nostrils on chilly mornings just like the cows. Thanks to the department's trusty workhorse, a warm and brilliant Harvard PhD named

J. Rowland Illick, we were beguiled by old fields, abandoned cellar holes, and Pleistocene glacial shorelines. It was good while it lasted.

Then came graduation and uncertainty. What to do next? Where to go? Back to the suburbs? No, thanks. Still, between bouts of despair that I might never find a place for myself, I was optimistic, somehow convinced that the world was my oyster, as the saying goes, even though I hadn't a clue how to eat it.

Like many a bewildered youth, I looked outside official channels for inspiration. I found it not in drugs, alcohol, or destructive rebellion but in Henry David Thoreau. I first read "Walden" in high school. Thoreau's manifesto of independent thinking and self-reliance helped me find the courage to be different, and it set me dreaming about living a life in the woods. I also took heart from the example of my mother's father, Burdett Eglin Brownell. I knew him as "Grampy." He was my hero and I loved him, although I never dared to tell him.

As heroes go, Grampy didn't look the part. He ate to excess, tended to look eight months pregnant, chain-smoked, snored mightily, and was prone after bedtime to extravagant displays of flatulence. Perhaps the tall glasses of milk he drank, along with an undiagnosed case of lactose intolerance, explained the exhaust. Grampy spoke his own language. He had odd pronunciations, such as "ignition" with a long first *i*, arguing that if you ignite something, then "ignition" should be pronounced accordingly. If he disliked someone, and he didn't dislike many, he called that person a "touch-hole." It's a suggestive epithet from an earlier time that literally refers to the firing orifices of muzzle-loading cannons and muskets.

Grampy had other, greater failings. A prodigious drinker in his youth, alcohol was a factor in the collapse, when my mother was five, of his marriage to my grandmother. The precipitating event seems to have been a house fire. According to a newspaper clipping that has survived, my mother-to-be was the hero. "Five Year Old Child Saves Lives of Family as Home Is Fire-Swept," the story begins. Joyce woke up to the smell of smoke and roused the household. All escaped alive, including upstairs tenants. The newspaper story did not make clear in those judicious days that my grandfather, full of beer or booze, had conked out in a chair, a cigarette dangling from his fingers. It's likely he had caused the blaze.

Later, too late to save his marriage but in time to save himself, Grampy found the courage to metamorphose. In middle age he shed his old bad-boy skin and crawled out a devoted public servant, an unabashed do-gooder, mostly sober at first and then, after diabetes presented him with the stark choice to either keep drinking or keep living, dry as the proverbial bone. He was a shy man who hated public speaking, yet he made friends easily and launched a modest political career. It began with him winning election, shortly after the Second World War, to Northville's village board.

Grampy was a strong, quiet man, more likely to act than to analyze, although he excelled at the kind of analysis that leads swiftly to thoughtful action. Although he lacked Thoreau's gift for words, by the time I knew him he possessed a superior talent for living. I know of no other man or woman who was as rooted in landscape (in his case, the Adirondack landscape), involved with its geography, and enmeshed, willingly and happily, in the lives of his neighbors, and with the flora and fauna, as he was.

His family tree (and mine by extension) was rooted on his mother's and father's sides in the southern Adirondack village of Northville. There his Brownell and Lawton ancestors had lived for generations, and there today they crowd the cemeteries. Forebears stayed put after the creation of the Adirondack Park in 1892 because, as we've discussed, this was Burroughs country. What they thought of the new arrangement—living in a park with rules rather than living on a frontier with few of them—I don't know. The important upshot was that my grandfather grew up in a homestead along the cold, wild, boulder-strewn Sacandaga River, in the southern Adirondacks. It's hard to imagine him taking shape anywhere else.

Most of the adults I knew groused about where they lived, finding it too hot, too cold, too something. Grampy spoke of home with pleasure, and he worked hard to keep it a good place to live. After cutting his political teeth on the village board, Grampy served as Northville's mayor and chief law enforcement officer. He was a man of principle. Open to multiple and inconvenient truths, he was a Rockefeller Republican who in the 1972 presidential race voted for George McGovern over Richard Nixon. He spoke with distaste of Nixon's unprincipled witch-hunting for communists during the McCarthy era. Once he fired a policeman who harassed a pair of men on motorcycles who looked like hippies, even though no one disliked long hair and outrageous clothes on men more than my grandfather.

Grampy's career, so much as he had one, involved cutting leather in small glove factories—factories that made Gloversville, New York, my mother's birthplace, the world's foremost producer of leather gloves from the late nineteenth century until sometime after World War II. As long as glove making persisted in upstate New York, which it did, barely, until the end of his life, Grampy possessed a skill that was always in demand, and the demand gave him freedom. He worked intermittently and only as much as he wanted to. More important were fishing, hunting, tinkering with mechanical things, helping friends and family, and poking around the forests and lakes of his native mountains. Outdoors, he often clenched a pipe in his teeth. He wore a weather-beaten felt hat and tended to dress in green. Today, the hat hangs on a peg in my writing studio. Sometimes I take it down and feel the sunbaked felt and gaze wistfully at strands of hair that linger inside. Those hairs hold the amino acid sequences of Grampy's DNA. One of his pipes sits nearby on a shelf. Ashes linger in the bowl. Thirty-two years after Grampy's flame burned out, their appealing smell summons delicious memories.

After my graduation from college, Thoreau and Grampy (I had not yet found Burroughs) remained, albeit posthumously, my close philosophical companions. I drifted into jobs as an interpretive naturalist, serving with the National Park Service, a county park system, and various conservation organizations. The work suited me, or at least it did for a decade. I got to be outdoors, mostly, and it was a thrill to teach people about birds, bees, trees, and other things that I loved. Astonishingly, I got paid for it.

Slowly, though, my hunger for congenial geography began to demand satisfaction. Everywhere I lived, from a barrier island off the coast of Pensacola, Florida, to a charming old farmhouse I shared with rats and flying squirrels in a 4,700-acre park in suburban Cross River, New York, I watched bulldozers chew up my nearby surroundings. I loved my home places yet hated them, not for what they were or had been, but for what they were becoming. I craved a refuge, not just for wildlife but for myself.

Eventually I gave up naturalist work for writing. Around the same time, during a walk in the woods on my thirty-fourth birthday, I met an irresistible woman, fell in love, and, straying from Thoreau's celibate path, married. Like me, Debbie loved wild places, loved sleeping on the ground deep in the woods, lamented landscapes purged of every species but our own, and hungered for adventure.

Hard, romantic years followed. For eight of them, we inhabited an identical number of spots on the map. We traveled for nearly a year in Australia and New Zealand, and, counting four moves to the same congenial town on the Mississippi Gulf coast near New Orleans, we uprooted a dozen times. We lived strenuously and joyously, except when we were miserable and broke. We explored the Downunderworld, hobnobbed with extraordinary wildlife and remarkable people, and served as migrant workers ("seasonals," we were called) for the National Park Service.

Friends and relatives fretted. Weren't we moving too often? Would we ever settle down? Truth is, we wanted a home. Yet to find one, we were compelled by our natures to wander. As the Tao Te Ching puts it, we sailed East to go West. To achieve a more stable geography in the long run, we had to go walkabout in the short.

What sort of paradise did we seek? Not the plain, upholstered, all-white, wall-to-wall-carpeted facsimile of God's heaven I once saw pictured on a backlit panel in a Mormon temple visitor center. Our notion of Nirvana was earthy. It included bugs and birds, flowers and trees, snakes and skunks, beavers and chipmunks, dirt and the occasional snowstorm, lightning bolt, and downpour.

We wanted to alight in such a place—to stop drifting like seeds on the gusts of chance. As nature lovers, we hoped to take root not just anywhere, but in, or along the edge of, a wild place. We insisted that the spot be governed by restrictions certain to prevent abuse. We had seen the landscapes of our youth despoiled by "development"—a curious word often meaning the reduction of a landscape from a habitat shared democratically by thousands of species to a place dominated ruthlessly by one. As newlyweds, we had moved south to work at Gulf Islands National Seashore, along Mississippi's Gulf Coast. Voters had just passed a referendum legalizing casino gambling. Month by month, we watched greed turn a vibrant world of bayous, pine savannah, estuary, and artsy seaside villages into a place of traffic; of overcrowded homeless shelters; of drugs, robberies, and pawn shops.

Our favorite place to spend rainy spring evenings in Mississippi had been a wetland next to the post office. There we took in the throbbing, symphonic orgies of narrow-mouthed toads and squirrel tree frogs. Today the place and its helpless inhabitants are no more. In their stead rises a housing development, giving shelter to cockroaches, ants, spiders, and blackjack dealers. Debbie and I grew despondent. Progress was plundering one treasured place after another. We found ourselves craving not just a home but a refuge.

We weren't antisocial types who longed to live in the middle of nowhere. The opposite was true. While wanting to live in, or on the frontier of, a wilderness, we also aimed to join a small but flourishing human community, one that would offer prospects for friendship, intellectual stimulation, art, music, employment, food, drink, outerwear, underwear, books, and barter.

We wanted to live in a part of the country or the world where the human population was stable or declining. In the United States, workers and retirees drift southward into the warmer latitudes like monarch butterflies Mexico bound in autumn. We loved the South but eventually ruled it out. Too many others were heading in that direction. We aimed our rusty station wagon northward.

We were in our early forties. Parents, siblings, and old friends were showing signs of age. The mirror didn't lie to us, either. Perhaps it was time to move closer to our points of origin: not to go home again, but to settle within a day's drive of the four sources of our chromosomes. We missed seeing our parents and siblings. We'd lost touch with irreplaceable friends who had watched us metamorphose from egg to crawling thing to pupil to adult. All but a few remained in the New York City suburbs where we had grown up.

Why not simply rent a moving van and go back where we came from? We could not. We would not. Real estate prices in our old haunts had climbed above reach. Familiar places had been "developed." Green spaces we had loved as children were buried beneath cavernous houses, shopping malls, tanning parlors, fast food joints, medical complexes, giant supermarkets, "superstores" of various sorts, and multilane highways. Facing the changes would bring heartbreak we could not bear.

We wanted to live within a half-day's drive of a major metropolitan area. That way, if we desired an escape from the woods or needed a toner cartridge for our laser printer, we could find it without fuss. The trick would be to keep a sensible distance. If we encamped too near a city, taxes and traffic would drive us away.

We wanted to live on water: on the shore of a lake or river or at the seashore. There we might swim in season; watch wildlife; cast for fish; and row, paddle, or sail.

We wanted to own a view no excavating machine could mar. To do so would require purchasing an extensive tract of land with a house in the middle of it or finding a place surrounded by land managed in a wild state. The government or the Nature Conservancy would make a better neighbor, we reckoned, than a speculator bent on churning acreage into profit.

Finally, we wanted a place where we could be happy. There was no way to delineate such a spot in advance. We'd have to blunder upon it, cry, "Aha!," and still be saying "aha" ten years later.

Were we searching for the unattainable, for the Shangri-la every latter-day homesteader yearns to find but rarely does? In dark hours we feared as much. We might search until decay and death caught up with us at some lonely bend of the road.

Only after we had shifted our search from Ithaca to Bar Harbor and from Maine to the Adirondack Mountains, identified paradise, purchased it (with considerable help from a bank), and commenced the Herculean labor of renovating the tumbledown structure standing on it, did we realize an item that should have been on our wish list but wasn't. We had neglected, in groping for a base, to focus our longings on a particular kind of house.

As a result, when luck came our way, we received what we asked for: not much of anything at all, a real estate agent's "fixer-upper." It was a drafty summer cottage, built without insulation or an effective heating system in one of America's coldest places. Only mice had ever inhabited it in winter. Verging on collapse, the house represented as much a liability as a prospective place in which to eat and sleep.

This was just the beginning. For the naturalist seeking shelter from the sleets and sorrows of outrageous weather, times have changed. In 1845, Thoreau's ten-by-fifteen foot cabin cost him, he boasted, twenty-eight dollars twelve-and-a-half cents exactly, including nails. Land came *gratis*. Thoreau squatted. He lived with no mortgage and suffered no taxes, not even, famously, the poll tax whose nonpayment earned him a historic night in jail.

Our place, by contrast, cost ninety thousand dollars. We laid out thirty thousand up front and borrowed the rest. The down payment came largely from money willed to us by Debbie's maternal grandparents. Producing the rest was trickier. Debbie had just started a new job, directing the activities program at a bustling "senior independent living facility," as they're known in the trade. Only one bank would consider a mortgage. As far as the institution was concerned, I, a writer and freelance naturalist, didn't have a job. My parents saved the day by cosigning.

One cold, gray March day, we walked out of a lawyer's office with a piece of paper granting title to the house and eighteen and a half acres. We tumbled into a Grand Canyon of expenses. More than $28.12 was needed to get this shack into shape. Beneath the peeling paint and sagging floors lurked hollow walls bereft of insulation, rotted floor joists, and supporting beams that had collapsed and decomposed. We'd known all this in advance. Yet romantics at heart, we'd gone ahead like Don Quixotes. When I wriggled under the house for the first time, I looked around and felt sick. Mushrooms sprouted from beams and joists. Wet soil mashed into my clothes. Moss grew in places where sunlight shot through cracks in the foundation. One patch of moss actually glowed.

Several months after the luminous moss was obliterated during a carpentry project, Ed Ketchledge, the grand old man of Adirondack botany, since deceased, told us the plant was almost certainly *Schistostega penatta*, or Goblin's gold. This remarkable moss reflects light through its chloroplasts, greening any glow that falls on it. The result is an impression, convincing but false, of bioluminescence, the name for the eerie glow given off by certain zooplankton, glow-in-the-dark fungi, and fireflies.

Up top, things were little better. Holes riddled the roof. Water dripped into buckets. The chimney leaked. In the attic sprawled a Sahara of black sand dunes—-the droppings of hundreds of generations of mice. Among them I found a cylindrical twist of hair and bone. It had likely been deposited there by an oversized weasel known as the American marten. The shaggy predator might have crept into the attic through one of several promising holes. Who could blame it? Until we arrived, the house had been inhabited by humans for only a few weeks every summer. The rest of the year, rodents ruled. Judging by the volume of their feces, enough to fill several large trash cans, the mice had made the most of things.

With the structure in such a shambles, why buy it? The question deserved attention. To see beyond our idealistic notions of living in the woods to the practical challenges we would face, we had done the sensible thing. We hired an engineer to give us his informed opinion.

The man appeared in the driveway one day, shook our hands, and tore off into the crawl space, his face etched with concern. He poked screwdrivers into rotting wood, examined breaks in the foundation, burrowed through tight places, and stalked gingerly across the roof. After an hour, the expert was ready to talk.

"Don't buy it," he said.

"Why not?"

"It's a money pit." One had to respect the man's frankness.

Debbie and I had heard the expression "money pit" before, but never in relation to a house we proposed to buy. Usually a mechanic applied the phrase to our car.

The man continued. "Really," he said. "Don't buy it. Get yourself a nice piece of land. Build something new."

I ruminated for a minute, then demanded explication. Where in the vicinity could we find a property half as appealing—one with a deep, dark river pouring over it, with a house close by but perched safely above the flood zone, with woods and a meadow, on a dead-end road, with state land behind it and two villages nearby, villages large and vital enough to provide jobs when we needed them, art, music, restaurants, consumer goods, cucumbers, and car parts? My mind raced, reviewing all the real estate we had examined from Maine to Mississippi. Yes, this house was nearly hopeless. Yet no piece of geography in our price bracket could rival this one.

To the engineer's credit, and despite his opinions, he listened. "You're right," he said. "This is a very unusual property, a desirable one. With a solid house here, you'd have a valuable asset. Knock this one down. Start from scratch."

The guy roared away in his pickup truck, leaving us a quandary and a bill. We struggled for weeks. Emotions soared and nose-dived. Finally we reached a decision. We'd go forward. We'd keep the house, decrepit as it might be. No matter what the engineer said, the old "camp" (as Adirondack summer places are called) had character. It wasn't feasible to knock the house down and live elsewhere while a new structure went up. For one thing, the bank wouldn't let us destroy a building they'd loaned us money to buy. For another, a tent and sleeping bags wouldn't do. We'd spent nearly a year roughing it around Australia and New Zealand, but the Adirondacks were not the South Pacific. Frosts come even in summer. The region is notorious as the coldest in the Northeast, and within the region, this is often the coldest spot of all.

The house would stay. Nevertheless, the engineer's report unsettled us. What to do? We did what most people do when faced with expert advice they don't like the sound of. We found another expert.

This one's name was Tom. A carpenter and jack-of-all-trades, he came out after we had signed the purchase contract. A delay in the owner's ability to produce a marketable title had voided the fine print, and this opened a legal escape hatch. For weeks Debbie and I agonized. One hour we saw great adventures ahead and felt happy we'd signed the papers. The next, imagining ruin, we thought of backing out.

Tom burrowed through the crawl space, padded over the sagging floors, and braved the seventy-eight year accumulation of mouse effluent in the attic. "Gotta do it," he concluded. "This place is a find. If you don't buy it, I will." Tom went on to explain how new beams and floor joists would fix the floors, and how new wiring and plumbing would turn the place from a nightmare into a dream. "You guys can do it," he said.

Which expert to listen to? Were Debbie and I charging like Tennyson's Light Brigade "Into the jaws of Death/ Into the mouth of Hell"? Or were we sailing on a fair wind toward Yeats's "Land of Heart's Desire," a golden realm "Where beauty has no ebb, decay no flood/ But joy is wisdom, [and] Time an endless song?" Seeing parallels between the decision facing us and the one we'd made years earlier to marry, we decided to step toward Yeats rather than Tennyson. We'd roll the dice and see how things turned out.

Each of us, Debbie and I, had a checkered past, one that might have driven a human structural engineer to declare us suited for demolition. I'd been "acquainted with the night," as Robert Frost put it, facing depression in my early thirties. Debbie had plunged into black depths in her twenties while suffering through a disastrous first marriage. Still, we'd chosen to turn away from the past and believe in the world and each other. After seven years of marriage, we were, it seemed, happier than the average couple. Life together continued to be exciting. So we took deep breaths and jumped into the money pit.

In the last nights before packing up our village apartment and moving eight miles to the house, we marveled over the piece of paper that would be a source of joy and a millstone around our necks for years to come. It granted dominion over eighteen and a half acres, "more or less." The acres teemed with living things whose forebears in the great majority of cases had inhabited the place for millennia. They had been given no say in the sale. We and our silent partners at the bank owned the land; so our lawyer assured us. But what rights, legal or otherwise, had the plants, the animals, the fungi, the microorganisms?

A branch of New York State government known as the Adirondack Park Agency (APA) oversees human activities in the 6 million acre Adirondack Park, which is a park like no other. The land is split nearly evenly between state-owned "forever wild" holdings and private parcels that consist mostly of big timber company properties but also villages and inholdings such as our own. Rules imposed by the APA specified the numbers of trees we could cut and setbacks if we wanted to erect new structures along the river. Still, to us the restrictions seemed modest. Our deed, filed in the Essex County courthouse, granted license to wreak all sorts of havoc. We could kill the majority of animals on the property—the majority consisting of invertebrates few other than highly specialized zoologists pay attention to. We could fell trees. We could turn most of the place into an ecologically impoverished putting green if we wanted to, as long as we did it in increments.

We had no intention of doing any of these things. Yet the power—a legal, if not a moral, one—unsettled us. As wildlife-loving naturalists, we had often criticized the way others used land. Now the time had come to be landowners ourselves, to see how well we could live up to our own philosophies. The years ahead would represent a trial and an experiment.

How would we treat our domain? After all, we'd already obliterated an interesting moss. Would we mow the lawn, or would we let the grass grow and watch as forest slowly reclaimed it? Would we cut trails or leave the woods as we found them? Would we practice live and let live outside the house but exterminate mice and spiders indoors? Would the birdsong of a spring day be interrupted from time to time by the roar of a chainsaw? These questions and hundreds more demanded answers.

In order to begin sorting them out, we hatched a plan. To the best of our abilities, we would inventory the property's wildlife. Using our know-how, and by consulting books, experts in various fields, and Internet resources, we would attempt to identify every last plant and animal, as well as every bacterium, every alga, every protozoan, every fungus, every slime mold.

Naming all the wildlife on eighteen acres anywhere is an impossible dream. The diversity is like the diversity of stars in the universe. Yet the more we pondered the effort, the more we became convinced it would lead in the direction of enlightenment, if not actually carry us the full distance. We believed we had no business managing our land, or entertaining ideas of being its stewards, if management or stewardship made sense, without deep immersion in the life already flourishing on it. We were biologists of the Burroughs school, after all. Our biological survey would help us overcome at least a little of the chauvinism toward other species we Homo sapiens tend to practice.

And there was another aim. By having a never-ending science project to work on, we would enjoy a running excuse to steal away from the roofing and the structural repairs, the plumbing and electrical work, to slip off into the creeping, crawling, flapping, blooming world that drew us to the property in the first place. Call it preventative psychiatry. For our very survival, and to maximize our chances of staying, it would be vital to maintain a strict regimen of fun amid the clambering over hurdles.

So began our involvement with the land and life we call "Moose Hill Farm" (moose for the biggest mammal we might hope to spy waltzing past the mailbox; hill for the knoll the house sits on; farm for the fruits and vegetables we would grow, climate willing). I bought a stack of index cards, and Debbie and I began making records. "*Abies balsamea*, Balsam fir, 2/26/00, abundant in woods behind house" and "*Poecile atricapillus*, Black-capped chickadee, 2/26/00, calling in woods" were early entries, scribbled a few weeks before the place was legally ours.

BIOLOGICAL SURVEY RECORDS:

Peromyscus maniculatus   Deer Mouse
3/5/00: Two found dead in a wastebasket in the house; clearly bi-colored tails and pronounced long, stiff bristles extending beyond cartilage of tail.

Castor canadensis   American beaver
3/6/00: Fresh evidence of wood gnawed and trees felled by beavers along both sides of river.

2

We Arrive

Sometimes I wonder if, in coming to the Adirondacks, I'm trying to live my grandfather's life for him all over again. His spirit, or at least my memory of it, exerts a Jupiter-sized gravitational force on me, one that pulled me back in middle age to woods and lakes I explored in his presence as a child. Here I am, tramping on paths he walked; driving roads he knew intimately and could pave with stories; fishing his favorite waters; living a rich, romantic, yet economically tenuous life with a bright, beautiful, strong, feminine woman who—as Grandma, my grandfather's second wife, did—beneath her lipstick and fashionable clothing hides a rugged, adventure-loving tomboy.

Why does my Grampy loom so large? The question never goes away. The answer, I suppose, is that I grew up in a household roiling with anger and despair. There were happy days, to be sure, but we spent all too many hours wallowing in unresolved conflicts between parents who both possessed a generous share of intellect, kindness, and practical skills yet who bickered at best and at their worst fought like cats in a barrel. I often occupied the unhappy middle ground in domestic battles. My mother coped with a difficult marriage, at least in part, by employing the Oedipal solution, favoring son over husband. My father resented the intrusion.

Into this maelstrom every year around Halloween (between my older sister's November 16 birthday and mine on October 28), my grandfather would arrive. He was a breath of bracing, balsam-scented air from the North. As long as Grampy lingered under our roof, all was sane. My parents put on a good show. And my grandfather had a way of putting everyone around him into a placid, reflective state of mind. He exuded goodwill and a touch of mischief, too. I admired him for the fact that he never set foot in churches except for weddings and funerals. Organized religion held no more appeal for him than it did for me. There wasn't an ounce of sanctimony in him. Most adults at least pretended to be pious. Not Grampy. Yet he was among the most moral, kind, generous human beings I've ever had the pleasure to know. Like John Burroughs, he didn't need a god on high threatening him with hellfire in order to act in a particular way. He acted how he chose to act, a self-authorized man.

Physically, my grandfather was rugged and impassive, much like the place where he lived. He was built, as he might have put it, "like a brick shithouse." He wasn't tall, but everything else about him was massive.

Nearly every adult I knew had inhabited at least two or three spots on the map, but Grampy was, as the naturalist John Burroughs once described himself, "as local as a box turtle." He turned his back on the Adirondack Mountains only once. As a young man out of work in the 1920s, he had taken up the hobo life, hopping freight trains deep into the South. Somewhere in Florida, he witnessed a race riot. You could press him for details, but none would be shared. This was out of character. When telling a story, Grampy never shied away from a gruesome detail that might get a rise, such as the time one of his coworkers nicked a coffin with a pickax when they were relocating graves at the time of the creation of the Sacandaga Reservoir, and a liquefied human being, green and unspeakably foul, poured onto the ground. When my grandfather-to-be had had his fill of the outside world, he telephoned his father in Northville. Elmer Brownell wired bus fare home.

The adventure left marks, literally and figuratively—garish tattoos on massive, oddly hairless arms, and emotional scars you could sense but not quite see. Grampy liked to joke. He was a kidder. Yet there was a distinct and appealing gravitas about him. He'd seen dark, brutal things. No cheap, superficial optimism for him. He knew the world abounded in sorrow as well as joy.

In my hunger to know Grampy better after his death, and to appreciate the elements that made him, I began digging into family history. My college friend Jim Alsina, a skilled genealogical sleuth, and my older sister, Maggie, helped make breakthroughs. I learned that Grampy's great-great-grandparents, Daniel Brownell and Hannah Hammond, had transplanted themselves to the town of Northampton, in the southern Adirondacks by 1797, when there is a record of Daniel serving as Northampton's town clerk. These first Adirondack Brownells were pioneers. Cold, forbidding forests, short growing seasons, and stony ground had discouraged American Indians from establishing permanent settlements in the mountains, or so archeology suggests. Tribes that inhabited lands around the periphery knew the Adirondacks intimately, but to the interior, they were visitors. When Daniel and Hannah turned up, Adirondack trees were just beginning to crash to the ground as homesteaders cleared bits and pieces of the great forest. We tend to think of the East as being settled and civilized before the Revolution, and the frontier lingering through the nineteenth century only in the West. Yet the Adirondack story turns this stereotype on its head. Frontier life persisted here through the nineteenth century.

I know little of my great-great-great-great-grandparents. Their reasons for forsaking the comparatively warm, rich soils of the New England coast and the Hudson Valley for the cold, stony ground of the Adirondacks are lost. Politics may have played a part. During the Revolution, Daniel's father, Joshua, was a Tory. At fifty years old, he abandoned his family and farm in Dutchess County, New York, slipped away to Canada, and joined the British Army. Daniel, then twenty-two, remained behind to face the neighbors, people for whom the name Brownell, perhaps, had come to mean "traitor." Daniel's sympathies seem to have been with the Colonials. His name turns up on lists of American Revolutionary War veterans, although the details of his service have so far eluded me.

Daniel Brownell was born in Dutchess County, in the Hudson Valley, in 1756. He descended from Thomas Brownell, a Yorkshire farmer, and Anne Bourne, daughter of a London grocer. Thomas and Anne, the first North American Brownells, migrated to Massachusetts aboard the ship *Whale* in 1638, eighteen years after the *Mayflower*. They settled on the Rhode Island coast and were Daniel's great-great-grandparents.

Daniel married Hannah Hammond, born in New Bedford, Massachusetts, in 1763. She and Daniel produced eight children. One was my great-great-great-grandfather, Orra. Hannah died in 1828. Daniel carried on, living to ninety-six—an impressive age in any time. He breathed his last in 1852, the year Franklin Pierce defeated General Winfield Scott in the presidential election and Charles Dickens, forty years old and at the height of his literary power, published *Bleak House*.

Daniel and Hannah lie side by side in the Olmstead Cemetery on Northville's Main Street. As kids, visiting my grandfather and his second wife, "Grandma Florence," we used to shortcut past their graves and those of other forebears. The attraction was ice cream at Hodlin's Market, the only lure powerful enough to draw me past those silent, lichen-spattered stones. My eyes were always drawn to the sod and my thoughts to the corpses that lay beneath. Gene Hodlin's warm welcome would help me summon courage for the run home.

Two hundred and two years, give or take, after Daniel and Hannah arrived in the mountains, my wife, Debbie, and I, under a luminous blue sky scrubbed by morning rain, climbed into a travel-weary station wagon and set off for our new digs. It was the last day of April 2000.

For several months, Debbie and I had been living in the village of Saranac Lake, seventy-five miles as the raven flies (nearly double that by asphalt) from the old Brownell haunts in Northville. We inhabited a second-story apartment in a building called the Santanoni. Saranac Lake's chief industry from the late nineteenth century until the mid-twentieth was curing tuberculosis, or trying to. The Santanoni, like a great many other structures in town, was originally a sanatorium.

We drove up Church Street, passed three houses of worship, said goodbye to the A&P and the Grand Union supermarkets, and turned right on Bloomingdale Avenue. Two potholed lanes stretched before us, flat and winding, threading their way between the steel-gray Saranac River and a parallel ridge of rock. Heaped along the base of the ridge sprawls the Saranac Lake esker, a calling card of the last Pleistocene glacier. Beneath the ice, rivers thundered, spewing sediment. Water sorts particles by size, something a glacier cannot do, so the glacial rivers dropped boulders here, cobbles there, gravel a little farther on, and sand more distant still. For quarrymen, such arrangements prove convenient and lucrative. Excavating machines have chewed into the Saranac esker for years. Six days a week except in winter, trucks loaded with sand and gravel rumble out of cuts in the formation, bound for the village and beyond.

For nearly six miles, Debbie and I followed the river, catching occasional glimpses of its chestnut-colored waters flowing placidly down a wide, gently tilted channel. Beyond, through occasional gaps in the trees to the east, we spied three mountains: McKenzie, or Saddleback, just under 4,000 feet; Moose, also just under 4,000, wearing a landslide like a crooked necktie; and Whiteface, summit elevation 4,872 feet, the sixth-highest mountain in the park. Forests dark with spruce and fir cloak McKenzie and Moose all the way to the top. Whiteface, by contrast, pokes its billion-year-old anorthosite crown above the tree line. An areola of Arctic wildflowers encircles the heavily trodden, lichen-spattered summit. In the last Ice Age, glaciers carved Whiteface into a stubby Matterhorn and scraped away its soils and plants. Eventually the forest came back, but landslides later peeled off big chunks of them. Light-colored rock thus exposed inspired the mountain's name.

The ease with which we motored to the Adirondacks in the final year of the second millennium, and the effortless journey we made to our prospective homestead in the first annum of the third, brought to mind the greater effort required to reach a point on the map here in earlier times. Getting here from the outside used to require a struggle or, at the very least, an adventure. Arriving in the late eighteenth century, Daniel and Hannah Brownell traveled by horse and wagon or in a cart hauled by oxen. The mountain roads were awful in those days, mere ruts in the woods, muddy in the warm months and otherwise buried under snow and ice.

In 1868, my great-great-grandmother, Elnora Graves, born on New Year's Day, 1847, and at that pivotal moment an unmarried young woman of twenty-one, traveled to the mountains to teach art in a Northville school. She arrived by stagecoach and horse-drawn sleigh. Elnora's odyssey began in Penfield, near Rochester, in civilized western New York. From the flat, pastoral country she had grown up in, traveling alone, Elnora reached her new home by traversing more than two hundred miles of farms and forests. Mountain lions and wolves still roamed the woods, and in spring and fall migrating passenger pigeons blackened the skies.

The final leg of her trip is described in a letter she wrote to "Dear Mother & all at home." The letter was passed down through the family and now sits before me. The handwriting is faded but legible, scratched in ink dipped from an inkwell. The date is Monday, March 23, 1868.

> [We] reached Fonda about half-past four in the morn—Went to the Depot & stayed until day light, then went to a Hotel & enjoyed a warm breakfast right well. Left Fonda about eight, reached Amsterdam about nine & for a while I was afraid the stage would not go to Northville as the road was so bad, but about eleven we started, had to leave my baggage there. After we had gone aways, the roads were so bare & going up Hill. All got out of the Sleigh and walked about a mile, only two ladies beside myself. We reached Northville about dark. The distance was twenty-two miles & the seats in the Sleigh were so narrow that one had to make quite an effort to keep on them, the roads being so rough. Of course I was a little tired. . . .

Elnora spent a night at a hotel, "had supper & breakfast, & Friday morn early was carried to Hope, about three miles, & in splendid style. (All for $2.00.)" She continues:

> Northville is [a] much larger place than I thought it was—a very pleasant village in the summer time, I should think, &

does considerable business. I have secured one of the pleasantest boarding places in N.—have a pleasant studio & my sleeping room right off from it. I have also a large closet, have a fire in my studio, all included for $3.00 per week—that was the best I could do—think 'tis very reasonable. Don't you all? . . . I commence next Monday the 30th. I think I shall get enough of Hills for they are seen where ever you look. . . .

The details are lost, but Elnora may have met my great-great-grandfather, Lewis Brownell, in Northville or in nearby Hope, a few miles deeper into the woods. Lewis worked in Hope Falls in his father's tannery and lumber mill. Then again, there might be another explanation. Perhaps Lewis, rather than a teaching job, drew her to the woods. Spending hours scrutinizing entries in an autograph book Elnora began keeping as a teenager, and that has been handed down to me, I found what might be a clue. A Leona G. Brownell, of "Penfield," Elnora's hometown, scribbles the old saying "Days of sunshine are given to all/ But into each life some rain must fall." She addresses Elnora as "Dear Aunt" and signs "Your Loving Niece." Did one of Lewis Brownell's brothers move west in pursuit of work and raise a family, including niece Leona, in or near Penfield? If so, a visit by Lewis might have led to a meeting. Eligible women were scarce in the mountains. Perhaps Lewis and Elnora's orbits touched as the result of matchmaking.

The Brownell tanneries and sawmill contributed to the deforestation that during the nineteenth century began to batter the mountains like a hurricane. Principally, softwoods were cut—pine, spruce, and fir for building lumber and hemlocks to provide bark for tanning. In places where these were cut, piles of branches tended to be left behind, and fires broke out. According to *Contested Terrain: A New History of Nature and People in the Adirondacks* by the distinguished Adirondack historian Philip G. Terrie, "one result of the combination of logging and fires was denuded mountainsides, and this in turn threatened the watershed." All the same, the woods must have seemed limitless in those horse-drawn days. Crossing the Adirondacks by road today takes only a few hours. Back then a traverse by road or river demanded days or weeks.

Leaving a comfortable home and supportive family in western New York to move alone to the Adirondack frontier, Elnora was taking extraordinary chances. Perhaps it helped that she had been toughened by experience.

Hunting for information about Lewis Brownell, I stumbled on a revelation: details, lost for more than a century, of Elnora's love life. A historian in Albion, New York, named Thomas Taber had collected letters written during and after the Civil War. The author of the correspondence was a young Albion woman named Cora Beach Benton. Cora was sending hometown gossip to her Civil War soldier husband, Charlie, fighting in the South with the Union Army. Included in the tidbits were items it gave me goose bumps to read 140 years later.

"Nora," Cora writes, referring to Elnora Graves, fell in love with Cora's brother, Howard "Hoddy" Beach. A letter dated March 7, 1864, informs us that Hoddy has given up his most recent girlfriend to take up with my great-great-grandmother, then single and seventeen. A letter from Hoddy, written April 21, 1864, posted from the Army of the Potomac headquarters near Stephensburg, Virginia, informs his sister, "Yes, if I live, [Nora] will become my Wife, we are betrothed."

Reading these words makes me lightheaded. If Nora had married Howard, I would not exist, nor would my children, my mother, and my grandfather. My father would have married someone else. The waves of change moving out from a single pebble cast on the waters of time lap on countless shores.

A May 1, 1864 letter from Cora predicts the affair between Nora and Hoddy will go nowhere. "They are both so young," Cora writes. "I do not think it will last; still it may." The end comes by November 13. On that day, Cora tells Charlie, "Howard has seen Nora . . . and I judge by the little he told me that that affair is all over. Poor girl, I am sorry for her, for she loved him very deeply."

One door closed while another, the one leading in my direction, opened. Nine months and a week after Elnora wrote her mother about her stage and sleigh journey to the Adirondacks, on the last day of December 1868, she and Lewis Brownell married in Penfield. The following day, Elnora celebrated her twenty-second birthday. Two years later the federal census found the couple living in the Adirondack hamlet of Morehouseville, in Hope township. Ten years later, they were still in Hope. But circumstances had changed. Now Elnora was the mother of four living children: in order of birth, beginning with the eldest, Elmer (my great-grandfather), Carrie, Nancy, and Harry.

I know little else of Elnora. In 1888, the year J. B. Dunlop invented the pneumatic tires that made our journey to the Adirondacks so smooth, she died on the fifteenth of May. Her headstone in the old Northville cemetery conveys minimal details. She was "41 years, 4 months, 14 days." She left behind children, two paintings that have been passed down in the family, a few letters, and an autograph book.

One of the paintings, an oil on a 17½ inch by 23 inch canvas, shows Niagara Falls from the American side, looking across the brink of the cataract to the horseshoe-shaped Canadian falls in the distance. An old masonry tower crumbles into the raging river above the Canadian, and small figures of men, women, and children stand scattered across the foreground. The nearest, standing behind a wooden rail, are a woman in a long white dress, with a beige bonnet and a brown shawl draped over her shoulders; a man in a black suit and stovepipe hat; and a young child in pants and jacket, apparently a boy. In the foreground the vegetation is indistinct and highly stylized. Elnora was not a naturalist, but her technique with brush and paint seems highly evolved, at least to my untrained eye. Final details: a white mist rises out of blue-green water into a pale blue sky. Billowing clouds drift in from the left, hinting at a coming change in the weather. The painting is unsigned. Grampy inherited it from one of Elnora's daughters and passed it on to my mother.

The other painting, also unsigned and with provenance assured by my grandfather, is executed on a 11½ by 17½ canvas purchased from "N.F. Reynolds, Artists & Painters Warehouse" in Rochester. It fails to engage the eye as the Niagara work does, yet for me this painting holds greater interest. The scene is of a dark forest, perhaps in the Adirondacks. A river pours from bottom center to middle center. Beyond a wooden gate on the left rises a big country house. Of simple gable design, the house has latticed shutters and a red roof that give it a Germanic feel. A rustic log bridge without side rails spans the river. The surface is decked with planks and wide enough to allow the passage of freight wagons and stagecoaches. There are no human figures. The style of this work is self-consciously Hudson River School, with more of the stylized, almost tropical-looking vegetation Elnora put at Niagara. Still, the season is clear. It's autumn. Orange colors some of the trees, which may be sugar maples.

For decades I'd never more than glanced at this second painting when something jumped out at me. The house may well be the old Brownell homestead, the house Grampy was born in, the house that still stands on the old road leading toward Wells from Northville. The size and shape are right, and the position relative to the Sacandaga River isn't far off. This was the place Elmer and Jenny Brownell inhabited for years before moving into the village. It may also be the house lived in by Elmer's parents, Lewis and Elnora, at the time of the 1880 census. If so, the gate would have been Elnora's gate. She may have carried her easel upstream along the Sacandaga, turned, and painted what she saw, embellishing a little, as artists often do.

The year 1888 was cruel to Lewis Brownell. In September, as the leaves turned color, four months after his wife's untimely death, their youngest children, twin infant girls Nora Fulton and Gail Hamilton (the middle names are counties their father represented in the New York legislature), died within days of each other. The cause is a mystery to me. The girls were buried beside their mother.

As we drove to Bloomingdale 132 years later, Debbie was a few days shy of her fortieth birthday. I was forty-three. Already I'd outlived Elnora. We had no children, yet our hearts were full. We'd become landowners in one of the most beautiful places in the world.

Acquiring private property inside most United States parks would be impossible, but not in the Adirondacks. These 6 million acres enclose not only the biggest wild areas and old-growth forests east of the Mississippi, but also villages and hamlets. Small towns such as Northville, where Lewis lived out his years as a widower, and Lake Placid, home of the 1932 and 1980 Winter Olympic Games, rise like islands in a sea of trees. The surrounding lands belong to the Adirondack Forest Preserve. A provision written into the New York State Constitution in 1895 declares that not a single tree on these state-owned lands may be cut. Paraphrasing the original wording, as is generally done today, the forest is termed "forever wild."

The road to Bloomingdale passed a farm with horses, a big vegetable garden, an old red farmhouse, and a paddock patrolled by llamas. We slipped between the school system's bus garage and a potato field, passed a cemetery and two antique stores, and then saw houses pop up on both sides. Domiciles were widely scattered at first but grew close as we proceeded. We passed a Catholic church, a firehouse, and a Methodist church. Just ahead, at a stop sign, Bloomingdale's most prominent edifices, St. Armand Town Hall and Norman's General Store, loomed over a four-way intersection.

Each building, in its way, tells the story of the village's turn-of-the-century glory. Norman's occupies a hulking wooden structure, long and narrow and two stories high. Its whitewashed exterior is prosaic, but the interior strikes the eye as a veritable sonnet to the glories of wood. Beaded pine paneling, burnished to an exquisite glow by age, covers walls and high-flying ceiling, and maple floors thump pleasingly underfoot. Building a structure like this today would cost a fortune. Norman's harks back to Bloomingdale's lumber boom, when old-growth pine, spruce, and fir succumbed to hordes of men with crosscut saws and axes, and towering piles of timber made their way down the Saranac and other Adirondack rivers to sawmills.

In those heady days, the community's prosperity seemed assured. The village elders changed the name in the mid-nineteenth century from Sumner Forge to the more tourist-friendly "Bloomingdale." A pair of wooden hotels rose in the heart of town, merchants opened shops, the population burgeoned, and an imposing wood-frame high school opened its doors, aiming to make scholars of local teenagers. A traveler following the Saranac River upstream from the foothills in 1880 would have found Bloomingdale a brash, bustling country town. Saranac Lake dwarfs Bloomingdale today. Then it was just a hamlet.

A boomtown requires a grand public building. The Town of St. Armand (pronounced ARE-mund) erected one smack in the center of Bloomingdale in 1903. The township consists mostly of wild country. Unless one counts anthills, yellow-jacket nests, and fields teeming with meadow voles, Bloomingdale represents its only sizeable concentration of life. St. Armand Town Hall seems out of place today, a ziggurat of red brick in a desert of vinyl siding and clapboard. A spire and four-faced clock crown it. The spire is the most prominent man-made feature for miles around. If you get lost in the woods, you look for it to give you direction.

Turning right, we passed an abandoned filling station with a hole in its roof and a dirt parking lot where once stood a hotel called the St. Armand House. Then came an old clapboard house that a century ago served as a boat livery and hangout for guides, a former hardware store now crammed full of antiques, and a plain wooden house that on its first floor houses Bloomingdale's post office.

A couple of miles later, we traversed the Saranac River on a one-lane bridge. Thumping over rough-cut planks and glancing upstream and down into oxbow swamps, we looked ahead. There sat our ramshackle palace. It crowned a drift of Pleistocene sand, the red roof scrofulous with sun damage and lichen, the porch sagging, the white paint peeling just about everywhere. A rusty weather vane proclaimed "Williams Camp." If we knew then what we know now, we might have turned the car around and fled. The house inspector was right. From a practical standpoint, the place shouldn't have been bought in the first place, and if some foolish notion had inspired us to acquire it, the logical next step would have been to drive a bulldozer in one end and out the other. But our leap forward wasn't about logic. It was about seeking home, about planting feet on a landscape haunted by fragmentary stories of ancestors, about giving the notion of putting down roots a try. The salvage effort that lay ahead would be monumental. Yet here we were. Whether we'd be around a year hence, or a decade, remained to be seen.

BIOLOGICAL SURVEY RECORDS:

Clintonia borealis   Clintonia or Bluebead Lily
5/16/00: emerging in woods across road

Taraxacum officinale   Common Dandelion
5/16/00: Flowering on lawn

3

The House

Where to begin? That was the first problem. The house's red shingle roof leaked in several places. The siding, which consisted of cedar shingles of relatively recent origin, had been painted white, but not well. The entire exterior peeled like a sunburn.

The foundation? Don't get me started. Two bedrooms added as separate wings in the 1950s had been built on top of cement block. The mason had neglected to first pour footings, so the blocks rested directly on wet, unstable soil. The soil was wet because the creation of the driveway had inadvertently dammed a gully and diverted water toward the house. Like water itself, wet soil expands when it freezes. Brutish Adirondack frosts had heaved the stuff this way and that, rearranging the blocks.

We soon learned that the absence of footings created another problem. Rodents could tunnel down, following the foundation wall until they hit soil, turn ninety degrees, and bore straight into the crawl space beneath our floors. When a house has footings, mice that burrow down find concrete flaring out from the base of foundation walls. It tends to discourage them.

The central part of the house was a bungalow built about 1922. It served as a "cure cottage," a house to get well in, designed for summer use by an ill man from Warren, Ohio. At the time, this part of the Adirondacks in general and nearby Saranac Lake in particular attracted throngs of TB sufferers, all drawn by the region's famous fresh mountain air. The air was, and is, spiced by the scents of pine and balsam fir. It was reputed to be curative, especially after a young tubercular doctor from New York City, Dr. Edward Livingston Trudeau, founded a sanatorium here.

At our place, the original cure cottage took on the functions of a house. It was held up—barely—by a so-called poured concrete foundation. The concrete had several big cracks in it through which one could see daylight. Mice no doubt savored the view. For a touch of country charm, the foundation also included air pockets and broken beer bottles. Was the beer swilled by the mason who, setting the style for the place, poured the foundation directly on the soil rather than on a footing? Then again, the mason may be blameless. When work comes your way in the Adirondacks, you've got to grab it. Perhaps he operated under orders to create a camp on the cheap.

Decades ago, in the absence of footings, rodents had established numerous ports of entry to the dank catacomb within the foundation. The foundation itself had had settled on the downhill side. This gave the house a subtle lean that grew less subtle the more you paid attention to it. Drop a ball on the floor in the house, anywhere, and it would roll briskly toward the river.

Finally, and here's the coup de grace where underpinnings are concerned, some energetic and no doubt benignly intentioned sage had seen fit to solve the chronic problem of moisture under the house (moisture is an understatement: more about this shortly) by taking sledge and chisel to the main foundation in two places. Two gaping holes were created, holes that gladdened the hearts of every shrew, mouse, vole, chipmunk, porcupine, weasel, woodchuck, raccoon, and garter snake in the neighborhood. The holes welcomed mosquitoes to a dark, moist, blissful place from which they could rise through lighted cracks in the floor to sip warm human Pinot Noir. Indeed, this being bear country, it's possible and maybe even likely that a sleepy bruin wriggled past one of the holes on an autumn day and put our crawl space to use as a den.

The walls of the house, held up by floors supported by joists that rested naked (without sills) on fractured concrete, sagged grandly. The result of one such droop was a crack between the fieldstone chimney and the adjacent framing. It presented a gap wide enough to admit considerable fresh air, daylight, and wildlife.

The plumbing? Don't get me started. According to the seller, despite their antiquity, the pipes and fixtures were all in working order. Yes, but with a hitch. We signed the purchase contract in late autumn. Nights had turned freezing. The pipes had been drained. We couldn't run a faucet or flush a toilet. All we could do was take the place or leave it. As the reader knows, we took it, and it took us, too.

Within days of moving in, we learned important things about our pipes. The supply line that fed the house from a drilled well 200 feet away snaked just two or three inches under the lawn. This would not do. Frost can penetrate four feet deep hereabouts during the winter, or so we'd been told. We also came to grips with the fact that the so-called jet pump that sucked water out of the earth and propelled it uphill and into the house would have to be replaced. It sat outdoors in a crude cement block structure about the size of the average doghouse. "Jet pump" has a modern ring to it, but this was an ancient piece of equipment, badly rusted, with bearings that screeched and whistled.

Hardly had we taken up residence and begun preparing to host my parents, who had cosigned our mortgage and were coming to cheer us on and inspect their investment, than the pump gave out. I wedged myself in the blockhouse, crowded with mosquitoes, spiders, garter snakes, and sow bugs. Wielding socket wrenches, screwdrivers, and a flashlight, I conducted a dissection. The pump itself was fine. Inside the motor that cranked it, however, I found a broken relay.

The relay was made of copper. Remembering a story I came across while researching my biography of the naturalist John Burroughs, I decided to emulate Henry Ford. The automaker, Burroughs, Thomas Edison, and Harvey Firestone were stranded one day in West Virginia when a fan blade broke on their Model T. Henry Ford, eager to demonstrate his prowess with tools and determined to get the vehicle rolling again so as not to generate negative publicity for his best-selling product, rolled up his sleeves and got to work. He drilled one set of holes in the stub and a matching set in the severed blade. Then, working carefully with copper wire, he sowed the fan back together. It worked! I did the same, boring holes with the tiniest drill I could find, then lacing thin bits of relay together with copper wire. I added a little flux and soldered the ensemble together. Presto! Apparently I'm no Henry Ford. The fix unfixed itself after half an hour.

I brought the broken part and pertinent information about the pump to a local plumbing supply house. There I expected to find, if nothing else, sympathy. It wasn't on offer. The man at the counter tried to sell me a new jet pump at a cost of more than two hundred dollars, even though I explained that we would be installing a submersible pump in a few weeks. The submersible would operate deep in the well. Barring a new ice age, frost would never reach it.

While the story I'm telling casts doubt on my ability to make sound decisions, in this case I did the sensible thing. I fled the plumbing supply store and headed to an electrical repair business in Plattsburgh, an hour away by car. There, in an old wooden building that had probably been welcoming distraught homeowners for a century, I found what I most needed: appreciation for my predicament and a replacement relay.

The part cost nineteen dollars. The man at the counter told me that if it didn't solve the problem, I should bring it back for a refund, and he'd loan me a secondhand pump at no charge. Thank heaven the world still has kind people in it.

Now we had water. It poured out of the kitchen and bathroom taps, filled the toilets, and gurgled out of the spigot over the bathtub. Then, after it filled the toilets, it kept filling them because debris in the system had damaged the seals. I replaced them, replaced them again, and replaced them at least one more time as bits of mineral and metal worked their way through the system. At last, the toilets filled and remained silent.

Out of this success came an ominous development. First one toilet, then another, then another (three were in place when we moved in) began to lose interest in emptying. Our friend Tom, the builder who'd helped convince us to buy the house, showed up one day to serve as Holmes to my Watson. We crawled beneath the floors into the dark mire and followed the old cast-iron sewer pipe to the foundation wall. On the outside, we picked up its course and with judicious digging traced the pipe's course in the general direction of the distant septic tank. Along the way, we uncovered ceramic pipe that picked up where the cast iron ended.

Egad! The line was broken in several places. In one of them the sluiceway was packed with material that smelled as awful as it looked. "Get a garden hose," cried Tom. We sprayed water into the pipe, but the mass would not budge. "Call Roto-Rooter!" came the next cheerful idea. I washed my hands in a bucket and grabbed one of the house's antique dial phones. Roto-Rooter promised to have a man on the scene first thing the next morning. In the meantime, Tom and I cut out the broken bits of ceramic line and replaced them with PVC, adding Y-shaped lengths at intervals to serve as inspection points and cleanouts.

The Roto-Rooter man arrived, gushing optimism. He would run a motorized reamer through the clog and have us flushing in no time. Four hours later, lunchtime had come and gone, and we'd gotten nowhere. Tom had a new idea. We would cut into the line down near the road. In a peculiar arrangement, the septic tank lay on the far side. While the professional man screwed his machine through the blockage from above, we amateurs would shove an old piece of galvanized pipe up the house's GI tract from below.

A few minutes later, Tom, who gets excited about things, shouted in my ear. "Watch out!" Right at face level spewed a giant, stinking sausage of historic, compacted excrement. Its diameter was that of a fire hose. The stuff shot out and kept on coming, and we dodged as much as we could.

The good news was that we had no idea whether we'd find a serviceable septic tank at the end of the line, and we did. It was nearly empty. No surprise. Why had the tank been placed so far from the house, across a plowed road beneath which the sewer line was vulnerable to freezing? Our guess was that because the original owners so loved their lawn, they couldn't bear tearing up the sod when it became necessary to stop pouring sewage into the river. (Nosing along the riverbank, I found our clay tile pipe, no longer connected to the system but still taking dead aim on the Saranac River. Ah, the good old days!) So they stuck the tank in a weedy patch across the road. Because the toilets were only flushed in summer, freezing wasn't a concern.

The house's plumbing cried out for updating. Still, for a short while we hoped to enjoy its rusty iron conveniences. Who could have anticipated the next disaster? Late on one of our first nights in the house, I heard a hissing. It came from a closet. I knew it was not a snake. Few snakes actually hiss, and none that does inhabits this part of the Adirondacks. Investigating, I opened the closet door. It was like stepping into a shower. Water blasted out of the ceiling, soaking all the household items we'd just tucked away.

Up in the attic where the pipes ran, I found a galvanized iron elbow spurting like Old Faithful. Time to shut down the water system. Again we were plunged back into sanitary arrangements more primitive than those of my forebears. Instead of an outhouse, we had a pit toilet, a mere hole in the ground a discreet distance from the house. Showering was done with a rig purchased from a camping supply store, a black plastic bag with a hose. We stood on a wooden pallet and doused ourselves, washing away vintage sewage or whatever else was aggrieving us at the moment. When the pump wasn't working, we bucketed water out of a second well on the property. This one had sticks and leaves and an old rusty bed frame in it, but the water was reasonably pure.

Growing up in the middle of the middle class, I'd always wanted to own a home someday. Now that someday had arrived, I wasn't sure it was a good idea.

On the happy side, our plunge back into the sanitary Stone Age brought communion with ancestors. I thought of Daniel and Hannah Brownell and how to them our ability to haul water in lightweight plastic buckets from a well would have seemed a luxury. At least in their early days, they would have lugged it from springs, streams, and lakes in heavy, clumsy wooden buckets, the burden itself weighing, then and now, more than eight pounds to the gallon. I remembered my grandfather's stories of growing up in a house without running water. His mother insisted he wash his face first thing in the morning, and in winter, this meant skimming the ice off a washbasin in an upstairs bedroom he shared with his five brothers.

Inside our dream house, Debbie and I spent our first night, the last in April, curled up in sleeping bags on the living room floor. A fire roared and crackled on the hearth. The night commenced with a bottle of wine and might have gone down as joyful and romantic had mice not intruded. There were a stunning number of them, and all night long they scurried and hopped and carried on as if practicing for a circus. We had roommates.

By morning, the fire had gone out and the interior of the house had plunged near freezing. Clearly, we needed a heating system. The house had none, save for ancient electric furnaces built into the walls in several places. Given the general state of things, we didn't dare trust the wiring. So one day when Debbie was off from her new job (a critical element in keeping us afloat during the financial storms of home renovation), we drove two hours to Burlington, Vermont, and bought a modern propane heating unit that looks like a woodstove.

I didn't install the heater straightaway. The floors in the house sagged badly, the situation so dire that when visitors appeared, we enforced a "no cluster" rule. No more than two adults were allowed to stand in the same place for fear the floors would collapse. When I ventured into the crawl space to prop up the spot where we planned to install the heater, I found myself wriggling through standing water covered by a skim of ice. No wonder the beams supporting the floor joists had rotted away. No wonder the decay had penetrated the joists and badly weakened them and was now eating into the subfloor.

Why so much water? We did some sleuthing and found two culprits. A wooded hillside sloped down to the house carrying surface and groundwater. There was no ditch or drain to carry the flow away. Also, when the house's driveway had been built, a driveway that began and ended on our dead-end road and swung with a flourish behind the house, a gully was dammed. The damming created a swamp, and the swamp drained very nicely straight under the house.

With cement blocks and two-by-fours, I made a crude fix and bolstered the floor to support the new heater. Soon we had the thing in place and the gas hooked up. The house, despite all its aggravations, began to feel cozy.

Major renovations might have dragged on for years, but we didn't have years. Summers are short in the Adirondacks, and they can bring hard frosts. Autumn would bring a deep freeze that would last for more than half the year. Winter would arrive in a hurry. We needed insulation in the walls, needed a winter-ready water supply, needed to replace beams and support the floors while it was warm enough to work outside, and needed the peace of mind offered by safe electrical wiring. So a plan was hatched. Our friend Tom was hired as crew boss. Hard labor would be provided by Debbie on her days off and on weekends, by two old friends, and by me.

The brothers Junker, John and James, had been pals of mine since I was three. Their parents were friends and neighbors of my parents, and through the parental grapevine the brothers had learned of our trials. At about the same time, in the midst of overwhelming demands on our muscles, psyches, and pocketbooks, Debbie had slipped into a depression and was calling me names. Hardly brimming with cheer myself, I returned fire in the form of ice. Things grew ugly. Couples divorce over much less. We faced dark, ugly days and frightening, hopeless nights.

Then arrived our angels from downstate. John had taken a week's vacation from his job. James's boss had granted him a week off without pay. The two arrived in James's van, which was packed with tools, work gloves, boots, electrical and telephone wire, light fixtures, food, beer, and more. They arrived on a Friday night, and each vowed to give us seven solid days of work.

And so we plunged into the most exhausting and productive period of our time here. We hauled our sore backs out of bed every morning and commenced our labors at about eight o'clock. John was usually working by seven. We'd step out on the porch and find him digging postholes down in the garden or working on the trench to the well. The earliest we ever knocked off was 9:00 pm. Once, in a rush to finish the waterline, we stayed on the job until midnight.

During those days, we nearly built Rome. A backhoe and operator were brought in to excavate for a dry well to disperse gray water from drains and to dig a six-foot-deep trench from the well all the way to the house. The last eight feet of the trench had to pass under the porch. James and I, working on hands and knees, dug it by hand over the course of a hot summer day. I'll never forget the happy moment when the deep trench under the porch broke through into a short one we'd gouged, while lying on our sides, in the crawl space.

We dug trenches with the backhoe and installed foundation drains along the uphill side of the house, and we backfilled the trenches one shovelful of crushed stone at a time. We ripped out electrical wiring and replaced it with new grounded Romex. We pulled out the old galvanized iron plumbing, too. While the rest of us did grunt work, Tom took his torch and sculpted us the rudiments of a shiny new system of copper. I expanded on his work in the years to come, replacing one antique line after another until the whole kit was properly caboodled.

In the midst of overhauling the plumbing, we made a further discovery. An old sewer pipe that drained a sink and toilet on the porch had a breach in it. For years, the toilet had been emptying its contents not into the septic system, but into the crawl space. Debbie and I discovered the problem with our noses. We were digging holes beneath the house for footings—part of a plan Tom had hatched to create two-foot by two-foot by one-foot-deep concrete pads, then to place jacks on them and coax the house's drooping floors back into place. That done, we could replace rotted joists and beams. To support the new beams, we'd install stout posts, and these would rest permanently on the pads.

Debbie and I didn't need three bathrooms, so the solution to the broken effluent line was easy. We ripped it out and in the process decommissioned the porch plumbing: a sink, a toilet, and a shower. Perhaps it was for the best. In the shower, a light bulb dangled from a live wire. No ground fault interrupting circuit protected a bather, feet in water and hand reaching up to switch on the light. It was the most peculiar bit of wiring we came across in a house full of peculiar wiring. Was this where the previous owners sent houseguests who stayed too long?

The roof would wait. For the first three years, I patched holes every time we discovered a leak. This approach worked well except in winter, when roofs around here are heaped high with snow, and slapping tar on cracks isn't possible. Winter leaks had to be tolerated until spring. Fortunately, all occurred on the porch.

The pace of progress, slow by most people's standards, was in part determined by our finances. We were broke, or close to it. Progress would have been downright glacial if it weren't for generous contributions from many quarters. Old friends Jim and Cecilia chipped in the money that paid for the new beams and floor joists. Debbie's Aunt Sue, who lives near Chicago, underwrote one project after another and in the end gave us two beautiful, top-of-the-line French doors to replace old leaky ones. She provided new kitchen cabinets, too, as well as a bathroom overhaul and a propane heater for our igloo-cold bedroom. She also paid a painter to treat the house's psoriasis. Our parents made generous and numerous contributions, too, both in labor and in cash.

Inside the house, things were also a mixed bag. Dark pine framed individual pieces of wallboard, and underfoot, western fir tongue-and-groove floorboards, the grain so fine it undoubtedly came from old growth, added vintage grace. Three handsome but decrepit French doors opened to the porch, and the porch itself was a nature lover's dream, big enough to eat and sleep on, with views toward Moose and Whiteface Mountains and deep dark woods we own across the road. Most appealing of all, the porch looked out over a lazy bend of the Saranac River. Our property included both banks. Not an electric light could be seen by night, nor a neighbor's house by day. What we saw we owned; either that or the state owned it, so it was ours in practice if not in deed.

But let's not get carried away with the porch. After all, we'd only be able to enjoy it when the weather was warm, which in the northern Adirondacks means June, July, August, and not much more.

Back indoors, the kitchen was bleak. The cabinets were metal, and the metal was rusting. The hot water heater had been jammed into a tight space between an old electric cooking range and a wall. Water pipes were exposed all over the place, the paint peeled, the floor sagged, the walls lacked insulation, windows had single panes and tattered glazing and leaked around the frames, the wiring was old and inadequate, and there was no heating system save for a few electric heaters we'd be frightened to turn on for fear of burning down the house.

To this, add an astounding accumulation of mouse excrement: little black grains in the kitchen drawers, in the cupboards, in the sink, all over the water heater and the countertops, inside the oven, on and under the furniture, in the bedrooms and bath, all over the mantle. They filled the crawl space, too, but in the muck and mire down there, they didn't stand out. Yet it was the attic, soon to be filled with cellulose insulation and effectively put out of existence, that held the lion's share. I spent the better part of a day with a big contractor's vacuum, sucking them out five gallons at a time. Had I rounded up all those little feces, they would have filled a bathtub.

If this were the West, we might have had a serious health issue on our hands. Mouse droppings can contain Hantavirus, a nasty bit of errant RNA that causes an often fatal disease known as Hantavirus Pulmonary Syndrome. The victim inhales dust containing mouse fecal material, develops a severe respiratory infection, and drowns in his own phlegm. Only one case had been recorded in the entire state of New York. Still, a slight risk existed. My precautions were surely inadequate, but I wore a dust mask and kept wearing it while dumping the contents of the vacuum outdoors.

Why so many mice? They and their forebears had occupied the house's site for thousands of generations before the first carpenter arrived on the scene. Even after the structure was built, humans intruded for a mere few weeks every year, while the mice never left. If squatter's rights prevail, I reckon mice are the house's rightful owners.

With rodents so maddeningly thick on the ground and on the floors and countertops, one might expect that predators of mice would also abound. They did. Scats in the attic caught my eye, ones that were an inch or more long, dark, twisted, and thick with hair. I'd never seen droppings quite like them before. Hitting the books, I found a description of marten droppings that fit the bill. American martens, arboreal weasels roughly the size of house cats, likely abounded in the nearby woods. Perhaps one had ventured near the house, caught a strong scent, and decided to investigate.

Soon we also discovered shrews in the house, and not just one species, but two. The first to turn up, perhaps hunting mice, was a short-tailed shrew. We'd caught inconclusive glimpses of them on several occasions, but eventually a live one turned up, rattling inside an aluminum box trap. Short-tailed shrews are about the size of mice but are not rodents. They're insectivores, meaning they belong to the order of mammals that includes moles. Among biologists, short-tailed shrews are famed for two things. They echolocate like bats, producing high-pitched sounds that bounce off objects ahead of them and reflect back useful information, and they produce venomous saliva. In one famous experiment, a biologist extracted the spittle of a single short-tail and with a hypodermic needle used it to kill 200 mice!

The other shrew that turned up inside was a masked, or cinereus, shrew. This tiny thing, hardly bigger than a bumblebee, popped out from under a closet door in my newly established office. I sat in amazement, watching it run the perimeter of the room, tracing the baseboards, until it reached the closet again and dove back inside. Some would have been horrified. I was delighted. The animal represented a new species for our biological survey.

Two other mammals turned up in the house in the early days. The first was a red-backed vole, a handsome rodent of local woods that perhaps strayed indoors for a look around. The second made ghostly footsteps in the central hallway one day when I was home working alone. If I'd believed in ghosts, I might have heard those footfalls, attributed them to a spectral source, and left it at that. But being a naturalist and a skeptic in all things metaphysical, I went sleuthing.

At first, I found nothing. Footsteps echoed no longer. But a bit of quiet waiting eventually turned up the apparition in the flesh. I'd left the fold-up stairway to the attic open, and a red squirrel had marched down for a look around. It was as astonished to see me as I was to see it. Uttering a chatter of alarm, it bolted back up the stairs and was gone.

The only other mammal to surface close to our sleeping quarters in the early days was in some ways the biggest deal of all. Just the other side of our bedroom wall, I found it drowned in a bucket that had filled with rainwater. The corpse seemed to be a vole's. A vole is a cousin of the Far North's famous lemming, a rodent with short ears and short tail. But what kind of vole? There were several candidates: meadow, red-backed, rock, and woodland. This vole took brevity of tail to an extreme I'd never before seen. Was it a woodland vole, or a close cousin of voles, a bog lemming (there are two species, both likely found here)?

I hit the books. I decided the animal was almost certainly a woodland vole. Yet this was a time to recruit expert opinion. I froze the deceased and mailed it to my friend Charlotte Demers, a small-mammal biologist at the Adirondack Ecological Center in Newcomb. She scrutinized, then voted for woodland vole, too. To be absolutely sure, she sent the well-traveled specimen off to a higher authority in Syracuse. He validated our judgments. The woodland vole proved to be the first of its species documented from our part of the Adirondacks. (No big deal. Woodland voles may be common here, but because they spend nearly all their time living in burrows, biologists and house cats find them notoriously difficult to catch.)

A single story perhaps best sums up the wildlife situation in the house. One summer night, we tried to fall asleep on our sagging mattress but were kept awake by scratching sounds. They came from inside a wall. An ugly smell hovered in the vicinity, especially around a metal space heater recessed into the sheetrock. Whatever was in there was scratching both metal and wallboard. It kept me awake on and off all night. Even Debbie, who sleeps like the proverbial log, was rattled in and out of slumber.

The following morning, I took action. I grabbed a screwdriver and extracted the heater. Inside its metal housing I found the mouse, emaciated and dead, along with the skeletal remains of other mice. The spot reeked of death. The wooden framing around the heater had two holes in it. Someone had nailed a metal patch over one of them. I found a scrap of aluminum flashing and nailed it over the other.

When the sounds started again a week or two later, I leapt into action. I took a utility knife and cut out a rectangle, six by ten inches or thereabouts, just above the heater.

Egad! I'm far from squeamish, but when a stench of mass death and decay poured out and flooded my nostrils, I nearly wretched. My journal tells the story: "It was a ghastly sight. Skeletons piled on skeletons, several inches deep, suggesting an illustration from Dante. The word Golgotha came to mind. The smell was awful. With a screwdriver at first and later with fingers, I counted out the skulls. There were 103, along with a pathetic assemblage of femurs, tibia, phalanges, articulated vertebral columns, and a fetid humus of decomposing hair and viscera."

We could have felt sorry for ourselves for having to inhabit such a house, but instead we pitied the mice. Something had to be done. A peek directly overhead in the attic revealed a hole in the horizontal two-by-fours at the top of the wall. An electrician had drilled a channel for a wire, then decided not to use it. A death trap waited for victims. Year after year, one curious mouse after another nosed into the hole, slipped, fell, and found itself on the charnel heap. There, after futile attempts to escape, they died of thirst or starved to death like all of those that had gone before them. This was muricide on a grand and gruesome scale.

The only thing I could do for the dead was show respect, and the only tangible way to do that was to make sure the killing ended. I crawled into the attic with hammer, nails, and some scraps of galvanized iron. Five minutes later, I was certain no mouse would drop into the pit again.

A few weeks later, I was running a new water pipe and to do so cut a hole in a living room wall. Egad! Here was a second death chamber, double the size of the first. Counting the skulls again seemed the thing to do, but as I neared 100, still not halfway through the pile, the spectacle and the stench got the better of me. I grieved for the poor animals, disagreeable as they were as housemates. Again, I mounted to the attic, found the lethal opening, and closed it.

Mice swarmed the house in greatest quantity, but when it came to the biggest furry animal discovered in the house in our early years, the prize went to a black bear.

Its entry was inevitable. My mother-in-law and her sister were visiting. Debbie had cooked a fish dinner, and not wanting to offend her relations with a bad smell, she had bagged scraps of flesh, bits of skin, and raw parings and stowed them in the mudroom. (A mudroom, for those not acquainted with the term, is a vestibule through which one enters a typical Adirondack house. It's a place to shed or scrape mud or snow off boots.) The July night was hot and sticky.

Our guests had gone to bed at one end of the house. Debbie and I were preparing to switch off the light at the other. Suddenly, from the direction of the kitchen, came the noise of a small object falling. Surely one of our pestiferous mice had knocked something off a counter.

Half asleep, I shuffled out to investigate. No sign of a mouse. Then from the mudroom came a thud. Switching on a light, I caught a glimpse of bulbous hindquarters, black and woolly, hurtling through a broken window screen. Yikes! A black bear had torn its way inside to get the stinking fish. Luckily for us, it was a fully wild beast and not a half-tamed animal accustomed to handouts. Fear drove it away as soon as I appeared, and happily for us, the fish remained inside the bag.

The list of mammals we'd seen inside the house was growing impressive. To it we soon added an ermine, or short-tailed weasel, that scooted into the kitchen one mild day. I had thrown open the doors and was standing at the counter making a sandwich from fragrant sardines when a long, slender shape streaked by. At first I caught only a blur of brown and white. Then there was the ermine in its perky entirety, attenuated of body and abbreviated of leg, gazing up at the sardines with dark, soulful eyes. When a noise came from somewhere in the house, the weasel turned and shot out the door.

For its important contribution to our biological survey, I figured the weasel deserved a reward. So I forked a sardine onto a rock outside. As if out of a jack-in-the-box, the ermine popped up, grabbed the prize, and was gone.

Species after species of animal appeared inside the house. To the best of our abilities, with the help of skilled friends, and within the limits of our time and energy, we identified and catalogued them. Highlights included a porcupine that took up residence under the unheated bedroom tacked on to the south end of the porch. In the middle of the pack was an arachnid, a long-bellied cellar spider, that our entomologist friend Wayne Gall picked out of the long, confusing list of candidates. And at the bottom of the heap, at least in terms of our appreciation, were two kinds of mosquito.

One mosquito is called *Ochlerotatus intrudens* ("intrudens" because it barges into buildings, no matter how tightly sealed). The other is *Anopheles punctipennis*. The first kept us up nights in late spring, skewering us again and again in the dark until years of effort with a caulking gun finally reduced their indoor numbers. So many of these have been squashed on the painted walls of our bedroom that their splay-legged corpses form a handsome pattern. The second astounds us every winter when it turns up in our bedroom on subzero nights, pestering for a drink. It's satisfying to catch mosquitoes alive, pop them in the freezer, and silence their maddening whining. I ship the corpses to Wayne Gall, who scrutinizes them when he has a chance and sends us the identifications.

Wayne also helped us with spiders. Two species turned up in our bedroom alone. The first was the long-bellied cellar spider. I collected it where a wall met the ceiling. This species of spider accounts for all, or nearly all, the old, abandoned webs cluttered with dust that we call "cobwebs" and that adorn every room of the house. The other was a shamrock spider, a big, bulbous thing that materialized one day, also near the ceiling. Shamrock spider females lay eggs by the thousand, so we quickly relocated this one outdoors. Wayne identified two more arachnids, both prowling the porch's window screens: a six-spotted orb weaver, prettily banded, and a gray crab spider, *Philodromus praelustris*, lacking a common name but fetchingly handsome.

From time to time we find pseudoscorpions in the bathtub—tiny arachnids, utterly harmless, that have proportionately giant front legs with pincers. We're fond of our pseudoscorpions. To date we haven't had the heart to freeze one and ship it out for identification.

Perhaps the strangest things we've named in the house have been bacteria. These, as we all learn in high school biology, outnumber all other life-forms. They flourish by the million on every square inch of our hides and from end to end of our gastrointestinal tracts. Unfortunately, they're impossible for a naturalist without an electron microscope and a faculty of microbiologists at his disposal to name. So we cheated. We bought yogurt of various brands, brought the containers onto the property, and catalogued the organisms identified on the labels: *Lactobacillus acidophilis*, *L. bulgaricus*, *L. casei*, *L. reuteri*, and *Streptococcus thermophilus*. Later, Debbie came down with strep throat, and we added *Streptococcus pyogenes*.

Of course, if our biological survey wasn't to be skewed toward conspicuous, supersized organisms such as ourselves; if it was to really confront the biological diversity of our property, our house, and our own bodies head-on, we'd need a team of microbiologists and a high-tech laboratory to do the work. As it is, we make the most of things with the resources at our disposal. But if we could give our bacterial life the attention it deserves, we might tally thousands of species—perhaps that many, in fact, simply within the spheres of our own bodies. If we added those on the roof, on tree trunks, on and under the water in the river, in the soil, inside and outside our flora and fauna, and even dusting the aluminum paint on the mailbox, we might catalogue species by the tens or hundreds of thousands. Or millions! Nobody knows how many are out there. The bacterial world is like the universe: vast and virtually unexplored.

And so we plod along, doing our best, documenting one star in our property's biological galaxy at a time. Our most recent addition to the biological survey is that hunchbacked, roly-poly, pincushion of a rodent known as the North American porcupine.

We had aspired to add a porker to our lists but failed repeatedly. On one occasion, a neighbor, who conveniently happens to be a biologist, telephoned. A porcupine had just left a tree in her yard and was heading in our direction. We had just sat down to dinner with guests, but all agreed there was nothing to do but let the food go cold and hurry off to investigate. The porcupine was gone. But as we started back toward home, it crashed out of the bushes, padded awkwardly across the road, and scaled a spindly American elm. The elm stood six feet off our property line.

Eventually, a porker turned up fair and square. I was marching back to the house one winter afternoon in failing light when my path converged with that of a low, bulky animal. We were both heading toward the house. Neither of us saw the other until we almost collided. Then, as I stood wide-mouthed, the porcupine, as startled as I was, barreled into the woods.

Tracks in the snow revealed that the animal was living under our mudroom. Soil had been patiently excavated, and the spiny rodent had made a comfortable bivouac. A month or so later, it abandoned these digs and shifted to a crawl space under the guest bedroom. There, the stoical beast made no trouble and holed up until spring.

I find it interesting that while porcupines feed conspicuously on bark, often girdling the trunks of trees and killing them, our porker commuted to and from distant food sources and left our backyard unmolested. What, then, was the animal seeking? Perhaps it wanted what we've found here: a home, a refuge, a place to sleep in comfort and safety, a base from which to venture out and explore the world with all its delights and dangers.

No incident in our early days drives home more powerfully the sense of our humble abode as a safe haven from life's storms, at least in my mind, than the afternoon I was struck by lightning.

I didn't take a direct hit. If I had, this book would not exist. A lightning bolt carries millions of volts, and the temperature along its path can exceed 36,000 degrees Fahrenheit, more than three times the surface temperature of the sun.

It was a sweltering summer afternoon, threatening rain. I was in the middle of a mechanical project, ripping apart the dash of our old Toyota station wagon so I could replace a worn-out ventilation fan. It wasn't easy. Mosquitoes were drilling me incessantly, and this was the kind of job where you reduce a complex mechanism to its miscellaneous components and wonder if the sum of those parts, after reassembly, will do what they're supposed to. I had to work with my body half in the car and half out. The sky was growing darker by the minute.

When rain began to spatter, I had to choose. I could walk away from the job and wait for conditions to improve, or I could devise a way to stay dry and continue. If I walked away, would I remember which part went where? That was doubtful. So I hauled an old beach umbrella out of the shed, an umbrella with a metal pole and sand-filled base. I cranked it open over the car's open door.

As I extricated the old fan, I felt like a transplant surgeon halfway through a heart replacement. At about this time, I heard a distant peal of thunder. The source was far, far away. I said to myself: If I hear another, I'll head straight for the house. During my days working as a National Park ranger on barrier islands in the Gulf of Mexico, I'd experienced the violence of electrical storms up close. Once, I'd been lightly shocked as a bolt struck ground near a boat I was in. That had been a close call. I didn't intend to invite another.

As it happened, I did hear a second rumble, and it sent me running for the house, but not quite in the way I had envisioned. I was just pulling the new fan from its box when a flash blinded me. At the same instant, two things happened. A great force of electricity surged up my arms, and an atomic bomb went off in my ears. As arms recoiled, I bolted for the kitchen. By this time rain was pounding down on the roof in torrents, and great booms of thunder echoed all around me. Wondering if I might keel over from a heart attack, I ran through the house shouting, "I've been struck by lightning!" I didn't know that Debbie was outside in harm's way, too. She'd heard the boom come from behind the house and hoped I was safely inside.

Once the initial excitement wore off, I felt myself wallowing in dread. It lasted for days. I pictured my charred, electrocuted carcass being hauled away to a funeral parlor. I pictured a memorial service a day or two later, with my grieving widow, sorrowful parents and sisters, and dear friends and relations gathering together to lament my loss. I pictured my burial. Yet here I was, dry and safe inside our crazy but lovable house, where the next bolt, and the ones after that, would have a hard time finding me.

Each day now more than ever seemed a gift, a bonus. I felt ashamed for all the complaining I'd done about rotten beams and shoddy wiring. Our house was a "very, very, very fine house," as Crosby, Stills, and Nash put it. I was grateful for its safe harbor. All the same, at times I still dreamed of handing in a change-of-address form at the post office. Debbie harbored lingering doubts, too. Would we stay? Time would supply the answer. As for the quandary of whether we'd see ourselves as stewards or mere humble citizens of the land, a response was taking shape. Wild things that had lived here far, far longer than we showed us at every turn that our kingdom was their kingdom, too. In fact, it was not a kingdom at all but something infinitely more egalitarian and interesting.

BIOLOGICAL SURVEY RECORDS:

Sorex cinereus   Masked, or cinereus, shrew
5/19/00: came into office, ran around, left

Clethrionyomys gapperi   Southern red-backed vole
7/21/01: caught in Sherman trap in house—we caught them routinely indoors through Dec. 2001

4

One Plus One Equals Four

Having longed so long for a home, I'd lost all sense of what it was like to have one. When circumstances changed, I found the effect of owning a house unsettling.

It became apparent that the process of converting a house into a home was, in a symbolic and visceral sense, a two-way street. While we were "putting down roots," as the expression goes, roots were insinuating their fibers into our own hearts, minds, and flesh. I had a feeling at times (an unsettling feeling that has not entirely gone away after a dozen years) that the Adirondacks, Bloomingdale, and the house itself were reaching into my core, seeking the far corners of my soul, groping for my heart, and sending tendrils of root into my marrow and neurons.

In one sense, I was imagining it all. In another, circumstances were granting me a preview of a time that will eventually come, a time when everything I am, my brains, bones, flesh, even my memories and thoughts, will surrender to Adirondack soil, will succumb to a gravitational force than cannot be resisted, a force that swallowed my ancestors willingly or screaming and kicking, and that gets us all in the end. I look around and see the ground I may one day be buried in. It makes me shiver.

Shake-ups can have salubrious effects, of course. They make you pull back a frame of reference or two and think. Why was I so queasy? Why were Debbie and I doing what we were doing? A few years earlier, it seemed we were born travelers, infused with the urge to wander— an inclination the writer Bruce Chatwin explicated through the lens of Aboriginal Australian nomadic life in his book *The Songlines*. Debbie and I had spent nearly a year camping our way around Australia and New Zealand. Despite rough patches here and there, at the end of the journey we would have gladly started over at the beginning. I've long recognized in myself a powerful, nagging hunger to travel far from home and keep on going.

Travel is addictive because if conducted in the right spirit, it makes you forever young. You constantly see things and meet people for the first time. Back where you came from, novelty is no longer available. Been there. Done that. Keep moving, and you're a perpetual child, a latter-day Magellan discovering the world with fresh eyes.

In the end, most of us cannot resist home's siren song. It's enough to make one question the existence of free will. Do we really have it, or, like the salmon that struggles through thousands of miles of open water and up rapids and spillways to reach its natal waters, there to mate and die, are we driven solely by biological imperatives hardwired into our genes? The salmon could settle for any one of a number of other streams along its exhausting way, yet it doesn't. Instinct drives it, and instinct will settle only for waters with the precise flavor of childhood.

Surely the same sort of process is at work in us. It may explain why people who grow up in mountains or at the seashore tend to spend their lives in mountains or beside the sea, even if the home environment of maturity lies an ocean away from the geography of youth. "Home is where the heart is," goes an old proverb. We seek what we love.

For some, only the authentic home environment suffices. That's the way it was with Thoreau. He stretched rather than broke the bonds of family and friends by building a cabin a short walk from the house he grew up in. There, by the shore of Walden Pond, he lived deliberately, as he famously said. Yet in the end the homing instinct exerted a more powerful pull than deliberation. Two years later, Thoreau was back under the roof of his parents, there to live until tuberculosis claimed his life.

The forces that drew me to eighteen acres of Adirondack forest and a house worthy of demolition, immolation, or decay drew their power from hidden currents. There was a love of wild places, of landscapes inhabited but not dominated by humans, that grew up with me in the suburbs and lamented the loss of the green places of my childhood. I wanted to return to them. There was also a craving for sanity, for serenity, for calm in a stormy world. My Adirondack grandfather was the single most important wellspring of those things during my youth. Even though he was gone in body, his spirit lived in me, at least in fragments. I longed to bring it home.

So here I was, back on the turf that had spawned a quarter of my genes. I felt like the human equivalent of a monarch butterfly that grows from egg to caterpillar to pupa to adult while making a journey back to ancestral meadows. The butterfly that returns to our yard in spring is in one sense not really returning at all. It has never seen this corner of the world or tasted the nectar of its milkweeds. Yet the flying thing with the stained glass wings knows exactly how to find its way. It has inherited the genes of Adirondack forebears, genes that in some fashion beyond our knowing compel the butterfly, hatched and metamorphosed somewhere in the South, to find the pink- and purple-flowering milkweeds of Bloomingdale.

In the early days here, there were times when I felt acutely at home and savored the sensation. One such time came late on a winter evening. Debbie had gone to bed, and I'd stayed up with the woodstove. When you heat with wood as we do, you don't simply adjust the indoor temperature by twirling a thermostat. You cut trees on your own land or acquire them from a logger. You take a chainsaw and buck the trunks into pieces of a length your woodstove can swallow. These you split into great piles of stove wood, which you must haul to your woodshed and stack. There they dry, ideally for a year or two, and there they wait in dry storage until you're ready to burn them. On this particular night, I had carried in enough wood to keep us warm through the night and following day. I'd loaded the stove, and now I was waiting for the wood to ignite. After the fire was roaring, I'd cut back the air and leave things that way—the fire burning slowly and releasing heat gently—until morning. If I shut down the air too early, the wood would burn little or not at all.

A great feeling of contentment came over me. I pulled up a chair, poured myself a glass of red wine, and sat before the fire, alone but not feeling alone, gazing not into flames, because they were hidden behind black-painted cast iron, but gazing idly about the room. Soon I had a book in hand and was reading. This was the good life. I was living it with a good wife, in a good place, in a good, honest way. I now realize these were dangerous thoughts, ones that were about to take my old life and stand it on its head.

When you're enjoying life deeply, you want to share it. When you're sharing it, and when you relish the sharing, you want to spread the bounty. For some people, this sort of thinking leads toward serial affairs or ménages à trois. In our cases, it tempted us in a direction far more erotic and risky.

Kids had never been foremost on Debbie's radar, nor had they loomed large on mine. We loved children and reveled in their company, but individually and as a couple, we'd always been satisfied to enjoy everyone else's—to eat our cake, so to speak, and have our freedom, too. But as we settled into domestic life amid a landscape of mountains, lakes, and rivers, and as we forged friendships with a rich diversity of neighbors, we developed an acute awareness of our biological window of opportunity. The window would soon slam closed. It looked out on Bloomingdale, which seemed an ideal place to have kids.

Should we? When we began rolling our gametic dice during our second winter in the house, Debbie was forty-two. I had recently turned forty-five. Kids would certainly rock our boat if we were lucky enough to have them. We'd have to stay put, at least for a while. With a house reclamation project well under way, staying put was our general intention. Still, it was nice knowing that if things got too tough, we could cut our losses and run. With kids, that wouldn't be so easy. Suddenly we'd find ourselves much more invested in home and community. Kids, too, would cost money, heaps of it, and demand of us a level of commitment that, just to think of it, left us breathless. The whole package frightened us. In the end, though, we summoned the courage.

Could we? That was another matter. Around the time we were getting launched, *Newsweek* magazine ran a feature about people in their forties struggling to have children. The talk of aging eggs and sluggish sperm and possible birth defects was enough to scare off the faint of heart. But Debbie and I tend to bone up on an idea, tally up the risks, and, if they seem reasonable, dive in headfirst. We were healthy, we ate well, and we'd taken good care of our equipment. Plus, although our parents had long since given up on our reproductive prospects, a few staunch friends, happy parents all, continued to drop hints.

Years later, I smile and wonder how much of a part, if any, was played by free will. Biologists such as Richard Dawkins make a persuasive case that we humans, who fancy ourselves so intelligent and sophisticated, are, like all living things, simply vehicles for delivering genes. In a sort of relay race, we pluck genes from the chromosomes of one generation, wrap them in new packages, and hand them on to the next. Of course, this is shorthand for a process that begins with youthful flirtation and Valentine's Day cards and runs in the end to the writing of sonnets, perfume, aftershave, singing, dancing, accomplishment of all sorts, intimate relations, babies, parenting, and the writing of memoirs.

There was no denying that our nest-building behavior had reproductive roots. Now those roots were sprouting aboveground. Where would the sprouting lead? There was only one way to find out.

As projects go, the attempt to conceive children is a good deal less strenuous than propping up sagging floors or rewiring a house, and it certainly proved more fun. There were moonlit walks and romantic dinners for two. There were deep looks into each other's eyes and long talks about hopes and fears. For us, though, the great breakthrough in fertility came during a monthlong holiday in Australia. There, welcomed by loving friends and immersed in daily adventure, we finally struck gold. I feel certain the lucky development came in a lonely corner of the state of Victoria, at a campsite beside the cold, rushing Suggan Buggan River. My gut told me, "This is it."

Debbie returned home carrying a backpack, a suitcase, a piece of carry-on luggage, and, we were soon to learn, a fetus. A home pregnancy test confirmed what Debbie suspected. She was on her way to the hospital for an official assessment when terrible cramps gripped her. These gave way to spasms and spasms to bleeding. It was a miscarriage, hard on both of us but especially on Debbie.

In the end, though, tragedy served a positive purpose. It gave us new resolve, taking whatever reservations we had about the direction we were heading in and throwing them out the window. We would give this our all.

My journal describes the second chapter.

The biggest news here is that Deb went to the doctor last Monday and got to hear the heartbeat of the 8-week-old fetus. All seemed to be going splendidly with this second pregnancy. Then the worst happened. An ultrasound exam attended by both of us on Thursday [Debbie could hardly contain her excitement and wanted to share it with me] yielded only blank expressions from the technician. She examined the fetus again and again without comment, and only when Deb's doctor appeared and blurted out the death sentence did we understand. . . . It all happened so fast. One moment we were counting on parenthood, and the next we were mourning the loss of a second pregnancy and wondering whether we'd ever succeed.

Weeks passed before we could bring ourselves to try again. Now Debbie threw herself whole hog into her biology, tracking the ups and downs of her core temperature as a means to predicting ovulation. She studied books, hounded her gynecologist and nurse-midwives with questions, and generally did everything she could to make our third time a charm. We'd decided against high-tech efforts at conception. This was going to work the old-fashioned way or not at all. We had friends who had lived rich, full lives without children. We could do the same.

On Friday, the 17th of January, 2003, I joined Debbie at the hospital for her next ultrasound. She was seven weeks pregnant and, after her recent experiences, feeling gloomy. Nothing could have prepared me for the moment when the technician, zeroing in on an amorphous blob of protoplasm in my wife's uterus, switched on the audio. Holy smokes! The machine amplified the percussion of a beating heart, one that did not exist seven weeks and one day ago. Now, having been set in motion by the union of an egg and a sperm, it commenced its lively pace of 152 beats per minute.

I was speechless. Later in my journal, I could only babble, "yes, yes, yes, hooray, marvelous, amazing, beautiful, love, love, love" and enthuse about "all the tributaries of my life pouring into half that heartbeat's chromosomes, and another fan of rivers flowing in through Debbie." The temperature that night fell to eight below zero. I didn't feel the cold.

In March, we received staggering news. Debbie and I had driven to Plattsburgh and crossed Lake Champlain on a ferry. In Burlington, Vermont, a doctor named David Jones had skewered Debbie's plump belly with an oversized syringe. It looked like a pump you might use to inflate a basketball. Watching simultaneously on an ultrasound machine, Dr. Jones steered the fearsome spike into the placenta that connected Debbie to our proto-child. The idea was to suck up a few bits of placental protrusions called chorionic villi. Debbie was brave. I winced but looked on, fascinated, as tiny bits of pink tissue swirled into the syringe.

The placenta is part of the fetus, not the mother, so by scrutinizing its chromosomes, someone schooled in cytogenetics can determine whether they are properly formed or not and whether they appear in the correct number, which is forty-six. Debbie and I, long in the tooth relative to friends who were bearing children in their twenties and early thirties, ran an elevated risk of difficulties. At the mild end, the test might reveal an abnormal triad, rather than a pair, of chromosome 21. This condition is known as trisomy 21, or Down syndrome. At the gruesome end, three of chromosome 18 might turn up, indicating a severe, developmentally hopeless condition called trisomy 18, or Edward's syndrome. Babies born with trisomy 18 cannot long survive, and about half die within two days of birth. The better-known amniocentesis reveals the same information as chorionic villus sampling (CVS) and a bit more, but it does so nearly two months further along in the pregnancy, when grim news is less pleasant to deal with.

The test would also tell one more thing. Unlike snapping turtles, which become male or female depending on the temperature at which each egg develops, we humans have chromosomes that spell out a child's gender. Two X-shaped versions of chromosome 23 deliver a girl. An X and a Y yield a boy. Which did I want? Which did Debbie? Neither of us gave a hoot. All we wanted was a child who was healthy.

One terrifying day, the gynecologist's office called with the news. The chromosomes looked perfect. Barring a last-minute crisis, we were going to be the parents of a boy.

In short order, the cat was out of the bag. Suddenly our frequent visits to the ob-gyn office could be carried out openly, and we began to broadcast the news. Our parents were shocked but delighted. The same held for siblings. Friends and neighbors either erupted in gladness or looked at us as if we'd lost our minds. Both reactions made sense to us. Adding a baby to our lives was something to cheer about, but at the same time, we were in our forties and somewhat set in our ways, and not all the adjustments would be easy.

I found myself worrying at times about baby care, especially because, as the work-at-home spouse, I was going to be doing a great deal of it. What did I know about caring for infants? Not a blasted thing. Truth is, on those rare occasions when someone thrust a little one in my arms, it usually looked up into my mustache and started to scream. I'd never fed a baby from a bottle, changed a diaper, or rocked a baby to sleep. But I countered my anxieties with thoughts of the orphaned songbirds, owls, raccoons, opossums, squirrels, and skunks I'd raised. Surely if I could foster a great-horned owl to adulthood with a mix of loving care and chopped-up, defrosted lab rats, and if I could form tender bonds with skunks, I could muddle my way through the early stages of fatherhood.

The test results came in March, but it wasn't until September that our son was born. During the intervening months we named him Edward IV, although with a vow that we'd always call him Ned. I grew up in a family with three Eds, and because none of us had a consistent nickname, things could get confusing. We loved "Ned," and soon we were cooing his name to him through amniotic fluid and Debbie's abdominal muscles and maternity clothing. I sang to him often and at close range. Perhaps Ned would be sick of my voice by the time he popped out, but then again, perhaps he'd recognize it and feel comforted. That was the theoretical basis on which I warbled.

Debbie had all the usual discomforts of pregnancy, including morning sickness (a polite name for wanting to retch), back pain, and a sense that her body was inflating at an alarming rate. Perhaps her biggest excitement during the ripening period, aside from the adventure going on inside her, came the day I marched off with a friend on a hike into the nearby McKenzie Mountain Wilderness. It was for a magazine story I'd be working on, and we'd be gone all day, navigating through a vast, wild forest with map and compass. Debbie was home alone, or as alone as one can be with a seven-month-old fetus in one's belly, when a black bear showed up outside the kitchen door.

We had not let occasional visits from bears ruffle our equanimity until this point. After all, they were wild animals and easily frightened, and no Adirondack bear that we knew of had ever attacked a human. Yet things would soon be different. A year from now we'd have a crawling baby wiggling around, and a year from then a succulent toddler. Debbie had had gory, unsettling looks at black bears gorging on the bloody carcasses of whitetail deer fawns when she worked as a National Park ranger in the Smoky Mountains in 1997. Both of us also knew the story of a young child at a Catskill Mountain resort who had been plucked from a stroller by a bear. The incident, which was recent history, proved fatal to both parties.

Debbie stepped out the door and yelled, "Shoo!" The bear bolted. It had been scarfing sunflower seeds from our bird feeder. But within minutes it was back. This time Debbie resorted to an old standby of country people who want to send a bear away in a hurry: she rummaged in a kitchen cabinet, pulled out a saucepan and a metal spoon, and bravely marched outside, banging.

The bear looked up, thought about things, and ambled into the woods.

Then it was back again. Now the expectant mother was nervous. Past encounters with bears, if they'd come to pots and pans, had kept the big, hairy carnivores away for weeks or months. This animal was reappearing inside an hour. Again, Debbie rapped the saucepan. Then she blew a police whistle and blew it again and again. The bear looked up. The bear stared. The bear went back to French-kissing the bird feeder. Not good.

After I staggered home on blistered feet, and after my parents arrived a few minutes later for the weekend, the bear came again. Arrival number four was dramatic and spooky. Materializing out of a leafy background like King Kong, the animal stood on hind paws, grasped a feeder gently between its forepaws, and delicately lapped out the contents. No matter how much clamor we made, it refused to leave.

That decided it. We would do what we should have done from the start: put the bird feeders away at the end of winter when bears come out of hibernation and not put birdseed out again until the first big deep freeze of November.

The following night, a bear demolished a compost bin we'd just built. A few swats of the animal's big paws, and the thing was a ruin. At about this time, I had to be away for two nights. Debbie manned the fort alone. She leaned a set of old wooden doors outside the screen door leading to the porch, aiming to make it harder for an animal to break in. She also had me give her a lesson in loading an old Winchester deer rifle recently given to me by my Uncle Bud. Debbie's father had taken her target shooting when she was a teenager, so she knew her way around guns. Her plan was not to kill or wound, but to squeeze off warning shots if a bear got frisky.

While Debbie wrestled with anxiety over bears, I grappled with a terror of my own. A journal entry I scribbled a few weeks before the big day gives a glimpse: "I have the feeling of approaching a great divide, one I'll cross, leaving the familiar world in which I've spent nearly forty-seven years and stepping forward, irrevocably, with no chance of turning back, into a new world. I'll be a father, and I can no more imagine what that will be like as I can imagine myself a fish."

It was a long, hot summer, at least by northern Adirondack standards. Frosts tapered off by the end of June and didn't start icing the landscape again until the second half of August. The occasional blazing day reached ninety degrees Fahrenheit. That would have felt cool during one of our summers in Mississippi, but in the Adirondacks, where we enjoy strings of summer days peaking in the seventies, a fifteen-degree spike brings on torpor. This was especially true for Debbie. She was hauling around a heavy and increasingly active cargo.

Debbie was uncomfortable and nervous. The nerves came after an ultrasound technician commented that fetal Ned at nineteen weeks had a twenty-one-week–sized head. Hat sizes of all the Edward Kanzes before him—my grandfather, my father the Junior, me the Third—run to extra-extra large. It was enough to make a prospective mother shudder.

The action began on a Wednesday night in September. As barred owls commenced hooting in the woods behind the house and kept up the ruckus all night, contractions started an hour before midnight. They came every ten minutes until 3:30 in the morning, making sleep for either of us impossible. At 3:30, the pace picked up. Now Debbie's abdominal muscles convulsed every five minutes, and the contractions grew longer, each lasting about a minute. Our bags were packed. I hustled them out to the car. I felt simultaneously elated beyond all reason and scared out of my wits.

Perhaps packing the car served as a kind of trigger. The contractions ceased. What's an expectant mother to do? We did what Kathy Kiernan, our excellent nurse-midwife, advised: we walked. For two hours we strolled up and down the road, soaking up morning sunshine and through bloodshot eyes looking at the mountains and the forests. It was all very dreamlike. Of course it was. We'd snatched only a few scattered minutes of sleep.

We unpacked the car, and contractions started again. Now they came every fifteen minutes. Then thirty. We were retreating, not advancing. Debbie felt discouraged. I didn't know what to feel. In the absence of clarity my emotions ran the spectrum from red to violet and back again.

Thursday evening, almost twenty-four hours after the first wave, a second of hard contractions began. They spaced themselves ten minutes apart until 2:30 in the morning, after which Ned kicked into a higher gear and the interval dropped to five. Had a photo of Debbie and me been taken at the time, it would have shown two people as white as boiled potatoes, swirling in a stew of high anxiety and happy anticipation.

At 3:30, we drove to the hospital. During the trip, my mind ran in circles around the idea that two people would enter the hospital and a couple of days later three people would come out. The only turn of phrase that seemed to do justice to my outlook at the time is that old standby of my sixties childhood, "It blew my mind."

Debbie's "water had broken," we were told. This meant the amniotic sac had disgorged its soup, and one way or another, a baby would be coming soon. We were also told about Debbie's cervix. As an expectant woman approaches delivery, this part of her internal anatomy begins to open up in order to let the baby slide out. Presiding midwives or physicians call out the number in centimeters, and as it grows, the hour of reckoning comes near. Debbie's number at the time of arrival was zero.

Poor Debbie was suffering considerable pain, and, as arranged in advance, an acupuncturist was called in at 6:30 in the morning, just as the sun in the sky was brightening. Sterile envelopes were torn open, and delicate stainless steel needles pierced skin. The pain eased.

At 8:00 a.m., we received good news. Debbie was dilating. "Three centimeters," we were told. That's not quite an inch and a quarter. While a significant number, it wasn't close to sufficient to allow the passage of an extra-extra-large head.

Things were proceeding, slowly. The nurse-midwife advised a drug called Pitocin. At noon, Debbie gave the word that she was ready for it. Pitocin would provoke faster and deeper contractions. Quickly it had the desired effect. Contractions sped up to every two minutes.

By this point, the jittery prospective father had pushed all doubts aside and gotten fully engaged. I hovered over my precious mama-to-be like a bodyguard, making sure she got what she needed, and what she needed now was pain relief to supplement the needles.

For four hours powerful contractions came relentlessly. Each would wake Debbie up, and then, under the combined effects of pain medicine and two nights without sleep, she would slumber. Long since, she'd been hooked up to a fetal monitor that kept watch on Ned's heartbeat. It looked good, but I could see concern growing on Kathy's face and wasn't surprised when Debbie's ob-gyn, Denise Ferrando, turned up, looking pensive. If I'd been a cartoonist at work in the room, I'd have drawn a circle over the doctor's head. Inside would have been the words "Caesarean section" and a question mark.

"Push!" ordered Kathy. "Push!" harmonized Dr. Denise. Somehow Debbie reached down into the depths of her being and summoned the energy. She was fully awake now. She pushed and she pushed. Her courage and determination were sights to behold. Then came history. Kathy, busily engaged at the end of the bed, cried out, "I see hair." I let go of Debbie's hand and hurried to look. It was the top of Ned's head! A few more shuddering, Herculean shoves and Kathy was tenderly pushing me into position, as I'd asked her to.

Slimy and wet and warm and wriggling and gorgeous, a very red Ned slid into my welcoming hands at 5:08 p.m. Debbie and I were parents.

Let me rewrite that last sentence. Debbie and I were parents!

From that moment on, events and hours sped by in a blur. But both Debbie and I remember one happening with crystal clarity: how one of us was cradling baby Ned at first light the following morning, and as we gazed out the window of the room where he was born, a window that looks out on a beautiful Adirondack lake, a bald eagle sailed by, its back looking just as black as the night that had ended and its head and tail as brilliantly white as January snow. We're not believers in omens, but if this was one, it seemed to portend good things for the precious little parcel we held in our hands.

Let me not give the impression that the onset of parenthood was all lovey-dovey bliss. No sooner had Ned arrived and Debbie, looking like a prizefighter who had just gone twelve rounds, taken her first sip of champagne than she fixed me straight in the eye. There was steel in her voice. "Ned's going to be an only child," she said.

Debbie's forty-two hours of on-and-off labor, culminating in a grueling home stretch even acupuncture couldn't ameliorate, were trying, but she and I knew we were, on the whole, immensely fortunate. My grandfather's parents, Elmer and Jenny Lawton Brownell, had had twelve children. There were six girls and six boys. One after another of the girls died in childhood until the last was gone. No one with a faint heart should step into the waters of human reproduction. My younger sister, Nora, named for her great-great-grandmother Elnora, carried twins to nineteen weeks. Three months after Ned's birth, Nora went into premature labor and delivered two dead but very human fetuses. Anne Elizabeth and Paul Joseph hadn't even stepped onto the stage when an infection attributed to an amniocentesis brought down the curtain. One day Nora and her husband woke up to filling their house with twins, and the next they were shopping for a cemetery plot.

After a few months of healing and breast-feeding and chapped nipples and regaining lost form, Debbie surprised me. She announced she was ready to do it all over again. She loved her baby and loved her new life. I loved them, too. In fact, if I remember any particular sensation from Ned's first year, it's of feeling I'd become a sort of fire hydrant. My valve had been wrenched open, and now all I could do was gush and gush and gush love, love, and more love. Suddenly I loved everything: my life, Debbie's, Ned's, our families, our friends, the birds, the trees. Wherever I gazed I saw radiance. Hormones? Genetic programming? Both? Neither? I didn't care. I held on and savored the ride.

And so, it wasn't long before history was repeating itself and we were making gynecologist visits together, driving over to Vermont so chorionic villi could be spirited out through an oversized needle, and bracing ourselves for a sea change. This time the chromosomes looked perfect, just as they had the first time, but with one critical difference. Instead of an X and a Y, there were two Xs. We were going to have a girl. In utero, we named her Tasman Victoria: Tasman for the Tasman Sea lying between Australia and New Zealand and Victoria for the Australian state that is home to dear and remarkable friends who helped inspire our new lives.

Tassie's birth played out the opposite of Ned's. Maybe it had something to do with her average-sized head. Late one evening, contractions started, and we called a babysitter who would stay overnight with our twenty-one-month-old. At the hospital it was determined that Debbie's water had not broken, and she was urged to hop into a warm tub. In no time nurse-midwife Kim Schoch arrived, probed Debbie, and beamed. There was no talk this time of centimeters. "Would you like to go over to the bed and have a baby?" she asked. Debbie beamed. I nearly fainted. I was expecting things to proceed slowly. Suddenly I seemed minutes or seconds away from becoming a double Dad.

Debbie pushed a few times, the cry of "hair" went out, and seconds later Tassie slid out into my hands. In no time I was squeezing scissors and crunching through the fibrous walls of her umbilicus. Debbie was forty-five and I was forty-eight. Thanks to family, friends, a marvelous midwife, a skilled and caring physician, first-rate nurses, and a Tasman Sea full of good luck, we'd gambled again and come up winners.

After Ned's birth there had been hard days and nights of interrupted sleep, not enough sleep, and generally overwhelming demands on our time and energy. The same held true again. Debbie had blue spells, as is common after the hard and often painful or nauseating work of carrying and birthing. I had my rough patches, too, and tended to vent my feelings in the form of black humor, much of it dwelling on bodily fluids, of which human babies are prodigious producers. Yet we soldiered on. In little time we were a happy family of four that could not imagine life any other way.

Mornings in those days I sometimes woke up with a sense of disbelief, a stark sense of life's overwhelming peculiarity. One day you're depressed, feeling like nothing good remains, and the next you're holding a healthy baby, and it's yours. One day you're on top of the world, ready to plunge joyously into the next day, month, and year, and the next, your doctor tells you have thirty days to live, or, as happened to a friend and neighbor of ours at about this time, a pickup truck creams your fragile, fuel-efficient sedan, and instead of thirty days, you've got thirty seconds as your lifeblood pours onto the asphalt. Then again, your literary agent may call, telling you a publisher wants your novel and is offering a six-figure advance, or, as happened to me recently, the economy nosedives and a hard-earned contract offer for a novel you've labored on for years goes up in recessionary smoke. Suddenly I felt, amid all my bounty, that it's a mad, mad world, and each of us is stuck in it for beautiful better and for liver-spotted worst.

I had other thoughts, too. At about this time I turned to my journal and wrote (I make only a few minor editorial changes): "Everyone has a dream life. By 'dream life' I mean not a life locked within the unconscious or semiconscious mind, but a life one dreams of in moments of supreme clarity, when all the worries and distractions of life evaporate like a fog, if only briefly, and one sees the place, the companions, the lover, the adventures of his deepest longings. Some of us manage to achieve this life, or at least a part of it, with a generous windfall of luck combined with hard work, discipline, dogged persistence in the face of setbacks, and the kindness of relations, friends, and strangers bringing about the happy result."

I was living a dream, albeit one with a collapsing house and pestilential insects. It was mine, and I had a healthy, beautiful family with which to share it. But was it real? Could it last?

BIOLOGICAL SURVEY RECORDS:

Homo sapiens   Human being
5/6/00: filling out this card
3/26/03: breeding activity—Debbie is 17 weeks pregnant! Chorionic villi sampling at UVM shows good-looking chromosomes—one is a Y

Ursus americanus   Black bear
6/29/00: ripped tree swallow box [a birdhouse] off utility pole—young birds, about to fledge, miraculously escape, seen with parents next morning, perched on wire near box

5

The Lawn

As naturalists and polymaths (Jacks of all trades, masters of none, as the saying goes), Debbie and I were interested in just about every aspect of our new home. Yet "just about every" means what it says. One thing that failed to hold interest was the lawn. After the snow melted that first year we found two or three acres of it: two or three acres waiting to be barbered by whichever of us was game to pilot the old but serviceable John Deere lawn tractor we found in the shed; two or three acres accustomed to tender loving care and regular applications, important in this region of wickedly acid soils, of lime.

For years, our place was known as "the Williams Camp" after the family that originally owned it. The property was famed, at least locally, for its expansive swath of neatly cropped grass and a lawn jockey that presided over it. The iron man had been given away to an admiring plumber shortly before our arrival, but the turf remained in all its regimented glory. The civilized part of the property had been managed like a golf course. We wanted a nature preserve. Therein loomed conflict.

The creation of a compost heap was linked in our minds to the idea that we would become productive vegetable gardeners. In our naiveté, little did we know how cold the place was, and how growing tomatoes here would not be like growing tomatoes almost anywhere else. But our resolve was steely. We'd acquire a rototiller and start turning our fairway into a patchwork of garden plots and weedy meadow. What we didn't till—the majority—we'd let go feral.

Taking a lawn and turning it into something more beautiful and practical can provoke neighbors to neurosis. A friend of ours in Mississippi, Don McKee, an avid birdwatcher, decided he'd rather have a wild meadow to please the eye and feed the birds than an expanse of cut grass. When he decided to let a portion of his yard bordering a wetland grow up to its natural height, all hell broke loose. The neighbors grew angry. They feared plummeting property values and a proliferation of venomous reptiles—cottonmouths, diamondback rattlesnakes, pigmy rattlers, and coral snakes. In the end, they sued.

Don supplied the judge and town officials with published materials explaining the science and aesthetics that inspired his project. In the middle of the fracas, chest pains sent Don to the hospital. Soon he was having triple coronary bypass surgery. But his recovery proceeded without a hitch, and soon Don was back at work on his defense. Tom Mann, a herpetologist at the Mississippi Museum of Natural Science, endorsed Don's efforts and scoffed at the idea of snakes running riot. Mann said that neighbors leaving out cat food probably encouraged snakes (by attracting rodents) far more than Don's unmown lawn. Don himself pointed out that the local high school's curriculum called for students to let plots of land in their yards go wild then record the rise in biodiversity. In the end, the judge tossed out the case and warned the man who filed the suit never to raise the issue again.

Our setting was wilder than Don's, and we anticipated little trouble. Still, we heard plenty of comments that were less than flattering, along the lines of "Do you need to borrow a lawn mower?" Neighbors told us that the Ohio man who sold us the place through a local realtor had no interest in meeting us when he came back to visit. He had loved his lawn, and we were ruining it.

The most interesting responses came from our late neighbor Bob LaPlante, a kindly man with a fatherly concern for our well-being. Bob had a deathly fear of snakes. I assured him that no rattlesnakes or copperheads lived within an hour's drive. He countered with two stories. One involved a loud hissing sound that couldn't be ignored one summer at his camp next to our place. Bob's father knew what to do. He brought out warm milk and poured it in a bowl. Out from under a pile of odds and ends slithered a rattlesnake, and Bob's father shot it dead.

The other tale is set in the woods behind our house. Bob was out walking one day when he came upon a giant snake about eight feet long. It was jet black with an orange diamond on its forehead—a serpent, I should add, unknown to science. The snake shook its tail. The tail rustled the leaf litter. From all directions wriggled baby snakes. One by one they disappeared into the mouth of the mama.

Both stories—a snake drawn out of hiding by milk and a mother snake swallowing babies to protect them—spring straight out of folklore. Yet years of working in parks and hearing far-fetched stories from people about wild animals, especially ones they fear, has taught me opposing lessons. On one hand, you can't believe much of what you hear. On the other, every story, no matter how crazy it may sound at first hearing, tends to rest in a grain of truth. We have no snake that hisses hereabouts, at least as far as anyone can tell. The nearest hissing hognosed snakes are at least one hundred miles away, and the nearest hissing pine snakes inhabit the New Jersey Pine Barrens. Although no snake is known to provide safe haven to young inside its own mouth, still, who knows?

Truth is, Bob worried for us. After our kids came along, he feared for their well-being, too. His own children had grown up and moved away. He became a sort of kindly uncle to ours, and we welcomed the attention. Still, we stuck to our plan. The tractor rested. The grass grew. Garter snakes became so numerous in the yard that on a warm day in spring, summer, or early fall, you could hardly walk a dozen feet without one slithering across your path.

Our kind of place.

As lawn metamorphosed into meadow, I pondered the reasons it had been created in the first place. We don't know when our land was first cleared, but it was sometime before 1922, the year the house was built. Our neighbor Sandy Hayes told us his grandfather had owned the property and used it as summer pasture for dairy cows.

Then came the Williams family, from Warren, Ohio. They bought the old Hayes pasture, had the camp built by Sandy's uncle, and, to keep the grass short, replaced the cows with a lawn mower. Better, they reckoned, to keep the place clear, to keep the wild woods at bay, than to stop mowing and let the trees march back and monopolize all the sunshine. Al Williams was an avid golfer, judging by a trophy we found in the house with his name on it. Perhaps he also wanted lawn, and lots of it, so he could practice his driving and putting and sit on the porch with his afternoon martini and gaze out on what looked like a nine-hole course. I'm guessing about the martini, but it's an educated guess. When we bought the house, it came furnished with a rolling wet bar, lots of cocktail glasses, and an astounding number of empty liquor bottles in the woods behind the shed.

In their desire to preside over a country club, Al Williams and his family typified the national temper. Nature is all right, but only up to a point. Around one's domicile, it must be beaten back and put in its place. A lawn is the usual solution.

First alone or with Debbie, and later with crawling, toddling, and walking children, I grew to appreciate the lawn-maturing-into-meadow as a field for exploration. As our experiment matured, we quickly set about cataloguing the plants.

Among the first to catch our attention were the ferns. I went crawling through a tangle of vegetation at the south end of the porch one day, seeking a song sparrow's nest, but found instead something equally interesting. It was a tall, lacy fern, its leaflets, called pinnae, as intricate as the finest embroidery. When I looked with a magnifying glass, the spore-bearing organs on the undersides proved crescent-shaped. Ah, lady fern!

There were others, too. The weirdest was an ugly gnome of a thing, barely recognizable as a fern, that I found growing on a slope where we were planting apple trees. It was a cut-leaved grape fern. Grape ferns bear grape-like knobs on their distinctive fertile fronds. The entire plant is small, covering only a few square inches that hunker close to the ground. The fern was thriving, I suspect, not in spite of the lawn but because of it. I feared for its future now that we'd stopped cutting the grass.

What we stood to gain from retiring the lawn tractor, or at least relegating it to a quick clip job every other year, was a reduction of work and noise and fossil fuel consumption, with a corresponding increase in wildflowers and wildlife. So it has proven. Debbie's favorites are the hawkweeds. By the middle of June every year a non-native species, the orange hawkweed (*Hieracium aurantiacum*), turns our ex-lawn into a sea of luminous tangerine. We didn't plant the hawkweeds. Their seeds blew in, perhaps decades ago, as biological immigrants. With the mower idle in the shed, up they sprang.

If I have a favorite plant that's flourished under the new regime, it's narrow-leaved gentian (*Gentiana linearis*). This is a peculiar native flower. Its blossoms, which appear in the heat of summer, never open but remain in a bud-like state until they ripen their seed and shed their petals. They and similar species are called "bottled gentians" because the flowers stay bottled up.

If there's a time of year when our former lawn attains a state of utter exaltation, it's autumn. This is the season when goldenrods, which have been rising unobtrusively all summer, suddenly flood the landscape with reflected sunshine. They're vexing to identify. In the early years, the only species I named on my own, with confidence, was the rough-stemmed (*Solidago rugosa*). But surely there were others. Depending on which botanist you consult, the Northeast is home to scores of golden-rods—or more than a hundred.

A recent visit by botanist friends Carol Gracie and Scott Mori, both of the New York Botanical Garden, helped sort them out. With the kids leading the hunt, Carol and Scott found four different goldenrods. None of us could be sure exactly what species we were looking at, so we uprooted one of each as herbarium specimens. Carol and Scott brought the collection to an expert colleague, David Weier, at the Garden. Weier generously scrutinized the plants and named them for us: rough-stemmed goldenrod, *Solidago rugosa*, the one I'd managed to figure out on my own; Canada goldenrod, *S. canadensis*, a common northeastern species; dusty goldenrod, *Solidago puberula*, which I'd never heard of even though we had it growing under our noses; and common flat-topped goldenrod, *Euthamia graminifolia*. It's all right to have goldenrods of any kind growing under one's nose because these are insect-pollinated plants. They produce relatively small amounts of heavy, sticky pollen adapted not to fly through the air with the greatest of ease but to stick to visiting insects.

With the goldenrods in autumn come New England asters, tall and stately and elegantly garnished with yellow-centered purple pinwheels. And with these come the year's last great rush of birds and insects. Goldfinches pick apart thistles and feed the seeds to their young. Overhead in skies of brilliant cobalt, hawks float dreamily southward, making the smaller birds below them nervous. Red-tailed bumblebees bustle among the goldenrods, gathering nectar and pollen, and on the billowing white blossoms of the sixty hydrangea bushes that border the driveway, monarch butterflies flutter down like autumn leaves.

Common milkweeds find congenial habitat in the old lawn, and as our kids grow, Ned and Tassie find more and more interest in them. First it was just the plants themselves—fleshy stalks that bleed a sticky milklike fluid if bruised, extravagant flower clusters suggesting purple snowballs, warty seedpods that swell and swell. Then the kids became caterpillar hunters. Once they fixed the image of monarch larvae in their minds, they could take almost any plant, scrutinize it up close (they don't need reading glasses like their middle-aged parents), and find even the tiniest caterpillars where none was first apparent.

Lately, though, it's the pods that supply the fun. The kids wait impatiently for weeks until the first bursts open on its own, spilling its seeds into the wind. Then it's a free-for-all of opening and teasing apart and tossing into the breeze. They love the fact that they're milkweed helpers, sending the chestnut-colored seeds with their silken airfoils off to conquer the world.

As the flora has diversified and made the grassy patch surrounding the house more interesting, the fauna has charged in exciting new directions, too. We document discoveries as we make them. One year on the twenty-sixth of September, in the evening, moose tracks were discovered in sand along our road by our biologist neighbor, Daun Dahlen. We all tramped down to see them. The tracks were made by a hoof cloven like a deer's, but this deer was the size of a horse. The moose had walked the road's edge, clumped across the wooden deck of the bridge over the Saranac, and vanished into the swampy patch of floodplain we own on the far side.

A day earlier, our friend and neighbor Diana Fortune had seen a moose, a bull, near her house at five in the afternoon. It may have been the same animal. Diana had been driving home, and the first thing she thought to do, before turning into her driveway and getting out of the car, was relay the details to us by cell phone. Unfortunately, we were out of town. Two bull moose had been killed locally within the last ten days—one on the Gabriels Road near the Bloomingdale Bog, a few miles from our place, the other a dozen or so miles away near Lake Placid. For weeks after we examined the tracks, we remained hopeful that the moose would saunter out of the swamp and back into view. Alas, it never did.

Moose sightings are a big deal here, unlike in Maine and New Hampshire, where the animal is again common. The last Adirondack moose was killed around the time of the Civil War. Then, in the second half of the twentieth century, populations to the North in Canada and to the east in New England rebounded, and moose began to trickle back. The first clear indications that they were breeding again in the Adirondacks came in the 1980s. Today, their numbers are slowly rising. State wildlife biologists estimate the current number in the park to be about 600 animals. That's not much of a population spread out over 6 million acres. But every year, more moose are seen, more are struck by cars, and, despite the carnage, more are born and survive to adulthood. If global warming doesn't pump up the numbers of the trio of parasites—a brain worm, a liver fluke, and a tick—that keep moose out of the South, we may find them a common sight by the end of another decade.

Near the opposite end of the mammalian size gradient, we have confirmed the presence in the yard of the hairy-tailed mole. First we saw their tunnels, which appear as linear bulges underfoot, and also openings where moles popped out, had a quick look around, and left behind a few telltale spoonfuls of dirt. Then one day in July I found a corpse in the garden. It had beautiful slate gray fur, dense and sleek, and oversized front feet, grotesquely splayed. The feet indicated that the animal was a mole rather than a shrew.

But what kind of mole? Two species are known to inhabit our piece of the planet. The star-nosed has a nose that lives up to its name, the points of the star being fleshy appendages that help the burrowing animal locate worms and other prey in the soil. The other is the hairy-tail. It has a bluntly pointed snout, like the better-known eastern mole that breathes terror into the hearts of gardeners to the South. Unlike the eastern mole's, its tail is thickly furred. Ours had a woolly tail. In our cold climate, it's hard to imagine a mole having any other kind.

What killed the mole? It might have been a house cat. Neighbors' felines prowl our property, and there's little to be done about it but shout and chase. I enjoy a purring puss on my lap as much as the next person, but as a naturalist and lover of wild creatures, I'm appalled by the estimated billions of wild birds each year pussycats kill, often merely for sport. Of course, cats slaughter moles, shrews, mice, garter snakes, frogs, toads, and plenty more, too. Still, cats were only suspects in this case. The mole might have been killed by any one on a long list of local predators, one that perhaps was frightened away after making its strike. Even old age could tell the story—old, for a mole, being something on the order of four or five years.

While gardeners in suburban Westchester County, where I grew up, often go to extreme and violent lengths to eradicate moles, their notions of them as incorrigible destroyers of bulbs and roots are in clear conflict with the facts. Moles, like shrews, are insectivores. They have mouths crowded with pointy teeth far better adapted for ripping into the flesh of tasty invertebrates than for gnawing anyone's favorite tubers. In the case of our hairy-tailed moles, scientists report a diet consisting almost entirely of earthworms, caterpillars of various sorts, insect pupae, adult insects, snails (including slugs), centipedes, millipedes, and sow bugs.

We're delighted to have hairy-tailed moles in our yard, aerating the soil, providing runways for shrews and voles and mice, and doing their bit to keep various insect populations in line. Once I had the chance to tell one so. I was standing near our shed when the ground began to quiver in front of me. Instantly my attention was fixed on the spot, and within a second or two, out of the ground erupted a mole with a fat hairy tail. I was tempted to reach down and grab it, but moles can inflict nasty bites when invited to. Instead I offered a warm "How do you do?" and watched, spellbound, as the mole squinted, sniffed the air, appeared to detect a scent it found offensive (undoubtedly mine), and turned tail— well-furred, of course—and plunged back down its hole.

Just as the underworld beneath our lawn throbs with the torrid lives of hairy things, so does the air above it. At night we see bats darting to and fro in the moonlight. (At least, we did see plenty of bats until a plague called white-nose syndrome, first reported from the Adirondacks and now spreading across the nation, began decimating their numbers.) They're asserting their air rights to our riverside acres—damp, fecund acres that excel in generating insects.

We rejoice in our bats, on one hand, and on the other they vex us. Unlike birds, bats—at least the kind we have around here—are all but impossible to identify on the wing, which is generally the only way we see them. One can usually say a bat is small and brown, but often that's the beginning and end of it. We have a friend who owns a high-tech rig uniting a sensitive microphone with a laptop computer. The computer runs software that deciphers the sounds, well above the range of human hearing, that bats utter while navigating and feeding. With this tool in hand, our friend can identify the species his computer hears.

Until we succeed in luring him here for an evening of batting, we must be satisfied with a single record in our file. It pays tribute to a red bat that flapped over the lawn in broad daylight. We saw it on the third of November during our first full year here.

The red bat is migratory, beating its wings northward in spring and southbound in autumn at speeds up to forty miles per hour. During migration, it is somewhat day active, and because our other bats are generally drab and brown, it's one of the few species the untrained aficionado can name at a glance. The red bat I saw on this unusually balmy November day was a handsome orange-red. It caught my attention as it fluttered over the house like an oversized moth. I followed it with my eyes until it vanished over the tops of the firs at the south end of the lawn.

Of all the animals that appeared under, over, and on our unkempt lawn during the early years, the one that pleased me the most was that American icon, famed around the world but little appreciated at home: the striped skunk.

Skunks are victims of bad press and nasty rumors. People seem to think they are quick to turn tail and spray their horrendously malodorous musk, and in suburban areas where skunks have little choice but to coexist with schnauzers and manicured lawns, skunks are blamed for assaults on family pets and ripping up manicured lawns. The truth? I've raised baby skunks and found them to be sweet tempered and particularly fond of being petted and scratched behind the ears. They spray, I suspect, only as the last of last resorts, a fact I became convinced of as a child when our family dog cornered, but did not quite catch, one without consequence.

As for abusing lawns, skunks are guilty as charged. But look beneath the surface of the crime and you find a motive that puts the whole business in a fresh light. Skunks dig in the soil for grubs. Many of the grubs that skunks devour are great pests of lawns and gardens. When a skunk rearranges a lawn, it's actually providing pest control services. Rather than be angry, the homeowner might want to reflect on the fact that the skunk, unlike the professional exterminator, never sends a bill.

I chuckle at the date of our first clear evidence of skunks on our property because it coincided with us having dear friends visiting from Australia. Our guests were two women, Beris Caine and Peg MacLeod, both approaching eighty at the time. Beris had visited us in 1997 when we were living in Townsend, Tennessee, at the edge of the Great Smoky Mountains. She had treated us like royalty in her country, and within the limits of our modest means we wanted to do right by her in ours. What would she most like to see? She didn't have to think long: a skunk. Beris had grown up in Queensland reading the comic strip *Pogo*. Ever since, she'd wanted to make the acquaintance of a real-live Miss Mam'selle Hepzibah, the passionate French skunk invented by cartoonist Walt Kelly.

We hadn't seen a skunk in ages, so we asked around. It turned out that a private campground just off the highway was notorious for its skunks, and if we went there after dark, we'd be almost certain of seeing one. We went. We walked. We saw nothing. Eventually the maintenance man, charmed by Beris's accent and enthusiasm, offered to drive Beris, Debbie, and me around the campground until we found what we'd come looking for. We took him up on the offer. Around and around we went, but alas, the Tennessee skunks had taken the night off.

For five years we'd lived in our Bloomingdale house, and for five years sign of skunks on the property had eluded us. But in honor of Beris and Peg's visit, a very welcome smell floated on the air near our shed one September day. The following morning, we found a spot a hundred feet away with the same bouquet. Three days passed. Nothing. Then we stepped out the door one morning to find a patch of lawn well mangled. Hooray!

Another five years on, we still look forward to our first actual sighting. If I could script it, I'd pick a sunny day in June and a mother skunk, her tail elegantly aloft, padding across the open space in front of the porch with a half-dozen miniature skunks behind her, all following in a row. I witnessed such a tender scene once, and it stuck with me—a black-and-white vision of nature at its most endearing.

Having a cleared area around the house rather than forest provides all sorts of opportunities to see things. We had a bobcat turn up on two consecutive winter days, for example. In the woods, this beagle-sized wild feline with its trademark short (as if bobbed) tail is virtually invisible. Its speckled coat makes for supreme camouflage. Also, bobcats don't run around as much as foxes and coyotes do. They're ambush hunters. So between their cryptic coloration and their tendency to stay put much of the time, they're devilishly hard to get a look at. When you do see one, it's usually for a millisecond—just long enough to be tantalized. Then the cat dematerializes right before your eyes.

The first day the bobcat appeared, Debbie and the kids watched it from the kitchen window. They contacted me by intercom over in my writing studio. As soon as they were satisfied with their own looks, I tried creeping over for a glimpse. Debbie said the bobcat waited until I was almost within view, then bolted for the woods.

The following morning, the cat returned and gave us a show. It had come the first time to dine on sardines I'd put out to feed a weasel that was visiting our bird feeder. Putting out fresh sardines the following morning did the trick. Debbie was again looking out the kitchen window when the cat padded out the door of our woodshed, which is open at both ends. She shouted, and this time I was there in a flash. I watched with her as an animal I'd caught glimpses of in the past but never seen clearly padded right before our eyes. It stopped to sniff the ground where I'd spilled a bit of oil from the sardine tin, walked past the bird feeder where a sardine banquet awaited, circled the south end of the house, and made for the river. This put the bobcat on a diagonal course straight across our lawn.

Together, the kids, Debbie, and I huddled on the porch. We shivered quietly as the cat, which moved with confident grace, strode across our view, paw by tawny paw, leaving slight drag marks in the snow. It descended to the road, walked over the bridge, turned east, and walked the snowbound riverbank downstream until it disappeared around a bend. Those five minutes of bobcat watching provided us with a thrill we'll long remember. It's exciting to live in a place where one can look out a window and see such things. Admittedly, a bobcat can't compare in size or danger to a lion or leopard, but it's a fierce creature all the same. Studies of Adirondack bobcats show that they routinely slay deer—a sudden leap, a rip into the jugular, the deer's knees buckle, and the compact predator, as lethal to its prey as the saber-toothed tigers of the Pleistocene were to theirs, crouches down for a bloody mouthful.

Another favorite sighting on the lawn stands out in memory because it seemed so bizarre. A survey card dated March 29, 2003, tells the tale:

> D. and I took a walk this warm morning, with the night's strong gusting westerlies subsiding to a light, steady breeze, when a bird flew up from the lawn in front of the house and landed in the top of one of the balsam firs near the well.

The wing beats, sharp and scissorlike, were like none other we'd seen here. . . . They were exactly like the wing-strokes of meadowlarks. A meadowlark in a fir tree? Yes! The bird returned to the lawn, where we watched it for a good while, and where we still found it bug-hunting in early afternoon.

Meadowlarks are birds of sun-scorched prairies and big open fields. Finding one here in a balsam fir, an iconic tree of deep, dark northern forests, seemed about as likely as spying a kangaroo.

Affirmations that we were doing the right thing in parking the lawn tractor appeared almost daily. Eastern bluebirds came and lingered, the bright blue males wooing the females with songs throbbing with passion. Twice in a decade they lingered and raised young, the unkempt grass far more valuable to them in terms of insect production than the tidy lawn it replaced. Woodcock came, too. These weird birds, the offshoot of sandpiper forbears adapted for life in brushy forest glades, announce their arrival every spring with loud single-syllable sounds uttered right at dusk. *Peent*, they seem to say. If you creep close to them, you learn that each *peent* is followed by a giggle.

At dusk, at dawn, and on moonlit nights, the male woodcock utters his sounds, turning like a windup toy after each one. And then, when he feels ready, he leaps off the ground, traces ascending circles on whistling wings, and reaches a height where, if you have been following him, you may lose his dark speck in the sky. At about this time, he utters loud kissing sounds, followed by great showers of tinkling notes. As he kisses and tinkles, he falls. At about the time it seems certain he will strike the earth and be killed, he pulls out of the dive, lands back where he started, and begins the display all over again. If all is going according to plan, somewhere out there in the dark edges of the clearing, females watch. They're shopping around for worthy mates.

On more than one occasion, a session of woodcock watching has kept us out long enough to see the stars switch on one by one. The night sky in the Adirondacks astonishes those who visit here from cities and suburbs. We have relatively few sources of artificial light and air that tends to be clear, especially when it's cold. Look up, and the Milky Way lives up to its name, pouring a frothy whiteness of stars across the indigo heavens. There's rarely any trouble spying Ursa Major, the Great Bear, the star pattern known as the Big Dipper giving away the greater constellation in which it's embedded. Trace a line through the outer two stars of the bowl of the Dipper, heading up and out, and you soon come to the North Star.

Our open view to the North puts us in a good position to view the northern lights, or aurora borealis. When we take the trouble, we sometimes see them, a faint greenish glow along the horizon. On better nights, their ghostly fingers rise up toward the pole star. If you gaze at them for a while and let your eyes fully adjust to the darkness, you begin to notice what look like diaphanous veils, swishing and swirling. These are a sort of hologram created by charged particles from outer space, deflected by the earth's magnetism.

Once, the aurora staged a show that lit up half the night sky. It was at a time when solar particles were showering the earth at a far higher rate than usual. A friend called and barked an order over the phone. "The northern lights are absolutely amazing. Drop what you're doing and get outside—fast."

For years, Debbie had had to put up with my complaining that any aurora display we watched together could not match the fabulous show I enjoyed once at Middlebury College, in Vermont, in 1975 or thereabouts. That night, the diaphanous curtains were multicolored, and they danced like spectral figures. This was my first experience of the northern lights, and it was grand.

Still, the extravaganza we witnessed one cold night in 2002 or thereabouts was the aurora of a lifetime. Rather than just brightening the sky in the North, these lights reached all the way to the zenith, and they were not of the usual lemon-lime variety, but flaming orange and red. The sky was on fire! We stood gawking for an hour or more. It was past midnight when we went to bed, and even then, it was hard to go indoors, knowing that what we were seeing was exceedingly rare and its like might never appear in our lifetimes.

The profound blackness of the Adirondack sky during new moons helps us get great looks at meteors, too. One November, friends who live in New York City but own a camp down the road told us they were driving up to take in the Leonid meteor shower. Astronomers predicted it, they said, to be unusually dramatic, the best Leonid (named for the constellation Leo, the Lion) to be seen for a century or more. The kids hadn't arrived yet, so without having to think much about logistics, it was easy for Debbie and me to arrange a rendezvous on our front lawn for 4:30 in the morning.

At 4:15, we dragged ourselves out of bed, brewed a pot of coffee, and hauled insulated mugs, lightweight reclining chairs, and sleeping bags out the door. Debbie and I slipped into our chairs and our bags, leaned back, and trained our eyes on the glittering sky. The Leonids lived up to the hype. Meteors streaked across the sky. It was a fireworks show in slow motion, the shooting stars coming steadily but not so swiftly that you couldn't see all of them. Some of the meteors left green, glittering trails that lingered a second or two. Others flared suddenly like a camera flash, then went dark.

Twenty minutes after we started watching, voices came from the darkness. "Are you there?" It was our neighbors, Barry and Stefani. They had brought sleeping bags and foam pads, too, and soon our party of four was assembled. We drank in the staggering vastness of the universe in all its star-spangled glory, noted the occasional satellite creeping insect-like across the sky, and marveled at the fireballs. Meteors continued coming until the sky brightened and erased them.

Of course, the celestial circus hadn't really ended. It was still going on, only now it was hidden from view by a curtain of daylight. The thought pestered me all day. What if among that space junk there was a meteor the size of the moon? It could pulverize all of the northeastern United States in a single blind and meaningless act. Or it might do the same to some corner of China, say, or Europe, bringing on a mass extinction of the sort that brought down the dinosaurs, leaving the rest of the world with just enough time to contemplate its imminent extinction.

There are things we're better off not thinking about. Sometimes the best way to avoid them, I've found, is to plunge hands deep into the soil. The purpose might be to grow vegetables, or install tulip bulbs, or dig for earthworms for a bit of fishing Huck Finn style, or simply enjoy communion with the fecund rind of the planet. Whatever the motive, something electrical takes place. Just like lightning blasting down from the sky in violent torment to ground itself in the calm, impassive earth, so fingers penetrating through humus and beyond bring one's psychic static down through the neck, out into the arms, and from there via one's digits into the serene place where all terrestrial life begins and ends.

To accomplish grounding at our place, we had a job to perform first: we had to break the sod. It wasn't easy. After we'd picked a small sloping spot near the porch for a kitchen garden and a larger flat spot near the road for our main vegetable patch, I rented a rototiller from a hardware store and attacked grassy turf seventy years in the making. The result was dramatic. The tiller bounced like a rubber ball. It lacked the heft and muscle to rip its way through.

Later that day, I was back from the hardware store with its monster machine. This tiller was to its predecessor as a plow and team of oxen is to a man or woman with a shovel—sure to triumph by sheer brute force.

Yet once again, the roaring of the engine and the thrashing of the tines had little effect. I nicked the lawn in a couple of places, exposing a few handfuls of dirt, but the turf came away the victor.

In the end, with a third, even more powerful machine rented from another source, I tore through thatch and roots and chewed my way to the soil. It took three passes over each rectangle of sward to turn green brown. Then in went my fingers, and I shuddered to contemplate the next obstacle between Debbie and me and our Adirondack agrarian fantasy. The dirt was so cold to the touch that I ached from more than a few minutes of contact. No wonder my Brownell ancestors, who arrived in these mountains as farmers, turned quickly to running sawmills, tanneries, a hotel, and a bottling plant. And no surprise that my great-grandfather, Elmer Brownell, a farmer and father of twelve, spent winters traveling snowbound Adirondack Mountain roads as a fur buyer. Extracting a living or even a mere subsistence diet from the cold, stony soils here was never easy.

One winter day, Debbie and I drove to Elizabethtown, the county seat, to rummage in land records. We wanted to trace the history of our land. Our most exciting discovery that day was that others before us had dreamed of raising crops on our cold, stony acres.

In 1850, our land, part of Old Military Tract number 164, was purchased as part of a 150-acre real estate transaction by Gerrit Smith. All familiar with the story of the abolitionist John Brown know that it was Smith, a wealthy land speculator and staunch opponent of slavery from Peterboro, New York, near Syracuse, who brought Brown to these mountains. Brown's job was to teach freed black families to farm. Smith planned to establish two settlements. The first, best known because it came to life on the land as well as on the drawing board, sprang up in the town of North Elba, near Lake Placid. It became known as Timbuctoo after a legendary ancient city in the Sahara. Our land was intended to be part of a second settlement until its future was shot down at Harper's Ferry. There, Brown—terrorist or hero, depending on your viewpoint—and a small war party killed an African American station master and launched an attack on a federal arsenal. The idea was to liberate and arm slaves and ignite a revolt that would spread like a conflagration across the South. It backfired. Brown and his coconspirators were captured and hanged. Smith, who had likely financed the raid, at least in part, checked himself into a mental hospital and evaded prosecution.

We live in a world of interconnections. Some of them blow straight into our vegetable patch. Cold air from the Canadian interior found its way to us repeatedly during our first summer, bringing hard frosts in July and August and turning robust tomato plants into ice-covered ghosts that putrefied by mid-morning. Potatoes we planted, which grew with great gusto in their first weeks of life, were promptly infiltrated by Colorado potato beetles. The insects first appeared as shiny striped adults. West winds, we're certain, brought them in from commercial potato farms a few miles away, perhaps after pesticide spraying began and the bugs realized they had to find new homes or die. Arriving like hostile paratroopers, they promptly began leaving smudges of bright orange on the undersides of leaves. These were egg masses. Almost overnight, the eggs gave rise to round little grubs that looked like blisters and devoured foliage like there was no tomorrow. Indeed, for any plant we failed to rid of the six-legged plague, there *was* no tomorrow. Because we were committed to gardening without pesticides, this meant an hour or two every evening scrutinizing every square inch of foliage for eggs and larvae and squishing what we found. By summer's end, I felt like a serial killer.

In the end, with the help of tarps, old bedsheets, stray bits of plastic, and one old shower curtain, we managed to cover our plants to keep them alive on frosty nights and to maintain sufficient pressure on the potato beetles so that we harvested a few tasty spuds for the table. It was a lot of work for not a lot of yield. All the same, we reaped a hidden reward that justified the labor and the suffering. The tilling and planting and cultivating gave us a deep and genuine sense of connection to the land. By eating lettuce, tomatoes, beans, peas, broccoli, cauliflowers, and potatoes that we grew, we brought the earth inside us. Our experiment in being part of nature, rather than its lord and master, was literally bearing fruit. It brought on good feelings. And we owed all of them to the fact that we were living in the Adirondack Park, not Yellowstone. Here we were players, not fans in the bleachers.

Sometimes, though, the feelings were not good, such as late on an August night when we were out in the garden in pajamas for the third consecutive session of hauling out tarps and old sheets, erecting defenses against another round of frosts. It is easy to romanticize rugged, wild places like the Adirondacks when you come, stay a week (or even an entire summer), and go. But as in the Grand Canyon, in the interior of Yellowstone, in the heights of Glacier National Park, and in the depths of Yosemite Valley, there is more than just beauty in such a place. There is that side of nature that stays relentlessly on the assault, that would take your life and your dreams and all you love and incinerate them in a fire, wither them in a drought, or render them ugly or useless through killing frost, pestilence, or the slow, erosional forces of struggle and despair. Few people live in the Adirondacks today, and still fewer lived here in the past. Why? It's a hard place. To endure, we'd have to summon the tenacity of a yellow birch, pushing roots into cracks in the bedrock.

BIOLOGICAL SURVEY RECORDS:

Viola sororia   Dooryard violet
5/23/06: Ned and I sprawled on the grass in front of the studio and scrutinized this one. . . . Beautiful little violet—lateral petals bearded, all 3 lower petals prominently veined

Pooecetes gramineus   Vesper sparrow
10/13/03: feeding along weedy road edge of meadow across road. Flew up and showed off white outer tail feathers.

6

The River

From myriad seeps, springs, rills, brooks, streams, ponds, and lakes, our river, the Saranac, gathers a bounty of water, fish, and flotsam and sends it pouring across the northern reach of the property. To the south and west, three deep, cold lakes that bear the name Saranac—Upper, Middle, and Lower—serve as catchments and picturesque staging areas for all the rain, hail, and snow that sift from the Adirondack sky year-round and eventually flow toward us.

Upper Saranac Lake, eight miles long, an array of summer homes and rustic palaces down the west side and mostly wilderness down the east, thunders over a rocky natural sluice into Middle. Middle, the smallest, formerly called Round, sits at the foot of Ampersand Mountain and is famous for its wild shores, wind, battering waves, and the occasional drowning. It drains via a meandering stream bordered by pickerelweed into Lower. Lower Saranac Lake, dotted with islands graced by tall pines and garnished with a smattering of elegant camps, feeds a current that winds through Lakes Oseetah and Flower, steals through Saranac Lake village, and takes looping, indirect aim for our place.

In the home stretch, the river collects effluent from two municipal wastewater treatment plants as well as herbicide, fungicide, fertilizer, and topsoil from a commercial potato farm. By the time we see the water, it has been stained black by tannins leached from decaying leaves and bark and heated to a comfortable swimming temperature (in summer) by shallow, solar-heated oxbows just upstream. The blackness is most apparent in early winter and early spring. Snow covers the banks at these times, and beside it the water, not yet frozen or thawed, looks like octopus ink.

From our porch we see the river as a horseshoe. It appears from around a bend, takes dead aim for the north end of our driveway, veers abruptly eastward, passes under a one-lane bridge, and bends sharply to the north and east. It continues on this general course until it slows to a broad ooze and empties into Lake Champlain at Plattsburgh.

The watershed of the Saranac covers nearly 392,000 acres. A good deal of it lies upstream of our mailbox.

I find it hard to observe the river here, or swim in it, without thinking of all the distance the water has traveled and the far greater distance it has to go. Topography and gravity drain the Saranac off our land and guide it to Lake Champlain, which, compared to our mountain lakes, looks like an inland sea. From there the contents pour northward past New York villages and farms on one side and Vermont villages and farms on the other into the big lake's outlet, the Richelieu River. The Richelieu (Champlain called it the *Riviere de Yroquois*) feeds the St. Lawrence, and the St. Lawrence—storied route to and from the interior for Indians in birch bark canoes and later for Cartier and Champlain in sailing ships—flows northward and eastward. The water that slides past our porch pushes through old, fortress-like Quebec City until the whole kit and caboodle empties into the Gulf of St. Lawrence. There, sweeping up from the South, the Gulf Stream picks up the flow, perhaps dotted with a few leaves from our maple trees, and sends it further north and east. A note in a bottle dropped at our house could conceivably wash ashore on my grandmother's home turf in Galway.

And that's not the whole story. The river's water is well traveled before it arrives in the watershed. Much of it has evaporated from the Pacific Ocean, drifted across the United States and Canada, and picked up acid and mercury spewed by North America's industrial heartland along the way. Just downstream from our place, the beautiful, apparently pristine Franklin Falls Reservoir provides some of the best walleye fishing in New York State. Sadly, the walleye are so tainted with mercury that the state conservation department advises that none of the tasty fish should be eaten. Doubters scoff, devouring them anyhow. "Something's gonna kill you eventually," one fisherman told me, arguing that concern over toxins in our fish is much ado about nothing. Cancer rates in the Adirondacks well exceed the state average. This may be one of the reasons—the attitude, as well as the mercury.

The river, perfectly still to the eye as if in one of great-great-grandmother Elnora's oil paintings, roils with irony. It's peculiar how something so active can look so passive. Yet any doubt about the river's relentless surge to the sea is swept away by jumping into it.

Our first summer here, when we were working long hours rescuing the house from ruin, we would take a swim in the evening. After a dunking or two, we worked out a routine. We'd leave towels and sandals on rocks downstream of the bridge, walk over the span to a grassy flat, and tiptoe in. The current would grab us and send us on our way. Passing under the bridge, we'd backstroke while admiring barn swallows tending nests on the girders. Sometimes baby swallows would peer down, wide-eyed, wondering what sort of manatees we were. Back in the sunshine, we'd haul out like seals on a sandbar, take in the mountains and the trees and the birds and the butterflies for a few minutes, and then climb to the sandbar's summit and dive back in. The current is aggressive in this spot. As we'd bob up from the cold, black depths, we had to kick and flail for all we were worth. Effort would bring us to the far shore and our towels.

Once I took the plunge alone on a dark night after a particularly hard, hot day of renovations. In the middle of the river I felt the current defeat me, just for a moment, and in that instant I caught a glimpse of a future that didn't have me in it, one in which I slid down into the inky torrent, inhaling it, brain cells switching off one by one, until some fisherman or forest ranger spied my inanimate form in an eddy somewhere, the following morning or the following week, and Debbie received the call that she dreaded. I felt not like a conqueror of nature, but what I really am: a pawn on its chessboard.

Fortunately, luck was with me. As quickly as I lost my advantage, I regained it. In seconds I was clambering out on the blessed rocks, still warm from the day's sunshine. Lights were on in the house. It hadn't been a particularly close call, yet I'd been unsettled. I have never looked at the river with quite the same innocence since.

Navigable rivers such as the Saranac have always served our own species as highways in and out of the region. While no evidence of permanent American Indian settlement has ever been found in the Adirondack interior, bits of flaked stone spear points, arrowheads, and primitive stone axes ground to smooth perfection in river grit testify to the fact that Indians visited here for millennia. No doubt at least one hunting or fishing party beached on our bank, perhaps lingering to spend a night beneath the stars.

Jay Yardley, the late first husband of our friend Fran Yardley, was excavating a trench on his property between Upper and Middle Saranac Lakes when he unearthed several Indian axes. They're of a type archeologists say were made several thousand years ago. My friend Clarence Petty, who died recently in his 105th year, sat down at our picnic table one day not long ago and unfolded a cloth. In it were stone points he'd found as a boy on an island in Upper Saranac Lake. Clarence told me that an archeologist had examined them and determined they were more than a thousand years old.

Sometime in the 1700s, the first Europeans paddled the inky Saranac. They were almost certainly trappers, French speaking, drifting down from Canada in search of beaver, muskrat, wolf, fox, and mink. Not long afterward, the Brownells established a foothold in the southern Adirondacks along the Sacandaga. Daniel and Hannah were the first to arrive, clearing a farm near the river. Their son, Orra, my great-great-great-grandfather, harnessed the thunderous power of the Sacandaga's east branch to spin the blades of a sawmill.

At about the same time, on the site of present-day Bloomingdale, a settler and blacksmith named Uriah Sumner started felling trees, hewing beams, and erecting the first sawmill on a cold stream flowing out of a vast bog. The stream was named for him. Sumner Brook drains into the Saranac a mile upstream from our place. The mill formed the nucleus around which a village grew. The village was called Sumner Forge until 1852, when the town fathers put their heads together (surely under the advice of the town mothers) and changed the name. "Bloomingdale" would appeal to tourists. Perhaps it worked. The following year, John Campbell built the first hotel in the village, and business was brisk enough that a second hotel rose up around the corner.

Continuity between people and place seems ever rarer in the modern world, but not here in the Adirondacks. A few months ago I enjoyed phone conversations with Bradley Brownell and Bruce Brownell, long-lost distant cousins of mine. They and I, and their children and mine, descend from Orra Brownell, born in 1795, who founded a sawmill in Hope Falls sometime after 1830. He is the same Orra Brownell whose name is written in an ornate, educated hand in an old family Bible passed down to me by my mother, who got it from her father. Today, Brad and Bruce run a lumber business in Edinburgh, just down the road from Hope Falls. It is a direct descendant of Orra Brownell's business. What's more, Brad told me that a sawmill still operates at Hope Falls. Who runs it? The answer comes right out of *Brigadoon*: a man named Orra Brownell.

We're all river people—not just my family, but yours and everyone else's. My Kanze and Jacobs ancestors on my father's side come from the Rhine, Main, Elbe, and Havel valleys of Germany. The Mullens and Quigleys who produced the half of my mother's genes that are Irish hail from the Owenglen, which flows into Clifden Bay in Galway. Rivers give rise to us. They flow with our history. It seems we have just as much business living along them and in them as beavers, muskrats, and otters.

The old millers and hoteliers along the Saranac are dead and gone. Instead of birch-bark canoes and mustachioed log drivers prodding rafts of old-growth trunks downstream to sawyers, as would have happened along the Saranac during the late nineteenth and early twentieth centuries, we now watch a procession of colorful aluminum, vinyl, Kevlar, Royalex, and carbon fiber piloted by well-washed folk in nylon and Gore-Tex. It's a recreational river now. Kayaks streak by in ones, twos, and threes, and canoes with adults on either end and kids in the middle pull up and picnic. Sometimes they converse so loudly that it sounds as if we have company on the porch.

The value of the river as a corridor for serious transportation is not entirely a thing of the past. One summer day during our second year here, we received an invitation from friends to go paddling on a distant lake. We wanted to go, but there was a hitch. The car on which we usually carried our canoe was propped up on jack stands. I'd started a brake job, and the auto parts store had provided the wrong parts. In an urban area, one would simply trade the bad for the good and get on with it, but here, parts must be ordered, and they take a day or two to arrive. We also owned a pickup truck at the time, an old Ford with problems. Into it we tossed the canoe and took off to meet our friends. We warned them. The truck might break down, so if we didn't show up, they were not to worry. Go exploring without us.

Nearing the village of Saranac Lake, a front wheel began to scream. A bearing had suddenly given up the ghost. What to do? It was a Sunday. No mechanic was working. As bystanders winced at the sound, I dropped Debbie and the canoe off by the river and limped the truck to a reputable garage. We'd call the mechanic in the morning.

No trouble getting home. Debbie and I shoved off and dipped our wooden paddles. We made a happy day of it, pausing halfway home to haul the boat out and swim and eat our snacks. Near the middle of the afternoon, we nosed the bow into an oxbow off the main channel and found ourselves approaching the backyard of our neighbor Sandy Hayes. Sandy was sipping a beer on a deck so close to the river that we could carry on a conversation.

"How's it going?"

"Great," I said. "Except for the fact that the car's jacked up in the yard, the truck died on the way to town, and we have no idea how Debbie's going to get to work tomorrow."

Sandy laughed. "Don't worry," he said. "I have a Lincoln in the garage. It hardly gets any use. You'll be doing me a favor if you drive it.

Keep it until you get things straightened out." We chatted about other things, and then Sandy had another thought. "You're going to need the car at your house. Connie and I will drop it off after supper." That evening, a convoy appeared at our place. For a week we piloted a big, shiny blue Continental.

This is what rivers do best. They deliver things. To the tube-building larvae of caddisflies, obscure insects known chiefly to trout and trout fishermen, moving water delivers bits of jetsam, dead and alive, on which they subsist. Two entomologist friends, both aquatic insect specialists, have identified nineteen caddisflies on our property. The insects are here in diversity and abundance because the ever-flowing Saranac makes deliveries to their makeshift underwater lairs.

Leeches like the river, too. The only one we've identified so far—there are surely several species—is straight out of a nightmare. We spied the first one on a submerged rock just before a swim. It was about the length of my longest finger and, despite its ghastly way of making a living, was actually quite beautiful. A line ran down the middle of the ringed body (leeches are annelids, like earthworms), and there was a row of spots down either side.

When I first set eyes on the big leech, it seemed to be lunging for things. Was it? I waved a hand nearby. The animal threw itself at me. Whichever way I fluttered my hand, it groped. By the time we left to jump in elsewhere, the poor thing must have been exhausted. I felt sorry for it and considered bringing it home as a pet. How to feed the bloodsucker? Debbie swam away when I suggested we take turns putting an arm in the tank.

Most of the river life is passive and innocuous where humans are concerned. Three aquatic plants, for example, grow rooted in quiet, sun-warmed parts of the bottom. Although I knew little about aquatic plants when we moved here, through diligent effort and the acquisition of a dissecting microscope and identification manual, I managed to work out what they are. One is a pondweed, a member of the notoriously difficult genus *Potomogeton*, which means "river neighbor." It takes the form of long, limp stems that yield to the current ("Go with the flow" is the stream plant's motto) and extend to six feet or more. The leaves clasp the stems, a fact that nudged me in my sleuthing toward *Potomogeton richardsonii*, also called Richardson's pondweed after its discoverer, the Scottish naturalist and explorer Sir John Richardson (1787–1865). Our botanist friend Mark Rooks took a sample I'd given him to a professional conference. An expert there agreed with our identification.

We have *Elodea canadensis*, sometimes called waterweed, in our stretch of river, too. It looks like a typical fish tank plant. More widespread is water celery, or eelgrass, whose genus name *Vallisneria* rolls pleasingly off the tongue. The species here is *americana,* appropriate because the stuff grows in waters across the United States and Canada. It's hard to imagine a plant more perfectly adapted to life in a stream. Vallisneria's leaves are green ribbons, long and supple. They flow with the current. When we're out on a backwoods brook in a canoe, trying to find our way, and the difference between upstream and downstream becomes hard to discern, Vallisneria shows the way. Its reproductive habits are extraordinary. Long, thin, spaghetti-like stems rise up from the river bottom, bearing female flowers at the top. The blossoms float. To make seeds, they must be pollinated. The goal is achieved by male flowers, which develop on brittle stems. The males snap off, drift downstream, and if all goes well collide with females. It's love at first bump.

As much as I'm drawn to plants, it's the river's animal life that gains most of my attention. The river stages a continuous show that includes the obvious but still delightful things one expects to find on an Adirondack Mountain stream—muskrats, beavers, great blue herons, eagles, fish—but also things one might not immediately expect.

Such as bears. One summer I devoted hours to cutting up white birch trees that had died near the water's edge. I'm not sure why the trees died—it might have been flooding of their root systems in a particularly wet spring, or it might have been insect pests or disease. At any rate, the trees, which rose out of a thicket of chokecherries, offered free heat for our house.

Deep in the chokecherries, which were a bit tall to be called shrubs but a bit branchy to be considered trees, I was running a chain saw when something unsettling dawned on me. I was surrounded by bear droppings. Ruby-red cherries hung thick on the limbs that year, and black bears, not minding their astringent pulp, had been wolfing them down by the bucketful. I had never seen so much bear sign in one place. Great piles of mushy blue-black stuff, abundantly studded with spherical BB-sized pits, loomed everywhere.

Where were the bears? I had no real worries about them. The big carnivores are fast and powerful and toothy but inclined toward herbivory, as the scat piles showed. A bear that challenged a man with a chainsaw would be a rare bear indeed. All the same, with such a bounty of food close at hand, I felt certain bears were close at hand, too, perhaps dozing the day away in a nearby shadow. One might expect animals as large as bears to be easy to spot, but the opposite is true. With its dark fur, a black bear can achieve instant invisibility by simply finding shade and ceasing all motion.

The kids and I have found bear tracks in mud by the river, and once we made plaster casts. Yet the most interesting bit of bear sign turned up one day when Tassie, then four, and I were out exploring. It was a fall day, and we were poking along the riverbank. I'd told Tassie about a hole I'd found in a steep patch of riverbank, a hole tracks indicated was a mink den. My little naturalist wanted to see it.

We reached the opening by climbing down to the water's edge, skirting some mountain ash and balsam, and then climbing back up to an undercut area just below the bank's crest. The soil was badly gouged. Something powerful and determined had tried to dig the mink out. But what? Two sets of deep and widely spaced claw marks told the story. A black bear had been following the river's edge. Perhaps it had caught the mink's scent. Well-washed mink hides that go into ladies' coats give off no odor, but the live animal is another story. Weasels stink, and the mink is a stinky weasel. The bank here is dense with clay, and the digging wouldn't have been easy. It seemed the bear had invested a minute or two of effort, then given up and gone in search of easier pickings.

While I've never seen a mink bound in or out of the den, we see the animals from time to time hunting along the river's edge. A mink is the color of rich, dark chocolate, which is to say, black at a glance but a marvelous, glossy brown on close examination. The eyes are bright and beadlike, the legs short, the body long and lithe like a snake's. Mink are fierce and accomplished predators. Once late at night when we were driving home, one leapt into the road from the river with a big frog in its mouth. On another occasion, I saw one carrying a vole.

The card for mink in our biological survey files records two notable sightings. First:

"Best looks I've ever had of a mink in motion—bounding on snow bank on far side of river, swimming across river, bounding up to the road and across into a thicket—I was amazed by the looping playfulness of the bounds—in the water the mink looked huge and we at first mistook it for a beaver!"

And second:

"Big, beautiful mink in water, on bank, and climbing out on ice to shake its fur dry, in river just upstream of bridge; gorgeous; at first I thought it might be an otter; then it dove with its rear end bulging above the water as it submerged and I thought it was a beaver; then it swam on the surface with its tail trailing behind and I thought it was a musk-rat; then it climbed out on thin ice and I could see that it was a mink." We contemplate keeping chickens, and I know that if the day comes when we build a coop and stock it with hens, mink will be seen by us in a new light. They and their cousin long-tailed weasels and ermines are famous egg thieves and poultry killers.

Far larger than a mink is a member of the weasel family we hoped to see on the Saranac from our first days: a river otter. A mink could be called semiaquatic. It lives near water and hunts in and along it. Otters are aquatic almost to the extreme. They live to swim and swim to live, fueling their substantial but supremely flexible bodies on such freshwater fare as fish, crayfish, newts, frogs, turtles, snakes, insect nymphs, and the occasional unlucky beaver kit or juvenile muskrat.

For years, winter, spring, summer, and fall, we watched for otters on the river without success. Then one morning on the thirteenth of Febru-ary, when Ned was two and Tassie still a babe in arms, Debbie looked out a bedroom window and shouted glad tidings. "Otter!"

Ned and I thundered in from the living room, joining Debbie and Tassie at the window. Down by the river, on an ice shelf extending from the north bank, a long, dark sausage of a mammal, its gait roly-poly, picked its way along the edge of the cold black water. I pointed to the otter so Ned would look and see it, commenting that the animal was frisky.

"Frisky," repeated Ned. "Frisky." And so our little boy added a new word to his vocabulary at the same time we were adding a new mammal to our survey. "Frisky," said Ned before he went to sleep that night, and "frisky," he said the following morning when he awoke.

The otter, meanwhile, having granted us a brief audience, slipped over the edge like a scuba diver and plunged into the Saranac's icy depths. For a fraction of a second it surfaced. Then it was gone. In about the time it takes to read this sentence, we'd had the first and last glimpses in more than a decade of a wild otter here, even though we live along a watercourse that abounds in them.

While otter sightings are rare, muskrat and beavers show themselves almost daily. It took a little practice to tell whether a particular large brown mammal slicing across the surface of the river was a muskrat or beaver, but after a short while, we had the hang of it. The tails of the animals could not be more different in size and shape—the muskrat's minimalist version slender and snake-like, the beaver's round and wide like the busi-ness end of a tennis racket. One would think telling the two animals apart would be child's play. But often it's dusk when we see an unidentified swimmer, and the tail blends in with the dark water or trails beneath the surface.

The trick is to look for a bow wave. A beaver, far larger than a muskrat, has a block head that plows through water with great resistance. Even with just the slightest hint of moonlight, I can usually make out the big ripple that precedes every beaver. A muskrat, by contrast, has a small, rounded head that makes love to the water rather than punishes it. If the tail makes itself visible, well, that proves the hypothesis.

Living beside a river teeming with fifty- and seventy-pound rodents that fell trees for a living brings frustrations as well as amusements. During the summer, when Debbie and I sleep in a bed on the front porch, crashes and booms sometimes wake us in the dead of night. Typically it's a series of snapping sounds very much like gunfire that hauls us out of our slumber. These are created by wood fibers giving way as a tree gnawed nearly through by beavers yields, sputtering, to gravity. Then comes a resounding thud. Sometimes we feel the sound as well as hear it. After ten years, I don't open an eye anymore. "Beavers," I think in my groggy state, then slide back into oblivion.

Beavers have plumbed the depth of our appreciation by attacking the handsomest bush on our property. It's a mountain ash. Because this one grew in full sun on the fertile and well-watered riverbank, it grew to great proportion and produced annual profusions of creamy-white flowers and scarlet fruits. Beavers loved the plant as much as we did, but theirs was a gustatory passion. The shrub started with a dozen or so trunks, and after a few years, only two or three were left. Then the rodents left the mountain ash alone. Restraint on their part? I doubted it. Studies of interactions between herbivores and plants show that when animals attack plants with their teeth, plants sometimes fight back by manufacturing compounds that make them distasteful. Could that be it? If the bush's solution was beaver repellent, it worked only for a time. Last year, beavers chiseled the mountain ash again. Now we are left with a single stem embedded in the bristles of neighboring firs.

Often when we go for night walks, we hear animals of substantial size splashing in the water and suspect they are beavers. The big rodents are active along both banks, mostly but not always at night, hauling aspen and birch limbs into the water and dragging them down to the bottom. "Busy beaver" is an apt cliché. These animals do not hibernate. To endure the long winter, a winter during which the river may be frozen over for two or three months, they jam enough sticks into mud on the Saranac's bottom to fill their bellies until springtime.

It's a huge job for a huge animal. I once saw a freshly killed beaver in the middle of a highway and out of curiosity pulled over to see just how big it was. Holding the tip of the beaver's tail near my Adam's apple, I was able to get the nose to clear the ground. I stand nearly six feet tall. That's a substantial animal! It weighed sixty pounds or more.

By contrast, a muskrat is puny. A muskrat is a kind of vole, and voles are generally mouse-sized creatures. Voles scurry beneath forest leaf litter and the grassy thatch of meadows, operating well below our psychic radar. People often call them field mice. The muskrat is a field mouse that has evolved into gigantic size, relatively speaking, and taken to feeding in the water.

How big, or how small, is a muskrat? They weigh two or three pounds, a big bruiser perhaps four pounds. An Adirondack beaver averages 45 pounds, and monsters up to 115 pounds have been recorded. A beaver may measure fifty inches from stem to turn, a big muskrat half that.

In behavior, two creatures that share a habitat could hardly differ more widely in behavior. The beaver, as we've mentioned, is provident, storing food during the summer months for the long winter ahead. The muskrat, as far as biologists can tell, is improvident. It swims straight into the cold eye of winter with reckless disregard for the challenges ahead. Or so it seems. But the muskrat has a trick up its thickly furred sleeve. While the unimaginative beaver subsists on the same old bark all winter long, the ecologically resourceful muskrat reinvents itself as a carnivore.

Most people I meet, if you ask them who leaves piles of mussel shells along the shores of Adirondack lakes, answer "raccoon." This is what my grandfather taught me. On this score, Grampy was wrong. Raccoons don't swim and dive much. Freshwater mussels form only a small part of their diet. To collect mussels in quantity, you've got to get away from shore, swim to the bottom, and rummage. This is muskrat behavior. Crayfish and insect nymphs also abound on the bottom, and muskrats eat those, too. All winter, while beavers are holed up in their cozy lodges, picking at stale bark they've dragged from the depths, muskrats are feeding in air spaces beneath the ice, filling their bellies with fresh freshwater seafood. In spring, when the ice melts and the muskrats move on, shell middens remain to tell the tale.

My favorite muskrat sightings occur when I blunder on one of the animals half in the water and half out, nibbling the bark off red-osier dogwood. This is a beautiful native shrub, one whose fruits provide a rich source of aviation fuel for migratory birds. I groan when I find deer eating it. But somehow a muskrat working on red-osier fails to irk me. I love to watch one hold a cherry-red stem in its delicate forepaws and twirl the thing like corn on the cob as it removes bark from one end to the other.

The smallest mammal typical of the riverbank is likely the water shrew. We've never seen one. The largest is the moose.

Moose are upland creatures during the cold months. Their diet then consists mostly of twigs and buds, and these, while rich enough to keep a 1,400-pound bull active all winter, are scant on sodium and calcium. When spring comes, moose migrate out of the hills down into wetlands. There aquatic plants—water lilies, pickerelweed, water celery, and more—abound in minerals the animals have been short on all winter. Our property includes good summer habitat. As the population of this giant member of the deer family rebounds in the Adirondacks, we hope to spy one strolling past our mailbox.

Birds also entertain us. March through December, when the river is clear of ice, we maintain a constant vigil, scanning the waters for ducks. The list of species we've seen is not long, but it includes the most glamorous of North American waterfowl, the wood duck. Nature can be ugly, such as on the occasion when a red squirrel raided a birdhouse in which a mother bluebird had just commenced sitting on eggs, leaving only bits of shell. But it can also supply great beauty, such as when one of us trains binoculars on an unidentified feathered object on the river and comes up with a "woody" drake.

In his breeding plumes, the male, or drake, wood duck appears too good to be true. There's something plastic about his good looks, as if he were a movie star of ordinary endowments who after three hours with makeup artists walks out wearing a patina of glamour. Yet keep looking at the drake, and you won't catch a false note. His colors—cherry red of bill-base and eye; rich chestnut of breast; metallic green of crest, crown, temple, and cheek, with black, white, and tan flourishes—harmonize to create a symphony for the eyes.

Most ducks nest on the ground, but woodies incubate their eggs in hollow trees. Our place abounds in fungi, carpenter ants, and anteating pileated woodpeckers. As a result, we have plenty of trunks to suit and therefore plenty of wood ducks. We see the adults and we see the babies. We see the birds arrive in early April, and we lament their departures in October or November.

Among other ducks to turn up, the most common are mallards. The drakes have brilliant green heads that shimmer in sunshine, and the females wear handsome brown-tinged camouflage. We also spy mergansers, the common and the hooded, both of which breed here. On a single remarkable occasion, two red-breasted mergansers turned up. Debbie and I saw red-breasteds often during the years we lived in the South. They nest in the Far North, generally well to the north of the Adirondacks, but when winter comes, most of them beat their wings for the coast of the Carolinas, Florida, and the Gulf of Mexico. Yet in early November 2004, on Guy Fawkes Day in the morning, as the season's first blizzard did its best to blot out our view, two ghostly shapes materialized on the river. They had the thin, elongated bills that typify mergansers, but even through the snow, the white neck bands and ragged napes that identify them as red-breasteds caught our eyes.

On another occasion three green-winged teal, rare birds hereabouts, turned up in a group of eleven common and two hooded mergansers.

Debbie is the duck expert in the house. She's taught me that any bird that drifts by merits scrutiny. It was her talented and educated eye that took the trouble one April morning to size up a big dark duck whizzing overhead. It turned out to be one of the most unexpected birds on our biological survey: a surf scoter. Surf scoters summer on lakes in Canada's Far North and winter mostly in the churning, briny fringes of the eastern seaboard. Yet a certain unknowable number drift north and south over the Adirondacks, and once in a very blue moon, someone like Debbie is looking.

The prize for weirdest bird along our stretch of river goes to an American bittern that spent a May afternoon in our yard stalking grasshoppers. There is nothing unusual about bitterns appearing along rivers or birds snatching up lawn bugs. It's the combination that was bizarre. Bitterns, short-necked but otherwise substantial members of the heron tribe, are famously secretive. Birdwatchers hearing their peculiar *oong-ka, oong-ka* broadcasts in marshes often search for them in vain. The bittern's camouflage is supreme. Brown and white streaks on the breast blend in perfectly with the stalks of marsh plants. Yet one ambled through our green grass, standing out like a billboard.

Thickets with trees rising out of them crowd up to the riverbank from the north and east, and they harbor a wealth of songbirds. We enjoy the musical presence of the chestnut-sided warbler, the common yellowthroat (also a warbler), the song sparrow, the alder flycatcher, and the gray catbird. The chestnut-sided is a favorite of mine. I love its intricate markings: a crown of gold, belly and cheeks milk white, ruddy streaks running down the flanks, and a back as boldly patterned as a stained glass window. The song is uttered in a breathless hurry. Roger Tory Peterson renders it, "see see see see Miss BEECHer" and "please please pleased to MEETcha."

The yellowthroat male wears a black mask and hardly ever shows his face. He sings *witchety witchety witch* so often and loudly, though, that you know he's around. The song sparrow offers snatches of Beethoven, the alder flycatcher a throat-sore *free-beer, free-beer,* and the catbird—well, the catbird says whatever comes to mind. The catbird is the Walt Whitman of our songbirds. In late spring and summer we see it occasionally but hear its free verse almost continuously, including, sometimes, in the dead of night. The catbird utters an occasional *meow* but otherwise improvises endlessly. There is no rhyme to its poetry, nor structure of any traditional sort. The bird simply starts whistling and warbling and doesn't stop until it has laid out its own "Leaves of Grass."

Out of the thickets rise the trunks and crowns of American elms. In spring, the trees produce round, papery fruits that look like coins. The fruits attract purple finches. The female finches look like sparrows, the males like sparrows that have been dunked in scarlet dye. Both male and female sing lively, fast-paced warbles. These serve to defend territory, allow the birds to keep in touch, and add cheer to overcast mornings.

Eastern kingbirds nest along the river, too. This is a treat because the elegant black-and-white flycatcher seems to be undergoing a regional decline. The year we moved in, Debbie and I laughed to watch kingbirds do what they always do—construct a nest of grass and sticks in the top of a tree. Yet these did it with a twist. The tree was a tall birch that had fallen over, and its trunk, still living and generating limbs and leaves, extended horizontally just a few feet above the water. The crown, despite the low elevation, met the kingbird's need for a treetop.

Debbie asked me if the kingbirds would reuse the nest. It was perfectly situated for us to view it from the bridge, and she hoped to repeat the experience in the future. I replied with a rickety generalization. Songbirds rarely recycle old nests, perhaps because a nursery that's been used teems with parasites. The kingbirds would likely go elsewhere. What happened? They refurbished the nest year after year for the better part of a decade.

The grandest birds we see along the Saranac are ospreys and eagles. The former always astound me, looking as they do when hunting fish like Cessnas that jerk to a halt in midair, then haul in wings for a nosedive. Down plummets the osprey in a tumble of brown and white. Up flies a spray of water, glittering in the sunshine. If the bird has succeeded, it lumbers away with a fish clenched in its rough-scaled toes.

Osprey sightings came frequently during our early years, while bald eagles turned up only occasionally. In winter we saw eagles along the state highway to Saranac Lake, clawed feet wrapped around tree limbs, piercing yellow eyes gazing down in hopes of spying a morsel of living, or formerly living, flesh.

Then eagles began breeding in the Adirondacks with greater success. As their numbers rose, sightings became routine at our house. For years we pictured a bald eagle gracing a giant white pine on our property across the river, but the picturing remained only a fantasy until 2008, when a particularly large eagle, very likely a female, circled down from the sky and landed on the spot. Bald eagles are chocolate brown for the first few years of their lives, with increasing amounts of white as time goes by. Generally after three years, but sometimes only after five, the birds molt and emerge with their trademark alabaster head and tail. The bird in the pine was an adult. From a distance, its head and tail looked like clumps of snow.

There's a special pleasure that comes from seeing a bald eagle sail over the roof of one's house on an autumn day. As Louis Armstrong sang, "I think to myself, what a wonderful world"—wonderful because such a magnificent creature sails our skies, and doubly so because life has granted me the privilege of living where bald eagles feed and breed.

Of course, if I were a duck, goose, or loon, and bald eagles killed and ate my young, I would see things differently.

Perspective is everything. This is especially true when it comes to snapping turtles. The reptile, one of the most loathed creatures in North America, has always been a favorite of mine. I've loved snappers ever since my father brought home a hatchling when I was a little boy. For a few weeks, the baby turtle made a fine pet. It was docile and sweet tempered and, despite excessive handling, never bothered to nip. Then we let it go.

My revered Adirondack grandfather had a few holes in his philosophy. Grampy loathed snappers. His idea was that the turtle was a monster that killed and ate fish (never mind that he did)—a competitor worthy of murder, not mercy. Once, we were fishing live bait and casting plugs on the Oswegatchie River when he spied a monster snapper basking. "Give me the spear," he said, referring to the Poseidon-style frog spear we kept in the boat in case bullfrogs turned up. Grampy brought the boat around and jammed the barbed tines into the turtle's Stegosaurus-like tail. "We'll make turtle soup," he said. I grieved for the big old turtle until it fell off as we dragged it back to camp.

It's a good thing I like snappers, because living on the river, with plenty of sandy soil hereabouts, we see plenty. In June, expectant mother turtles claw their way out of the drink, cross roads (where they're often crushed by steel-belted radials), and seek out bits of roadside sand that meet their exacting specifications. There they plant themselves like backhoes with stabilizers and with their back feet quickly get to work.

If a particular hole doesn't fit the bill, and it's hard for a human to know why one suffices while a dozen fall short, Mother Snapper tries again until she finds just the right grit, moisture, or temperature. Then she lays. Out of an opening called a cloaca (it's Latin for "sewer") beneath her tail pop spherical white eggs that look like Ping-Pong balls. The sperm that fertilized them may have been collected from a donor years earlier. Females copulate when the getting's good, then store what they collect.

The egg chamber is like a squat wine bottle, narrow at the neck and wide at the bottom. The typical number of eggs placed inside falls between 20 and 40, although the record clutch is 104. Temperature decides gender. Snapping turtles have no sex chromosomes like humans do. Eggs in the upper part of the cluster tend to be warmed most by the sun and yield females. Eggs from the bottom stay cool and generally produce males. If a raccoon, fox, or some other predator doesn't find the nest, hatching takes place in late summer or early fall. We know when the young turtles are out because shocking numbers are flattened by automobiles.

We see huge snappers nesting at our place, some of them probably weighing twenty-five pounds or more and measuring a foot or more down the upper shell, or plastron. Even when approaching closely, I have never known one to snap. I am certain, though, that if pressed, a snapper will live up to its name and do so at lightning speed. The turtles are mild mannered in the water, and we have no fear when we swim.

Snapping turtles are accused of drowning and devouring ducklings. They're guilty as charged, but not to the degree that their detractors think. One study found that more than half of the diet of the turtles in the research plot consisted of plants such as sedges, pondweed, and cattail. I once dissected a big snapper that came to the edge of a frozen pond during an autumn thaw and got frozen. Its belly contained only tree leaves.

The only other turtle we see in the river is the painted. It's a puny thing by comparison, the males smaller than the females and neither as large as a dessert plate. Painted turtles, named for red or yellow highlights around the margins of their shells, appear early in spring. It's a ritual at our house to scan the banks for the year's first. The black, polished shells reflect sunlight and at a glance look like shiny rocks. The rocks hurl themselves into the water with a *thunk* if you approach them. Snapping and painted turtles have a business partnership. Snappers cozy up to painteds and let them eat algae and leeches off their backs. Hangers-on are a particular issue for snappers, which don't bask in sunshine as much as most turtles do.

Frogs are declining all over the world, but at our place, they still flourish. We hear them more than we see them. When snow still lies on the ground and ice lingers on lakes and ponds, their annual concert commences. It continues, each species following the next in sequence, until the summer lovemaking of green frogs gives way to the amorous August stridulations of crickets and katydids.

The first number on the program is performed by wood frogs. We find them dotting the roads on rainy nights in April, their skin black when they first emerge, tan with black masks later on. Mainly, though, we hear wood frogs. At a distance, their calls suggest quacking ducks.

I learned the identity of these "ducks" in my teens. There was a pond in the woods, hidden from the trail until you crested a ridge. In March and April I would hear what sounded like hundreds of ducks as I approached, then cross the ridge and find the pond silent. Neither a mallard nor any other kind of waterfowl would show itself. I was baffled. Then one year, taking time to investigate, I crept close and waited for ten minutes. One by one, submerged frogs bobbed to the surface, their throats swelled, and the quacking started up again. The joke was on me.

Next in the ancient opera—which has undoubtedly played along the Saranac for millennia, since the last ice age interrupted a run of millions of years—comes the spring peeper. If the spring thaw comes late, we may hear wood frogs and peepers start up the same night. Generally, though, wood frogs have been quacking and cackling for a week before the first peeper pipes. On a mild April night, one takes the meteorological hint, inflates its tiny throat like bubble gum, and belts out a squeak.

A male peeper could sit comfortably on my thumbnail. A female might require twice that space. We tend to think of male animals being bigger than their female counterparts, yet in a variety of groups, notably the hawks, falcons, eagles, owls, and frogs, sisters dwarf brothers. In frogs, female superiority of mass may have evolved because girls grow to produce and carry massive loads of eggs. A boy's role is more humble: to be a FedEx man for small volumes of sperm. Both females and males wear a trademark X on their backs. It inspired the frog's species name, *crucifer*, meaning, according to my battered old copy of *Webster's Collegiate Dictionary*, "one who carries a cross."

Spring peepers are conformists. Once one starts to pipe, a hundred or a thousand (counting them would be impossible) join it. Collectively, they sound like sleigh bells. It's a festive sound. In me, it always inspires a happy feeling that the long, tenacious Adirondack winter is finally losing its grip.

It's not surprising that wood frogs and spring peepers produce home-grown antifreeze. Both emerge from hibernation early. Sudden plunges in temperature below thirty-two degrees Fahrenheit are commonplace, so for the frogs to endure here, they need a physiological trick to get them through short, hard frosts as well as long winters. The adaptation is a marvel of simplicity. The frogs make themselves sweet. Glycogen is converted into glucose, a simple sugar. Glucose suffuses the body, lowering freezing temperatures, retarding the formation of ice crystals, and helping the frogs hold on to vital moisture.

After wood frogs have gone quiet, not to be heard again for a year, and while peepers are still noisily peeping, northern leopard frogs begin to sing. Their serenades must be highly seductive in context—we see leopard frogs more than any other kind of frog, so without doubt there is a whole lot of loving going on. Oddly, the frog's love song is virtually identical to a human sound with antierotic effects. It sounds like snoring, and not snoring of a subtle sort, but full bore and loud.

Despite the ugliness of its voice, the leopard frog dazzles the eye. Every time I see one I stop in my tracks, the same way I might be temporarily immobilized if the world's most beautiful woman were to appear in front of me. I nearly stepped on a leopard frog this afternoon. It rocketed out of high grass and landed inches in front of my feet. I've seen thousands, including dozens this past week, but still I was spellbound. Saranac River leopard frogs are the prettiest I've seen. Their background color is a luminous gold that shimmers when the sun strikes it. Superimposed on the gold are the black spots, some round, some oval, which give the frog its name. This is a substantial animal. It dwarfs the wood frog and the peeper, measuring as an adult about four or five inches long. The hind legs are beefy and attenuated, adapted by evolution for the high jump.

Next up are American toads. Toads are not just similar to frogs; they *are* frogs. All over the world, frogs that have adapted to a largely terrestrial life have developed, often independently, adaptations such as thick skin resistant to desiccation and toxins to help fend off predators. A toad may be more closely related to the nearest frog than to the nearest species of "toad."

American toads, squat and warty, are our ugliest amphibians. Fortunately, nature has compensated them with the most beautiful of Adirondack amphibian voices. Most often at dusk but sometimes at high noon, the males inflate white, pebble-grained throats and slowly release air. Out come sonorous trills that go on and on for ten, twenty, or even thirty seconds. In his poem "The Song of the Toad," John Burroughs proposed that that the American toad "Makes vesper music fit for kings/ From out an empty bubble." Burroughs finds enough in the toad's voice to occupy four eight-line stanzas. He concludes, "Blessings on thy warty head:/ No bird could do it better."

Compared to the toads that immediately precede them in courting along the river's lazy bends and stranded oxbows, green frogs mate without fanfare. They emerge from the wet muck in which they hibernate, hop on rainy nights to favored breeding waters, and there the males, which have brilliant yellow throats in spring, stake out territories and call. The voice of a green frog is often compared to the plucking of a banjo string. We have friends and neighbors who play banjos, and I have to say that while I've used the banjo string analogy myself, I have yet to hear that instrument sound anything like a green frog. What, if not a banjo, does the voice suggest? The typical call is a single, guttural note, repeated often. If it sounds like anything, it's the noise made when a finger rubs against a latex balloon. Green frogs occur along the Saranac in great numbers. In May and early June, when they're at the height of their breeding rapture, they fill the night air with a pleasing cacophony.

A green frog looks a good deal like a bullfrog. Both are big and both are green. One way to tell them apart has to do with features called dorsolateral folds. These are creases, one running down either side of a frog's back. The green frog has them and the bullfrog doesn't. Both species, as it happens, tend to be green.

Hard on the slimy heels of the green frog comes the gray tree frog. It sounds something like a bleating sheep and something like the territorial call of the red-bellied woodpecker yet not exactly like either. "Gray tree frog" can be a misnomer. This frog is often gray, but, possessing a chameleon-like ability to change color to match backgrounds, it may also appear brown or green. Males blare with shocking volume. Their voice is a flatulent sort of trill, a veritable Bronx cheer. If you're walking past one when it starts up, you may jump. It's nothing for a gray tree frog to blare 1,000 times in a single hour.

We hear gray tree frogs every evening from late May until early July but almost never see one. It's remarkable how a creature can make so much noise yet be so hard to glimpse.

While green frogs and gray tree frogs are going full bore, another voice joins the chorus. It's subtle at first, and Debbie almost always picks it out of the din before I do. This frog is present in far lower numbers, and its voice is less demanding of attention. *Knock-knock*, it seems to say. *Knock-knock-knock*. This is the fervent plea for feminine attention of a mink frog.

A mink frog doesn't look like a mink. It's green, not brown, and its skin is slimy, not covered by thick fur envied to a lethal degree by socialites. The amphibian acquired the name "mink" because it smells like one, which is to say, not very nice. A real mink, if you get close to one, reeks of musk. The smell brings to mind a public toilet in desperate need of cleaning.

It's a sore point that we live on a river full of fish, yet we know little about the ones that are here. A few miles downstream, in Franklin Falls Reservoir, there are walleyes of great size and number, and it's likely that at least a few of them come and go past our house. Men, women, and children come from far and wide to cast lures and bait in hopes of catching them. Out-of-state license plates appear on a substantial portion of the cars that line the nearby road. No one seems to pay much attention to the New York D.E.C. warning that Franklin Falls walleyes are tainted with mercury and unsafe to eat.

Walleyes are sometimes called walleyed pike. Pike are predatory, and so are walleyes, but that's where the similarity between these unrelated fish ends. Pike are built like barracudas: long and narrow, vaguely cylindrical, and sharp-pointed at the forward end like a spear or pike. Walleyes are a kind of perch and, like their cousins, are flattened laterally and broad in the middle as viewed from the flanks. According to my old copy of *Webster's Collegiate Dictionary*, "wall-eyed" means "marked by a wild irrational staring of the eyes." To be sure, a walleye's eyeballs can look a bit rheumy, and there's something clueless in the way it looks at you. Yet these things can be said of most fish. I'm not sure why the walleye was singled out.

Because we've not yet gotten around to surveying our piece of the Saranac in an organized way, our only proof of the existence and diversity of its fish has come from the occasional report from a fisherman, the odd corpse that washes up on a bank, and bullhead fry we've seen swarming in our oxbow pond. To date, we have only three species listed in our records: rock bass, a native member of the sunfish family with blazing red eyes; brown trout, an exotic species introduced long ago from Europe and caught by a man I noted "seemed experienced, bright, knowledgeable, sober"; and a rainbow trout, a native of the Far West, brought East more than a century ago. The rainbow was hauled in one mild May evening by a teenaged boy.

Suckers are in the river, too. I know because once I found a dead one in springtime. The fish was so odiferous I decided to nudge it into the current and send it down the Styx. Only after I got back to the house and consulted a field guide did I realize my mistake. Two suckers inhabit Adirondack waters, the white and the longnose, and the features that separate them are subtle. Only with the fish in hand might I have identified its corpse.

Nor can I say which kind of bullhead we have. They're almost certainly brown bullheads, but yellows swim within the realm of possibility. Bullheads are cousins of catfish, named for their big heads and for stiff, sharp spines hidden in their dorsal and pectoral fins. Being "horned" by a bullhead is an Adirondack rite of passage. When an unwary child tries to pull one off a hook, the bullhead does its best to drive a spine deep into a tender palm. I was horned several times as a child. Mild infections resulted from the puncture wounds, infections not serious enough to require a doctor's attention but painful enough to deliver a lesson.

Everything I know about bullheads and bullheading I learned from my grandfather. On several cherished summer occasions during my childhood, he took me out on Adirondack Lake, near Indian Lake, to fish after dark, and there was never any question about the quarry. The first time, Grampy rigged each of my two poles with two hooks and sinker. I pushed on night crawlers and dropped the lines over the side. You could see when you had a bite because the pole tips would jerk violently, and you could see the pole tips because a gasoline lantern, hissing and casting a blinding glare, hung from a bracket slipped into an oarlock.

I got horned that first time and got thoroughly worked over by mosquitoes, too. Vivid in memory after more than forty years are the fish slime and worm excrement that caked my hands and the rest of me, too, as I swatted bugs that pierced my skin. Grampy would keep the fish in a tub in a shed overnight. There, raccoons couldn't get to them, and there in the morning the bullheads would remain alive, pushing their whiskered mouths out of the water to gulp for oxygen. Some would make grotesque croaking sounds. My grandfather would sit down at an old rickety table with an ancient pocketknife and clean dozens in no time at all. He had a knack, which he tried to teach me once but I never mastered. You made a few incisions, crunched through the back of the bullhead's neck, and with a single pull removed head, skin, and entrails. Then the corpse was dropped in a pan of water. There, the headless, skinless, gutless fish would swish its tail, still trying to swim.

Time spent in my grandfather's company and the eating of bullheads were opposite sides of a single coin. He froze the fish a dozen or more at a time in blocks of ice and wrapped the blocks in newspaper. Come to visit, and a block would soon be thawing in the sink. If he visited our house, a package or two would find its way in from the car. My parents had little interest, but my sisters and I relished the treat.

Perhaps because I tended to revere my grandfather, the eating of the bullheads he brought us represented a communion far more meaningful to me than the consumption of grape juice and wafers at our local Methodist Church. It was the body and blood of the Adirondacks we were consuming, delivered to us by the strong, wind-chapped hands of a man ordained by the sun and moon. Perhaps these occasions primed me to develop a personal philosophy more in line with Burroughs than with Muir. My grandfather was genuinely humble but never pious, someone who literally lived in the midst of nature as a full participant rather than a passionate dilettante who flits in and flits out. Whatever those whiskered, bottom-feeding bullheads were made of, he was made of, too.

Big fish feed on smaller fish, or at least many of them do, and nearly all, large and small, feed to one degree or another on invertebrates. The river swarms with them, and we have only begun to know their names. Part of the trouble is that we are generalists, practicing casual science. Identifying animals from groups too small or obscure to examine on the run often requires the attention of specialists. Luckily, we know a few, and the few we know are generous with their time.

After ten years of living here, we still hadn't identified any of the crayfish that scuttle along the river bottom. A decade was long enough, I decided. So one May afternoon, Tassie and I plucked two from the water and slipped them into a plastic container. There, the larger of the two promptly dismembered and ate the other.

The following day, the little crustacean, mud-colored and barely two inches long, joined us in the car for a 300-mile drive. We were heading to a county park near New York City, where I was scheduled to lead a bird walk. It so happened that the park naturalist and museum curator who had recruited me, Jason Klein, is a self-taught crayfish expert. He didn't know what was coming.

The expedient thing to do would have been to dunk the crayfish in alcohol or freeze it in a block of ice. That would have ensured a perfect specimen for Klein to scrutinize, and it would have eliminated the need for transporting a captive and maintaining it in cool, oxygenated water. I ran the options by Tassie. "You can't kill it, Dad," she said, frowning.

She was right. The protocols for our project call for the sacrificing of live specimens only as a last resort. The crayfish would take its chances on the Taconic Parkway.

In a lidded plastic container in which I changed the water at every opportunity, the crayfish endured the drive and the two days that passed before I showed up to lead the walk. Would Klein be there? I wasn't sure. He was new to the job, and his wife had recently given birth to their first child.

Happily, the car ahead of me pulled into the parking lot, and out Klein bounced. Seizing the moment because you don't bump into crayfish experts every day, I ran to the trunk of my car, hauled out the container, and thrust it in Klein's hands. He peeled back the lid. Out between his fingers came the crustacean.

In about a second and a half, we had an identification. "*Procambrus acutus*," said Klein. He spoke in the casual tone some of us might employ to say "robin" or "blue jay." He went on. "It's a male." I was delighted and impressed. On the underside of the tail, Klein pointed to a pair of delicate appendages called swimmerets. These angled toward the head and were modified, he said, to carry sperm.

I asked if *Procambrus acutus* is known by a common name. This stumped Klein for about fifteen seconds. He closed his eyes, and out popped the answer. "White river crayfish," he said.

And so a white river crayfish was added to our survey. Back in the container, it survived two days of family visits with frequent water changes and a few nibbles of roast turkey from Stop N' Shop. I blew oxygen into the water with a soda straw. During the ride back up the Taconic, Tassie and brother Ned conducted a serious discussion about the crayfish's name. Eventually, they decided. The crustacean would be "Lucky."

Tassie wanted to keep Lucky as a pet, but by this time I was committed to our original idea that the animal go for a long ride, then return to the exact piece of river bottom from which we'd abducted him. Monday night at midnight when we unloaded the car, Lucky was still frisky. So he remained Tuesday morning.

I managed to find the precise spot where we'd found Lucky. As Tassie watched, I placed our spineless friend on the doorstep of his burrow. The crustacean scuttled calmly into the hole. What, if anything, we wondered, did the crayfish make of his extraordinary adventure? Perhaps the 600-mile road trip seemed like just a dream.

Because ours aspires to be a complete biological survey (an "all-taxa biological inventory," or ATBI, as they're called these days), our interest in the crayfish extended beyond his chitinous exoskeleton to things that he eats. The river bottom teems with the juvenile stages of various insects—the larvae or nymphs of winged creatures known in their adult stages as dragonflies, damselflies, mayflies, stoneflies, caddisflies, mosquitoes, and more. Identifying them posed a problem. We lacked the expertise required to sort out creatures so ubiquitous, diverse, and obscure. To make progress would require skilled help.

We found it in an old friend, Wayne Gall, and in a new acquaintance, a graduate student named Luke Meyers. Gall (a deliciously Dickensian name for an entomologist) worked as chief insect man at the Buffalo Museum of Science when we first got to know him. He has since moved on to the New York State Department of Health. Meyers was working on a master's degree at Colorado State. He'd grown up a few miles from Bloomingdale. When we introduced ourselves to him, he was chasing insects with a butterfly net along our stretch of river. As soon as we learned that his mission was to survey for stoneflies, we invited him to trespass at his pleasure, morning, noon, and night—as long as he shared his records. This he was eager to do.

And so our insect list, while light-years distant from being complete, contains an impressive array of species that rear their young in the river. Gall launched a caddisfly inventory on a sticky August night in 2000, our first summer in the house. He set up a white sheet on poles down by the river and illuminated it with a black light. Later, after a cold beer on the porch, he led Debbie and me (this was B.C., before children) to see what the rig had attracted.

The sheet was crawling with life. Gall zeroed in on the caddisflies, slender things with translucent, veinous wings that fold like pup tents over their backs. There was no question of identifying them on the spot. The insects would have to be killed, transported to Gall's lab back in Buffalo, relaxed (you relax an insect after it's dead by humidifying it, which allows rigid body parts to be moved without breaking), prodded into standard posture, skewered with pins, mounted on a white board, and finally examined with a dissecting scope. We consented to the procedure, which was the only way of finding out which caddisflies we had. All the same, we felt queasy. If Gall was an assassin, we were the shady characters who had put him up to it. Truth is, Gall loves bugs more than anyone I know. The hard realities of his trade trouble him a little, too.

Weeks later, a letter arrived from Buffalo. "Dear Ed," it began. Several sentences later, Dr. Gall got down to business. The sheet and the backlight had yielded the following specimens: *Cheumatopsyche petiti*, two males;

genus *Hydropsyche*, species uncertain, seven females; *Lepidostoma costale*, one male; genus *Lepidostoma*, species uncertain, four females; *Limnephilus sericeus*, one male; *Limnephilus submonilifer*, two females; *Nectopsyche albida*, four males and two females; *Oecetis cinerascens*, one male; genus *Platycentropus*, species uncertain, one female; *Pycnopsyche lepida*, one male and two females; *Pycnopsyche limbata*, nine males and a lone female; and finally, two females of the genus *Triaenodes*, species unknown.

We were off and running—with caddisflies. Luke Meyers picked up the baton next. He stalked the banks with a net by day and a black light trap at night and recorded ten more kinds of caddisflies. He found other things, too. With the help of Janet Mihuc, an entomologist and ecologist who teaches at nearby Paul Smith's College, he supplied us with records for six kinds of mayfly and four of stonefly. Two of the stoneflies, *Isoperla cotta* and *Isoperla frisoni*, were first-ever records for New York State. The night the e-mail came in from Meyer's office in Colorado, Debbie and I popped open a couple of Saranac Brewery black and tans and toasted the good news.

Meanwhile, even as we celebrated, minute by minute, thousands of gallons of water continued to rush over our land. The Saranac never rests. As long as we live here, this courier of life and death from near and far will bring interest and entertainment.

The event that best illustrates the river's ability to deliver things transpired on a cool, crisp October day. Debbie, Ned, Tassie, and I were taking a stroll. I was lingering behind, the kids were in the middle, and Debbie held the lead. "What's that?" she said, pointing to the Saranac. An answer was hard to come by. The brown object bobbing with the current might have been a dead animal or a chunk of debris. It was larger than the average loaf of bread. Heavy rains had swollen the river. Things wash into the current, especially at such times. Debbie scrutinized it with binoculars. "I think it's a decoy," she said. "Or part of a decoy."

My interest was piqued. I sprinted back across the bridge and clambered down a steep pitch of bank to where an eddy sweeps things toward shore. The object might not come close enough to grab, and I wasn't about to risk my life in the frigid water and current, so I searched for a long stick. With it I would try to coax the mysterious flotsam onto the bank.

Luck was mine. The brown blob in the water slowed, turned, and came straight at me. I got ready with the stick. When the moment was right, I reached out. Soon the object was cradled in my hands.

It was a decoy! But it looked ancient. The head was gone, and any paint that might have covered it was worn off. Judging by size and shape, the decoy was meant to represent the body of a Canada goose. It had been chiseled from a coarse-grained softwood, probably northern white cedar. The carver had been clever, using the wood's grain to create the impression of feathers. The decoy was expertly made, handsomely symmetrical, the work of skilled hands. It felt as heavy as a rock of similar size, the wood waterlogged to a point where it had nearly lost its buoyancy. This work of art had been lost a long, long time. Perhaps it had spent a half-century or more embedded in mud, waiting for a flood to pry it loose.

Debbie and the kids were excited and full of questions. How to answer them? My old naturalist friend Dennis Walsh had been pestering me for years to look up a man named Paul Casson. For years, Casson had owned and run a plant nursery in Bedford, New York, not far from where Walsh taught school and I had grown up. Casson had retired to the Adirondacks. Walsh thought his old friend and I had so many things in common that it was imperative we get to know each other. Walsh mentioned that Casson was an expert on the subject of decoys, a subject that had never interested me.

Until now. Debbie, the kids, and I drove to meet Casson and his wife, Edith. Both are painters. They live in a small, comfortable house surrounded by greenery. We were hardly in the door before Casson asked for the decoy. He sat down at a table and began telling its story.

"This is a Canada goose, but then, you've already figured that out. It's a type of decoy that was carved along the St. Lawrence River between the 1890s and 1920 or so." He ran his fingers over the wingtips, which were carved into the body. "This is good work. The carver knew what he was doing. It's likely he was Canadian. Decoy makers on the north side of the river tended to cut in some of the feather detail, while the ones on the American side tended to do it with paint." We discussed the fact that because a wooden effigy of a bird can't fly, this one had either been carved in Canada and brought here or carved in the Adirondacks by one of the many Canadians who settled in the region near the time the decoy was made.

Casson produced a measuring tape and wrote down numbers. "Would you like a head for it?"

Three weeks later, the Cassons appeared at our door. Paul reached a hand into a bag and pulled out a wooden Canada goose head. It had glass eyes and was black and white, just like the real McCoy. We grabbed the body, which had dried very, very slowly by the woodstove. It had lost much of its weight but otherwise looked as good as when we'd found it. Casson's carved head fit it perfectly.

Meanwhile, the Saranac flows on, delivering all sorts of sustenance to the fish and the caddisfly nymphs, the birds and the crayfish, and the humans fortunate to live along its banks. Idyllic? Not entirely. In the spring of 2011, after a winter of monumental snowfall and an April of record-swamping rains, our humble river turned mighty. One day it rose an inch per hour, flooding the road to our house under more than three feet of water and turning a neighbor's place into an island. We live thirty feet above the floodplain on a knoll, so danger never pressed, at least not directly. But life as we knew it changed. Mail and newspaper deliveries ceased. No longer would UPS or FedEx trucks bring stuff from the outer world. The school bus wouldn't come. For weeks we had to hitch rides through the waters in our neighbors' pickup trucks, or, on those many days when the waters grew too deep and the currents too fierce even for trucks, we made crossings by canoe and kayak.

Life became a word problem. Four people go out across the river in a canoe. One comes back immediately in a kayak, leaving the canoe on the other side while the other three head off to work and school. When the other three come back to the far side, the one who paddled the kayak crosses again, leaving the kayak and helping the other three return in the canoe, which had been left on the far side. Working out the placement of canoes and kayaks, which we neighbors shared freely with each other, taxed our brains. Meanwhile, the ground where our septic tank and leach lines are buried grew saturated with floodwater. Flushing toilets became an impossibility. I marched into the woods and dug a hole, and for several weeks there was much toting and emptying of buckets.

Mostly the flood brought inconvenience, but nothing more. Still, minor scares came often enough to stir the adrenaline. One day, for example, Ned prepared to go to school while Tassie, feeling not quite chipper, made a convincing case to stay home. In the morning, all four of us crossed to the outside world (where we'd left our cars before the waters rose) by canoe. On the homebound leg, Tassie sat in the bottom of the boat, snug and safe in her flotation vest, while I kneeled behind her and stroked the surging waters with a double-bladed kayak paddle. It worked well. With wind and current in our favor, we soon reached home.

At three in the afternoon, Tassie and I set out again, this time to meet the school bus bringing Ned home. Now we had to buck wind and current. I was barely getting the better of them, muscling toward a slot between two trees where I would swing sharply into a race and reach calm water, when a gust seized the boat. Suddenly we were slipping backward fast, the wind forcing us sideways toward a barely submerged guardrail. A broadside approach might have swamped us, so I swung the bow downstream as fast as I could. The canoe shot over the rail. On the other side we found quiet water and paddled out. But the complexion of the enterprise had changed. I would take no chances with our kids in those cold, rushing waters. After meeting the bus, we remained on the far side, running errands for three hours until Debbie was back from work. With two adults paddling, we powered the canoe safely home.

For nearly a month, the river remained too high to allow a car safe passage. Some days I found myself wishing we lived somewhere else. Yet there was also something enriching about the experience. Like the character Pierre, who requires more than a thousand pages of *War and Peace* to grasp that true happiness cannot exist without suffering, discomfort and inconvenience had given us a greater sense of our own good fortune. We were high, we were dry, and we had stories to tell.

BIOLOGICAL SURVEY RECORDS:

Potamogeton richardsonii   Pondweed
6/27/03: found in about 2 ft. of water in our stretch of Saranac River, just off downstream end of big sandbar on n. bank; i.d. with help of Gleason and Cronquist; confirmed 7/2/03 by Mark Rooks and colleagues at Adirondack Park Agency; beautiful stuff, long, as fluid as the water, plants 2 meters long and longer

Tringa solitaria   Solitary sandpiper
5/11/01: one bird feeding all day and evening along muddy riverbanks just downstream of sandbar—gorgeous!

1. Summer 1959, in front of my grandparents' house in Northville. From left to right: my sister Maggie; my mother, Joyce Brownell Kanze; my grandfather Burdett Brownell; me (age not quite three); and my stepgrandmother, Florence Brownell. Photo by my father, Edward J. Kanze Jr.

2. Left to right: Maggie Kanze, Florence Brownell, newborn Nora Kanze, Burdett Brownell (Grampy), and the author (age four) at the Kanze house in North White Plains, summer 1961. Photo by Edward J. Kanze Jr.

3. Left to right: Wayne Hammer, Ed Kanze, Nora Kanze, and Burdett Brownell. Wayne and Grampy are cleaning bullheads after a night of fishing as grandchildren look on. The photo was taken at the Hammer camp on Adirondack Lake, near Indian Lake, ca. 1965, by my father, Edward J. Kanze Jr.

4. The author (about age ten) and Jeff Ille, with fish they caught with grandfather Burdett Brownell in Black Lake, near the Oswegatchie River, ca. 1967. In the background is the Northville school on Third Street. The fish were frozen and brought home for show.

5. The author with two great-horned owls he raised while working as a naturalist at Teatown Lake Reservation, Westchester County, 1982.

6. The author working as a National Park Ranger, Baker Island, Acadia National Park, Maine, August 1999.

7. Gazing out over Keene Valley from the Porter Mountain ledges, the author and his future wife, Debbie, contemplate a crisp fall day. September 1991. Photo by Jeffrey Parsons, used with permission.

8. Grampy (my grandfather Burdett Brownell, 1904–1978), second from right, at a meeting of the Northville Rotary Club, ca. 1965. Grampy was Northville's mayor for eighteen years, from 1953–1961, 1963–1969, and 1971–1975.

9. My grandfather Burdett Eglin Brownell, about age sixteen, poses for a rare portrait, ca. 1920.

10. My great-grandfather Elmer Brownell used this double-barrel shotgun to provide food for his family. Beside the gun appears a mitten Elmer wore while driving horse teams and sleighs through the Adirondack Mountains in winter. Elmer was a teamster and fur buyer. Note the wear on the palm where he held the reins of his teams.

11. My great-grandfather Elmer Brownell with his granddaughter Joyce Brownell (my mother), ca. 1930. The photo was taken in front of Elmer and Jenny Brownell's house on Third Street in Northville.

12. Burdett Eglin, Carrie Brownell Eglin, Floyd W. Abrams (guide), Nancy Brownell Shipman, and Walter Shipman at Abrams's cabin at T Lake, near Piseco, ca. 1910.

13. Tassie, Debbie, Ned, and Ed Kanze visiting the site of Floyd Abrams's cabin at T Lake, deep in the woods west of Piseco, September 2012.

14. My great-great-aunts Nancy Brownell Shipman (1876–1962) and Carrie Brownell Eglin (1873–1956) in Northville, ca. 1944.

15. Lewis Brownell's house at the corner of First and Bridge Streets, Northville, ca. 1890. Lewis stands at the top of the stairs, Carrie sits jauntily at the top of a banister, and Nancy sits in a chair on the porch.

16. Niagara Falls, painted by my great-great-grandmother Elnora Graves Brownell sometime before her death in 1888. Private collection.

17. An Adirondack scene, painted by my great-great-grandmother Elnora Graves Brownell, sometime between her arrival in Northville in 1868 and her death twenty years later. Private collection.

18. Edna Kanze Gordon ("Aunt Dolly") at Stony Wold Sanatorium, Lake Kushaqua, ca. 1944.

19. Photo of Stony Wold Sanatorium, Lake Kushaqua, near Onchiota, New York, ca. 1944.

20. Ed, Ned (age twenty-one months), and Debbie Kanze leaving the Adirondack Medical Center in Saranac Lake with newborn baby Tasman, June 2005.

21. Tassie, Ed, Debbie, and Ned Kanze at home on their porch, ca. 2008. Photo by Carol Gracie, used with permission.

22. My guiding work sometimes takes me far afield. That's Ayers Rock over my shoulder. I was leading a 2011 Smithsonian Journeys trip to Australia and New Zealand.

23. Tasman, Debbie, and Ned (left to right) enjoying a sunny winter skating party on an old oxbow of the Saranac River. Whiteface Mountain rises in the background.

24. The Saranac River near our house. The photo was taken in February after the ice began to break up.

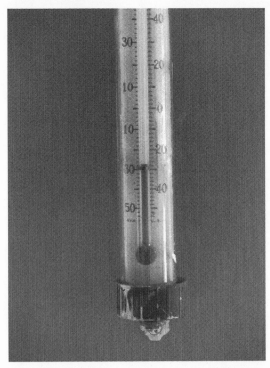

25. Our porch thermometer registers twenty-eight below zero Fahrenheit. On the coldest nights, we've seen temperatures dip to forty below.

26. Snow falls at the end of April, and we're still busy feeding the woodstove that heats the house. Cutting, splitting, hauling, and stacking wood to fill this shed keep me busy.

27. The proximity of Moose Pond to the Adirondack property we purchased helped compensate for all the sacrifices we had to make to rescue a house from the verge of collapse.

28. Every year, female snapping turtles like this one come out of the river to dig nests along our road.

29. Our property along the Saranac River abounds in native wildflowers. Here, one of the prettiest, cardinal flower, blooms at the beginning of September.

30. The author in his Adirondack writing studio, 2013. Photo by his daughter, Tasman, then seven.

7

The Woods

E very morning, or at least every morning when the temperature outside is above freezing, I grab a cup of coffee and step out on the porch to take in the view. What I see cheers me. There's the quaint winding road we live on, a sturdy one-lane bridge paved with planks and reaching over the river, the river itself, a smattering of utility poles draped with electric and telephone lines, perhaps a bird or two on a wire, a swath of sky, a distant hill, and several hundred thousand trees: red maple, sugar maple, quaking aspen, American elm, white birch, yellow birch, black cherry, chokecherry, American beech, balsam fir, white pine, red spruce, northern white cedar, and tamarack.

Trees rule the landscape, making all other life forms here seem like accoutrements. Adirondack forests, among the most extensive and best-preserved temperate deciduous woodlands in the world, stand vibrant and diverse, impenetrably dense in places, rich in old-growth. They stretch on forever, or seem to. Trees crowd up mountains to their summits, or nearly so, and they push down into every gully, basin, and ravine, their roots splitting rocks as they go. The species that flourish are hardy. The balsam fir, for example, an abundant conifer at our place and throughout the mountains, has been shown through laboratory study to withstand temperatures of one hundred below zero Fahrenheit. Thermometers never sink that impossibly low (forty below zero is the coldest we've seen at our house), yet if they ever do, our firs will be ready.

We in the world's cold places make little use of the word "jungle." Yet it's jungle here, although no one calls it that—jungle so thick and leafy a half-ton moose could stand a few feet distant from you on a trail, and unless it moved, you might never see it.

Someone might argue that what I call Adirondack jungle isn't really jungle at all. It lacks elephants thundering around on the ground and monkeys cavorting in the trees. But hold on. Mammoths and mastodons surely trampled the wildflowers here for millions of years. Then, just the day before yesterday in geologic and biological time, overhunting by Indians, climate change, a mysterious plague, or some combination of factors drove them to extinction. The Paleo-Indian hunters who cast the first human footprints in Adirondack mud would have found elephants here. Surely they killed and ate them.

As for monkeys, look in the mirror. The biologist Jared Diamond points to the overwhelming majority of DNA we share with chimps and bonobos and dubs humans "the third chimpanzee." We are more closely related to chimps and gorillas than red-eyed vireos are to white-eyed vireos, and no one would dispute that vireos are peas from the same pod. Monkeys? Here they wear hiking boots.

The dominant color of the Adirondack Mountains is green. The richness and variety of that single hue astounds the observant eye and makes the tourist gasp. I once had the pleasure of leading high government officials from the Persian Gulf nation of Qatar on an Adirondack nature walk. Qatar is a parched, desert land. It was thrilling to immerse these men in our humid, leafy woods and watch their eyes bulge. They were agog at the green. Even a jaded (in this case, the word is especially apt) local can hardly set foot in the forest without being overwhelmed by the staggering quantity of leaves.

A cheap but satisfying thrill is to climb to the summit of a mountain in the central Adirondacks, look out in every direction, and see nothing but forest—the dark, glossy green of balsam fir, the luminous yellow-green of sugar maple, the cool frosty green of white and black spruce, the deep blue-green of white pine, the wavering light-and-dark green of aspens trembling in a breeze. Leaves stretch north, south, east, and west. They reach to the horizons and spill over the other side. There are billions of them.

I fell in love with the verdure as a child. My parents would drive my sisters and me up to Northville to visit my grandparents. We lived in Westchester County, about thirty miles north of New York City. Up the Taconic Parkway we'd cruise, pushing ever deeper into an ocean of trees. The car would feel like a submarine. Just north of Mayfield, as we crossed into the Adirondack Park, the woods closed in on both sides of Route 30 and the immersion became complete.

We'd arrive in Northville on a sultry Friday afternoon. I have vivid memories of driving down streets that tunneled through leaves, the dappled light filtering down nearly as green as the leaves themselves, the air thick and fragrant with the moist exhalations of stomata. Our destination was an island of brick: the Serfis Glove Shop, a Northville institution, housed in an old 1888 schoolhouse on Main Street. The shop was not a store where gloves were sold. It was a factory. Cowhides were hauled in one door and boxes of finished gloves left by another. Serfis's enterprise owed its existence to the forest, although I didn't comprehend this at the time.

My mother would cajole us out of the car and lead my sisters and me into a room filled with women, sewing machines, and the mingled smells of cowhide and machine oil. One of the women was Grandma Florence, my grandfather's second wife. She'd rush up to greet us in a paisley dress and flurry of arms and lipstick. Soon the machines would stand idle, and all the womenfolk would be fussing over us, saying how big we were, and how good-looking, and how much we looked like our parents, and how delighted everyone was to have us visit. This was my first taste of celebrity.

The glove shop—a factory in miniature—consisted of two parts. Upstairs, women stitched leather into finished gloves. Downstairs, the men, one of them my grandfather, laid patterns on hides and cut out the pieces for the women to sew. They used "shears," as Grampy called them, which were nothing more than heavy iron scissors. They explained the muscle and sinew that bulged in his hands. I was witnessing history. The Serfis Glove Shop was among the last of scores of small glove factories that flourished in the Adirondacks through the second half of the nineteenth century and the first half of the twentieth. Today, the building is gone, demolished to make way for new town offices, and the industry is gone, too. Gloversville, just down the road, once a world capital of glove making, is a ghost of itself. The old factories have been razed or sit empty, succumbing to decay.

Grampy and Grandma were typical of their time and place in that they plied their skills in glove shops when work became available, and when it dried up, they lived off the land. Grandma was nearly as expert and passionate a fisherman as Grampy was. They knew how to loaf and play and find other sources of income when there wasn't any work.

Most adults I knew didn't know how to relax. By contrast, taking it easy never posed a problem for my grandfather. Mind you, he was industrious. As Northville's mayor and chief lawman, he was the most responsible adult I knew. Yet when the opportunity for leisure presented itself, he seized it without guilt or hesitation. More than anyone I've ever known, he relished sitting outdoors on a summer evening, telling stories, listening to stories, puffing on a pipe, and watching the sun go down and the bats come out. He relished idle time indoors, too, rarely traveling with a book but rather picking up the nearest one that presented itself and reading it cover to cover. As a reader, he was an opportunist.

Much of my grandfather's leisure had a practical side. His fishing and hunting filled a giant chest freezer in his cellar. There was food to last through lean times. And he was a compulsive tinkerer and inventor. He devised a Rube Goldberg device to winch a heavy boat on top of his car without exertion. To open his garage door, you pressed a knot in the door frame. As kids, we loved the secret switch he'd installed behind the knot, although I doubt it would have fooled a burglar. Greasy thumbprints gave it away. My favorite device was a hidden switch that opened the cellar door. Behind lay the big freezer, filled with frozen fish, venison, and popsicles. You descended a dark set of stairs in the garage, reached the next-to-last step, and kicked your heel against the riser behind you. A buzzer blared so loudly it terrified us as children. To the left, a door that had no knob or handle popped open. Popsicles were soon in hand.

After World War II, when the glove industry began migrating to the Philippines, my grandparents and many of their neighbors found themselves high and dry in a sea of trees. Among the trees was the one—a titan of the North Woods—that had brought the glove industry to the mountains in the first place.

The eastern hemlock, *Tsuga canadensis*, is not, as its name implies, kin to the notorious poison hemlock, *Conium maculatum*. As every schoolchild learns, perhaps apocryphally, capital punishment in the form of "hemlock tea" ended the life of the Greek philosopher Socrates. Legend has it that the drink was brewed from the beautiful but lethal poison hemlock, a water-loving herb native to Eurasia. Poison hemlock has been introduced to North America and grows widely here. It's rare in these mountains, at least where I roam, but I've seen it along a trail near Speculator in the central Adirondacks. It looks a good deal like wild carrot, or Queen Anne's lace.

The hemlock tree, by contrast, is a handsome, soft-needled member of the pine family. It flourishes in shady ravines and valley bottoms where the soil is rich and deep. I've made a tea that is rich in vitamin C from its needles and lived to tell the tale. The part of the hemlock most valuable to the glove industry was the bark.

Scratch a fingernail on a hemlock trunk, and a red-brown color is revealed. This is "tannin," a catchall term for a group of bitter, astringent compounds that occur widely in tea leaves, coffee beans, wine grapes, and the bark of oaks, hemlocks, and northern white cedar. Tannins from Adirondack hemlocks supported a leather tanning boom in the mountains from the mid-1850s until 1894 or thereabouts. Loggers marched into the woods, sawed or chopped through giant boles, and sent old-growth hemlocks crashing to the ground. Next, "bark-peelers" moved in with spuds, long-handled iron chisels forged by blacksmiths. With the tools, they pried off the tannin-rich bark, which in turn was loaded on sleighs and wagons and hauled by draft horses to riverbank tanneries deep in the woods. Rivers brought tanneries the water they consumed in great volume, and they carried away toxic effluent. Tanneries turned streams green, made them stink, and purged them of life.

In her detailed history of the Adirondack tanning history, *Hides, Hemlocks, and Adirondack History*, author Barbara McMartin includes a firsthand account of what it was like to peel hemlock bark. The source was an old man, Truman Hayes, who died in 1969, but not before dictating his memories of life in the hemlock woods in 1880. "The spring I was 16 I was working in the barkwoods for Mr. Ross. As I remember it there were twenty men, five crews, four men to a crew. Each crew had to keep count of the trees he peeled during the days. There was one always more or less racing to see which crew peeled the most trees. From sixty to one hundred trees was a good day's work. . . ."

Each man had his role. Hayes's cousin, Ed Hayes, felled the trees with an ax. Then Truman chopped off the branches, and another cousin, Eugene Hayes, sliced the bark in four-foot lengths and on the log's crown slit it end to end. Finally, Charlie Hayes, Truman's brother, slipped his spud beneath the bark and pried it off in sections. For this labor, carried out from 6:30 in the morning until 6:00 at night, six days a week for six weeks, the men received a grand total of $5.00 apiece.

For the bark peeler, the hardest part was apparently not the labor but the bugs. Truman Hayes recounts:

> The plague of the bark peelers is flies: big flies, little flies, and all kind of flies except peaceful and gentle flies. There were the mosquitoes constantly yelling "Coming, coming," and they were by the thousands and millions and each one trying to stick his bill into you first, and deepest. And then there were the billions of black flies who never told you they were "coming" but commenced work at once. They would crawl into your eyes, ears, nose, and mouth, in fact any opening they could find. And then there was another small fly, so tiny you could hardly see him. We called him "All jaws." After a few billion had bit you your flesh would smart as if it had been burned.
>
> Insect repellent didn't exist or wasn't available. At night, so they could sleep, the men built smudge fires that filled their log huts with smoke.

For me, these stories strike home. At the apex of a pyramid built on the backs and blood of bark peelers and tannery workers sat my country squire of a great-great-grandfather, Lewis Brownell. I know little about Lewis aside from his formidable résumé. He owned, at various times, a sawmill and lumber business, two tanneries, a hotel, a bottling plant, and one of the grandest houses in Northville. His obituary, published the day he died, May 12, 1909, is headlined "Hon. Lewis Brownell Died This Morning: Prominent Northville Man Succumbs After Long Illness—Well Known Mason."

Little about Lewis has come down through the family, but his obituary fills in some of the blanks. "His popularity," it reports, "had been manifested upon two different occasions when he was nominated for the office of member of [New York State] assembly and elected by handsome majorities." The tribute goes on to say that Lewis was "of a jovial, pleasing disposition, and made many friends, all of whom will greatly miss him."

Lewis died nearly a half-century before I was born, and by my time, all but one of his children were gone, too. Still, in 1960 or thereabouts, when I was three or four and my family was in Northville, I shook the right hand of the lone survivor. She was Lewis's daughter, Nancy Brownell Shipman, my grandfather's Aunt Nancy.

Aunt Nancy's hand was a frightening thing to a small boy, withered and translucent, poor in flesh but rich in implication. It had been grasping objects since 1876. Aunt Nancy had long, snow-white hair. She beckoned me to the bed, saying, "Come here" in a singsong voice that had undertones of power and lunacy. Fear glued my feet to the floor. My mother nudged me. "Go ahead," she said. "It will be all right." Nancy fixed me with a dewy eye and clasped my little paw in hers and said something nonsensical. Somehow, though, she radiated goodwill, or so I vaguely remember. She was a mythical figure from a long-lost past. Yet instantly I loved her, and I cherish the memory of our only meeting.

Aunt Nancy represented a bridge to nineteenth-century forebears. In that brief handshake, I reached across time and touched another world—a horse-drawn, oil-lamp–illuminated world alien to me in countless ways, yet peopled by men, women, and children to whom I was related.

Aunt Nancy's father, Lewis Brownell, was born in 1840, three years after New York State geologist Ebenezer Emmons made the first recorded climb of the Adirondacks' highest peak. Emmons named the 5,343-foot pinnacle after the sponsor of his survey, New York Governor William Marcy. Lewis's father was Orra Brownell, born in 1795, a second-generation Adirondacker and son of Daniel and Hannah. Orra was born in

East Greenbush, outside the mountains, and sometime during childhood he made the move with his parents and siblings to the woods. Orra married Nancy Harris, a Scot. Sometime in the early nineteenth century, he built a sawmill on East Stony Creek, at Hope Falls, a few miles north of Northville.

On my desk sits Orra's Bible, handed down from my grandfather. It's a massive, leather-bound job with pages yellowed or missing and edges tattered. The binding is falling apart. On the inside cover appear two notable inscriptions. One is scratched in ink with an old steel or quill pen. It reads "Orra Brownell . . . Book . . . Hope." The other is marked in pencil. "Commenced," it says, "to read the Bible through, Jan 1st 1891, Carrie Brownell, and Finished it age 17 yr. 1 mo. Dec. 1891." Carrie Brownell, born 1873, was Lewis's daughter and Aunt Nancy's older sister. Carrie was a slender beauty. She married a well-to-do Northville bank cashier named Burdett Eglin, Grampy's namesake. Aunt Carrie, as my grandfather called her, died in 1956, the year I was born.

I know little of Lewis Brownell's youth. He grew up in the backwoods hamlet of Hope and likely spent considerable time hunting, fishing, and cavorting in the wilds when not helping his father at the sawmill. He was born May 16 in Northville, the tenth of twelve children (eight boys, four girls). The 1860 census for Hope lists Orra Brownell, sixty-five, a farmer, as the head of a household consisting also of Nancy Harris Brownell, sixty; Lewis Brownell, twenty; "farm labor"; Frances Brownell, eighteen; and a Henry Lwquick [sic], thirty-five, perhaps a farmhand.

Orra Brownell was an entrepreneur. By 1855, he was operating a tannery as well as a sawmill, getting in early on the leather boom that resonated through Adirondack forests from the mid-1850s until the industry collapsed in about 1894. In 1855, the tannery was known as Orra Brownell and Sons. Lewis was only fifteen at the time. Elder brothers Robert, twenty-eight; Orra Jr., twenty-five; John, twenty-three; and Ira, twenty-one, were likely the ones implied in the name. Yet by 1868, command of the operation had shifted to Lewis. Did he gain control through force of ambition and aggression, through keen intellect, or did his siblings just lose interest and step aside? I haven't learned. I do know that in 1868, the family tanning business was known as "Lewis Brownell and Company," and that in 1875 it was called "Lewis Brownell and Brothers," perhaps reflecting an insistence on the part of family members to share in the name.

Tanning, during its brief Adirondack heyday, proved lucrative for those at the top. It earned Lewis Brownell a stately clapboard house on the corner of Bridge and First Streets in Northville, and undoubtedly it played a major role in his being elected a Hamilton County judge and later, in 1888 and 1889, a representative for two one-year terms in the New York State Assembly.

According to Barbara McMartin, the hides that were salted, shipped hard as boards, soaked, softened, scraped free of hair, fleshed, and ultimately steeped in Adirondack hemlock tannins came almost entirely from overseas. Cattle ranches in Central and South America supplied nearly all of them, with the majority coming from Argentina and Brazil. First by sailing ship or steamship, then by barge or rail, then over the last leg by horse-drawn wagon or sleigh, raw cowhides found their way to the tanneries. The economics of the enterprise don't seem to add up, yet somehow they must have. At Hope Falls in 1860, reports McMartin, the Brownells consumed 1,800 cords of bark, sold $84,000 worth of leather, and turned a profit of $25,580. By 1880, the profits had nearly doubled. Lewis Brownell's fortunes swelled accordingly.

A peculiar thing began to happen as I immersed myself in family history. I began to feel unnervingly close to my ancestors, particularly (and I'm not sure why) to Lewis; his wife, Elnora; and their children. We have more in common than genes. They woke up in the morning with the same appetites as mine, blinked at the same sun, navigated life's twists and turns with the similar hopes and fears, and at night, under the very moon I now gaze upon, they went to bed with the same mix of satisfaction, angst, longing, delight, and dread. I grew up in a house with an Elnora painting of Niagara Falls hanging over the fireplace. Perhaps that's part of it, too. A gulf of eighty-eight years stretches between my great-great-grandmother's death in 1888 and my debut in 1956, but still I think of her with tenderness.

One summer day a decade ago, I stood in the Northville cemetery and wept at the foot of her grave. I grieved, too, for her and Lewis's dead children: for Fred, the firstborn, who died on the twenty-fourth of February, 1873, aged eight months and three days; for Lewis, who died on the sixth of October, 1877, aged two months and twenty-six days; and for another Lewis, a second brave try at producing a namesake, who died on the nineteenth of November, 1885, aged two years, six months, and seventeen days. The modern mind reels at those losses. Despite the family's wealth, life was hard. Contagious illnesses raged through the countryside, and at the time doctors could do little more than prescribe bed rest and whiskey. A son of Lewis and Elnora, Elmer, who lived to adulthood and was my grandfather's father, died twenty-one years before I was born.

Born in 1876, Aunt Nancy, like brother Elmer, survived the plagues. Unlike him, she lived through much of the twentieth century. It pains me knowing that all the experiences of her life—her early years, her adolescence, her romantic life and marriage to artist Walter Leroy Shipman, their childlessness (a choice? a bitter twist of fate?), and decades of adult life in New York City and Northville again—are lost and forgotten, save for an album of photos and a gold watch with "WS" engraved on the back.

The watch ticks quietly on my desk as I write these words. It belonged to Walter Shipman, who died in 1918. I know Walter mainly from photographs. He had a round, kindly face and a big dark mustache. One photo shows him standing at an easel in a room full of easels and artists in New York City. In another, circa 1910, he appears with his wife, sister-in-law, and brother-in-law at a cabin deep in the woods. The letters "FWA" are carved in one of the cabin's logs. A man who appears to be a guide appears in the photograph, too. Two sources came forward and identified him after I published the photo in an Adirondack newspaper. He was Floyd W. Abrams, who ran a wilderness lodge and guiding service near Piseco, a day's journey by horse-drawn carriage from the Brownell sisters' homes in Northville.

Elmer Brownell's double-barreled shotgun, an old hammer-lock model with Damascus steel barrels made by beating coils of wire with a hammer, was given to me on my sixteenth birthday. It came as a surprise. Grampy had promised to give me a .22 rifle when I turned sixteen. It was a gun he had given to my grandmother during their brief marriage, and he had promised to keep it for her in the expectation that a male grandson might come along. My grandfather was a man of few words, yet he spoke loudly to me in his own way when he handed me my grandmother's Remington. I admired him for honoring a decades-old promise to a woman who scorned him, and for doing so without uttering an unkind word. Then out came the shotgun. Elmer Brownell had used it to bring home meat for his family. My grandfather put it in my hands. This was a powerful moment. The artifact, reeking of the past, was mine to keep, Grampy said, and mine to pass on. I couldn't speak. My grandfather didn't say much, either. Suddenly I was no longer just a kid. I was a link in a chain stretching back into the past and forward into the future.

As I roam Adirondack highways and byways in the twenty-first century, I think of Elmer Brownell, bundled in furs and woolens, shotgun by his side, driving a horse-drawn sleigh from village to village through miles and miles of trackless snow, night coming on, surrounded by a vast and inhospitable forest that spreads in all directions, miles from the nearest house, jagged flakes stinging his face, longing for a warm fire, a strong drink, a hot meal.

Elmer was a "teamster." Today teamsters drive giant tractor-trailer rigs, but at the turn of the twentieth century in the Adirondacks, they piloted freight wagons and sledges pulled by horse teams. In winter, Elmer held the reins with wool mittens, one of which has come down to me. It's far too snug for my extra-large paws but seems designed to fit a man's hand, size small. The yarn is knitted to a thick pile over the palm and thumb. It includes strands of yellow, charcoal-gray, olive, and salmon. The mitten is badly worn in one place—across the upper palm, where Elmer's hand would have clutched a rein. His work consisted of buying furs from trappers in mountain villages. With a full load, he'd turn and head for Albany. There, the pelts were handed over to the France-based furrier, Reveillon Freres, or so says family lore.

I wish I'd known Elmer. To me, my great-grandfather is little more than a cipher, a thin man in a few old photographs, smiling behind spectacles and a mustache. I hold his mitten and shotgun in my hands and wish they could tell tales. My mother recalls hearing from her own mother that Elmer attended a Methodist seminary but was thrown out for drinking. He was, my grandmother said, witty and bright, a marvelous storyteller who could hold listeners spellbound. Elmer cultivated his oratorical gifts while away on fur-buying trips, picking up and dispensing stories while meeting with trappers and gathering up pelts.

My mother remembers her grandfather as an empty husk. When she visited the Brownell homestead as a child, Elmer sat silent and expressionless in a chair. His wife, my great-grandmother Jennie Lawton Brownell, would shoo away the children. "Don't disturb Grandpa," this tiny, generally sweet-tempered woman would say. If a boy ignored the command, Grandma Jenny reached out and gave a stinging smack. Elmer Brownell died on the sixteenth of September, 1935. He was about sixty-five; my mother was not quite seven. The obituary reports, "He had been ill a long time." Elmer Brownell had had his share of sorrows. His mother died when he was in his teens. Each of his six girls had perished in childhood. His son Graves, a soldier in World War I, was gassed while fighting with Company G of the 105th Infantry in France and Belgium. Graves married and had children, but his lungs were ruined, and he died in his fifties.

The great Adirondack forest that provided the logs for Orra Brownell's Hope Falls sawmill; that supplied the hemlock bark for Lewis Brownell's tanneries; that produced the beaver, muskrat, fox, otter, and mink who yielded their lives to the trappers who sold their pelts to Elmer

Brownell; and that gave my grandfather his first full-time job when he left school at fourteen to cook in a backwoods lumber camp—the same forest that thrilled and terrified me during childhood visits to the North Woods—swallows people if they're not careful. Just as the English explorer Percy Fawcett vanished without a clue in the Amazon, people go missing and stay missing here, too.

One summer when I was a child fishing in the Adirondacks with my grandfather, another boy, eight years old, went for a walk in another part of the park and never came back. Despite a massive search that went on for weeks, no sign of Douglas Legg was ever found. There was speculation that he had been abducted or murdered by a member of his own family, but these were mere rumors. More likely he got lost, perished of exposure, and become dinner for a scavenging bear.

Sometimes the missing are found, but too late. Twenty years ago, my brother-in-law, Andy, and I climbed Mount Marcy, the highest of the so-called Adirondack High Peaks. Its summit rises 5,344 feet above sea level. The early October day was sunny and mild, and the weather forecast at Adirondack Loj predicted agreeable conditions. But mountain weather can change suddenly. We were caught in a blizzard near the top, out on bare rock. Only because we brought winter clothing in our day packs did we stumble down the mountain alive. The following spring, I read a newspaper story about a hiker found along the trail we'd walked. He had gone in several days before us and was lying dead or dying, only a few feet from the path, when we passed him. The man had hiked alone, broken an ankle, and moved off the trail to find shelter and make a fire. The night turned bitterly cold. Unsuccessful in sustaining a blaze, the man had died a lonely death of hypothermia.

Adirondack forests consume buildings and history, too. One recent morning, Debbie, the kids, and I made a visit to Lake Kushaqua, about a half hour's drive north of our place and well back in the woods. In 1902, a massive tuberculosis sanatorium opened there, the pet project of the wealthy feminist and philanthropist Elizabeth Newcomb. In its prime in the twenties and thirties, the institution housed more than one hundred patients. It employed a substantial staff, included about twenty buildings, had its own train station and power plant, and supplied the dining room with produce from its own farm.

Stony Wold interests me because my Aunt "Dolly," my father's older sister, Edna, spent three years curing there during the Second World War. Time at the "san," as Aunt Dolly always called it, proved formative as well as curative. A chemist trained at Barnard University, she went on to a distinguished career in biomedical research, much of it spent with the National Institutes of Health in Washington, DC.

In my image of Stony Wold, an image cobbled together from my aunt's stories and letters and my father's memories of a 1944 visit there, the place bustles. Trains come, go, blow their whistles, and spew steam. Doctors and nurses march between patients, dictating every facet of their lives. The scent of antiseptic hangs heavy in the rooms and hallways. In the clamorous kitchen, cooks whip up the next meal.

What we found was silence. It was August. Songbirds had either fled or were engaged in the silent work of fattening up for southbound journeys or bulking up to stay alive through the winter to come. Only the occasional piping of a blue-headed vireo graced the air as we walked up a gravel road with friends who rent one of the sanatorium's last surviving cottages.

Stony Wold's Tudor chapel still stands, spruced up as a private home. The rail station is gone. Gone, too, are all but one of the other cottages and utility buildings. We were directed off the road and led to a flat where the ground underfoot was packed hard. Exotic spotted knapweed grew lavishly, its purple flowers adding cheer to a place otherwise devoid of it.

Charlie, one of our guides, led the way to an embankment. Beyond, pushed over the brink by heavy machinery, lay great heaps of rubble, the last remains of Stony Wold. The buildings were razed in 1975 after the land became part of the Adirondack Forest Preserve. In another century, they will vanish all but entirely. The forest reclaims its own.

Meanwhile, my aunt's experience of the place lives on in her letters. One of the first, postmarked October 24, 1942, begins "Dear Mom." She writes, "I'm starting to settle down to this bed routine at last. I may even learn to like a bed pan in time. . . . This morning I got my physical exam. The doctor said it was very 'uninteresting.'" She goes on to say that her husband—she and my Uncle Morey had been married only two years when the diagnosis of TB was handed down—will be coming for a few days. "I hope he brings his woolies. It's awfully cold." Another letter, posted in January, reports, "It is so cold that the rails snap."

Fresh air was considered a vital part of the get-well regime. In a letter dated November 16, 1942, Dolly explains. "I'm not so good at writing letters lately. It gets so cold here when the windows are open that I stay under the covers. By the time they shut the windows & the place warms up enough to come out, it's time to open up again for the next rest hour." Bed rest and balsam-scented Adirondack atmosphere—lots of both, even when temperatures dropped to forty below zero—were a mandatory part of every patient's daily life. Dolly adds, "Nothing new happens up here. I spend my time sitting, eating, lying down & sleeping. Some life."

In the next letter, to my father, dated November 24, Dolly reports, "It's so cold here I hope I don't get well enough to go outdoors until Spring. Last night it was 10 below zero. Coca Cola bottles [put] on the window sill to cool froze and exploded."

Eating was part of the cure, too. Food was supplied in abundance, washed down with milk at midmorning and midafternoon. The rich diet, consumed with almost no exercise, put on girth. Dolly writes her mother on January 5, 1943: "Did I tell you that I gained another 3 lbs.? That makes a total of 8 lbs. since I am here. It is really beginning to show now especially around the fanny. I'll soon have a figure like Stinky's." Stinky was the family's cocker spaniel.

"Boy is it cold here!" a February letter begins. "It was 37 below zero this morning at 9 o'clock. I don't know how cold it was last night. There has been a wreck in the train somewhere and we haven't had any mail." Good news mixes with bad. "They have fired the dietician," reports a March 28, 1943, letter, "and the meals are much better. We had roast pork for lunch and chicken salad for supper. I hope it keeps up."

At times the treatment seemed worse than the disease. "Yesterday morning," Dolly reports on May 19, 1943, "I had another gastric. This means they wash out my stomach in an effort to find some TB bugs. It seems to me they are going a little too far. If they are having so much trouble, why don't they just decide I haven't any? Maybe they think they ought to do something for the money it costs to stay here."

Nearly five months later, on October 13, Dolly is glum. "I now have a 5 lb. bag of lead shot that I have to put on my chest over where the T.B. is when I lie down," she writes her mother. "It's supposed to keep the part from moving. It's an awful nuisance." For a time, the letters are brief and brave, full of undertones of sadness. On November 4, she writes, "I don't know how long I'll have the weight or how long [I] will have to stay in bed—several months at least, I'm afraid. My last X-ray didn't show any change since I was back in bed. My next one is next week—then I'll find out if the bag is doing any good. It certainly keeps me from doing anything but read."

Tuberculosis patients, even those who survived the disease and the cure, had setbacks. On November 19, Dolly tells her mother,

My last X-ray wasn't very good so they decided that I needed something more than staying in bed and using the shot bag.

Monday they started pneumothorax—they inject air into the chest cavity to collapse the lung so it rests and can heal. . . . It hurt a lot and I ran a temperature the first day, but since then I have felt fine. The only part that bothers me is that I have to lie on bedside a few weeks until it gets started. I'm not sick but it is supposed to be quite a strain on the lung for a while if there are any adhesions and I have to be very quiet. It won't be more than 3 weeks.

The letter concludes: "Don't worry about me. I'm all right but you can see yourself that I have been here a long time and it was time to do something more than rest."

A November 26 letter to the younger of her two brothers (my father-to-be) tells more. "No more cracks about the sandbag please. I don't use it anymore since they have been giving me the air. I got another dose this morning. I always feel as if they were pumping up tires; they check the pressure and everything." My aunt's passion for science in general and human biology in particular were not dimmed by her forced retreat from research. On the first of December, she writes her mother, asking for books to be sent. The list consists of texts on physics and physical chemistry, a work on the chemistry of the brain, and an introduction to physiologic chemistry.

Like many TB patients, Dolly had financial worries. They are rarely mentioned, but a December 3 letter to her mother gives a sense of things: "I expect to stay at Stony Wold to finish the cure. I know it is cheaper than most places and even cheaper than at home where I would have to pay a private doctor to give me pneumo twice a week. Pop [her father] shouldn't worry about helping out. . . . Stony Wold will let Morey [Dolly's husband] pay half my board now and continue paying the rest after I leave. I guess Morey will do that and then things will be easier."

Dolly's health improved. Just before Christmas 1943, she was granted freedom from incessant bed rest and allowed to move back to an upstairs room. "This room is also warmer and nearer the bathroom," she writes her mother, "so I don't have to walk as much. I am supposed to take it very easy—that is no sudden movements or outbursts of laughing or coughing. Those things would cause sudden pulls in the adhesion and would be bad. Otherwise I am fine." Dolly expresses frustration that she and Morey, who was in the Army but not overseas, can't be together at Christmas. "Some of the other girls here have husbands in the Army and get permission to leave here and meet them over Xmas. They aren't even going to let me get up to dinner or go to the Christmas party this year so I would certainly never get permission to leave here."

Still, Dolly accentuated the positive. She rejoices in the fact that Sonny (a nickname for Robert Kanze, the older of her two brothers, both younger than she) is in the Army in Italy and far from the fighting and that my father will be able to visit her before he ships out to fight with the Tenth Armored Division in France and Germany.

The last letter that survives, dated January 15, 1945, shows Dolly's spirits rising and humor brightening her prose. "Dr. Henning is on the war path," she writes, "and wants everybody to stay in bed more so we have to lay low until he calms down again. His Mother-in-law has been visiting. We think that probably has something to do with his bad mood."

By this time, Dolly was liberated from bed much of the time and allowed to work a few hours in the sanatorium's laboratory. The letter ends: "I have been working all morning since I got back and it doesn't bother me. I had an X-ray this week and it was good so I guess the running around didn't do any harm. Love, Dolly."

Eventually, her films ran as clear as the brooks pouring down mountain slopes into Lake Kushaqua. Dolly was discharged. In September 1945, she boarded a southbound train and turned up on the 16th without advance notice in her parents' living room in North White Plains. By extraordinary coincidence, my uncle and father returned home from their respective theaters of the war, separately and without warning, on the same joyous day.

My aunt came to the Adirondack Mountains for her health and Debbie and I and my pioneering Brownell ancestors to start new lives. But the majority of people who come here don't intend to stay. They arrive to immerse themselves not in brine, as tourists at the seashore do, but in the trees. By some estimates, the annual number of visitors to the park approaches 10 million. They have been coming in a steady stream since 1849, when an outdoors-loving man of the cloth named Joel Headley published the seminal North Woods travel book. It was titled *Adirondack; or Life In The Woods*. The author advocated Adirondack fresh air and hearty adventure as antidotes for modern ills. This book was followed in 1869 by a perhaps even more influential tome, William Henry Harrison Murray's *Adventures in the Wilderness; or Camp-Life in the Adirondacks*. It launched an Adirondack tourist rush and inspired the author's nickname, "Adirondack Murray."

Among Headley's readers was William James Stillman, an artist, writer, woodsman, and Renaissance man who, in August 1858, brought the most famous camping party in Adirondack history to sleep beside a remote pond. Plenty of celebrated camping groups came later—most notably, 1916 and 1919 parties that traveled in Model T Ford convoys, literally electrified the woods, and included Thomas Edison, Henry Ford, Harvey Firestone, and John Burroughs. Yet none left such a lasting impression as Stillman's.

Joining him to hunt, fish, play, and ruminate deep in the forest and far from the madding crowds of Boston were Ralph Waldo Emerson, poet, philosopher, and mentor of Thoreau; Louis Agassiz, the Swiss geologist and biologist and perhaps the most celebrated scientist of his time; James Russell Lowell, a distinguished poet; and several others. I've heard it said that Thoreau was invited to come but decided against it when he learned Emerson would carry a gun. It's a good story. Yet Stillman is the horse's mouth on this. Although he tells the familiar tale, it's Henry Wadsworth Longfellow the poet, not Henry David Thoreau the naturalist, who contemplates an armed Emerson and backs out. Stillman quotes Longfellow: "Is it true that Emerson is going to take a gun?" The answer came in the affirmative. Hearing it, the poet made his feelings clear. "Then somebody will be shot!" he told Stillman. Longfellow stayed home.

Emerson's account of the expedition comes in a poem titled "The Adirondacs" [sic]. The stanzas brim with romance and echo the sentiments of Headley and the time. A short way in, Emerson writes:

> Ten scholars, wonted to lie warm and soft
> In well-hung chambers daintily bestowed,
> Lie here on hemlock-boughs, like Sacs and Sioux,
> And greet unanimous the joyful change.
> So fast will Nature acclimate her sons,
> Though late returning to her pristine ways. . . .
> Up with the dawn, they fancied the light air
> That circled freshly in their forest dress
> Made them to boys again. Happier that they
> Slipped off their pack of duties, leagues behind,
> At the first mounting of the giant stairs.
> No placard on these rocks warned to the polls,
> No door-bell heralded a visitor,
> No courier waits, no letter came or went,
> Nothing was ploughed, or reaped, or bought, or sold;
> The frost might glitter, it would blight no crop,
> The falling rain will spoil no holiday.
> We were made freemen of the forest laws,
> All dressed, like Nature, fit for her own ends. . . .

Emerson captures the essence of the Adirondack tourist's fantasy then and now: that these vast woods represent an Eden where one may live in states of grace and bliss. It's an easy fiction to maintain when one doesn't have to make a living here, to endure twelve months in the cold, dark woods rather than twelve days of summer, to remain like a porcupine or bear rather than flit in and out like a hummingbird that skims nectar from Adirondack wildflowers while actually spending the lion's share of its life in tropical Mexico.

Still, Emerson, deep thinker that he was, saw through even his own hyperbole to the bedrock truths lying beneath. Romanticizing the wilds while demonizing the city was too facile for him. He knew better:

> We flee away from cities, but we bring
> The best of cities with us, these learned classifiers,
> Men knowing what they seek, armed eyes of experts.
> We praise the guide, we praise the forest life:
> But will we sacrifice our dear-bought lore
> Of books and arts and trained experiment,
> Or count the Sioux a match for Agassiz?
> O no, not we! Witness the shout that shook
> Wild Tupper Lake; witness the mute all-hail
> The joyful traveler gives, when on the verge
> Of craggy Indian wilderness he hears
> From a log cabin stream Beethoven's notes
> On the piano, played with master's hand.
> 'Well done!' he cries; the bear is kept at bay. . . .

Emerson presages the mix of savagery and sophistication that the Adirondack region has marketed to sophisticated travelers ever since.

Our great forests, so wild, so primeval in atmosphere, so thickly draped in lichen and moss, are perhaps best enjoyed with a rugged hike up billion-year-old bedrock. The trail will lead through ancient forest and across streams that have scoured their way down mountainsides since the Pleistocene. Then, at day's end, steaming coffee or single-malt Scotch can be sipped as one stands before the dragon's mouth of a hundred-year-old fireplace, followed by a glass or two of cabernet, a sumptuous meal on old china, a rich dessert, maybe a warm brandy, and finally, the crowning glory, sliding between crisp sheets onto a plush mattress, where the contented traveler lies inflated and contented as barred owls hoot and brooks babble and he, or she, subsides gently into a world-class sleep.

Immersion in the bosky can also be had camping in the backcountry. In important regards, there's no substitute for roughing it, for planting one's back on terra firma and gazing up at a trillion billion stars or, less poetically, sprawling on the hard plank floor of a rustic lean-to or cocooning inside a tent. Having enjoyed the Adirondack around-the-clock experience in all its permutations, including in my grandparents' travel trailer and in a motor home my grandfather cobbled together from an old yellow school bus, I am not embarrassed to say that a blend of extreme wildness and extreme comfort most closely approaches the sublime. Sure, the backpacker hews closer to primitive nature. But he also eats dehydrated food or pasty stuff out of cans, spends mornings and evenings slathering himself with insect repellent, and sleeps fitfully as mice cavort all night in the lean-to. Or, as in "The Princess and The Pea," a root that looked harmless while the tent was pitched makes its presence felt through closed-cell foam or self-inflating mattress pad, and the night brings nagging discomfort if not outright torture.

My friend Jeff Main and I once backpacked to the remote Cedar Lakes in the central Adirondacks. Finding all the lean-tos filled, we decided to sleep out under an indigo sky strewn with stars. I drifted off to sleep in a state of bliss, only to be awakened an hour before sunrise by a cold, pelting rain. I dug a tarp out of a pack, threw it over our bags and as much of our faces as I dared cover, and tried to get back to sleep. As I recall, Jeff dozed, but I writhed until first light and then hauled out and built a warming fire. An experience like this makes for a better story than a night of pampering in a high-end lodge. Still, there's something to be said for comfort.

If a single day in my own Adirondack life can be said to combine in near-perfect proportions the agony and the ecstasy, the sweet and the sour, that make time spent here enthralling, it's the one when my old college friend Jim Alsina and I climbed Mount Redfield. The mountain is named for William Redfield, who was part of the historic 1837 expedition that made the first recorded ascent of Mount Marcy.

The day began with the clanging of an alarm clock. Jim and I had spent the night on a sleeping porch at his family's camp in the woods near Keene Valley. I doze poorly when I know I have to shine early, and this was one of those occasions. It was 5:00 a.m. on the twenty-third of August, dark, cold, raining steadily. Yet we climbed out of sleeping bags like caterpillars out of chrysalides, tiptoed downstairs so as not to wake the rest of the household, grabbed packs and snacks, and were off. The forecast predicted clearing skies.

Jim and I planned to walk more than eighteen miles (more if we got lost, a distinct possibility) and climb one of the most remote Adirondack peaks. If we executed our plan, Jim would make personal history. Forty-six peaks in the mountains top 4,000 feet, at least according to the original survey. Since the 1920s, it's been a mark of distinction to climb all forty-six, despite the fact that fewer than half the summits can be reached by trails. Jim had climbed forty-five. His final conquest, Redfield, its summit 4,606 feet above sea level, was named for a distinguished meteorologist of the early nineteenth century.

The windshield wipers of my 1964 Ford worked hard as we drove an hour through rain and fading darkness to the trailhead. After parking, there was no time to waste. We laced on boots, wriggled into packs, double checked supplies of food and water, and plunged at a brisk pace into the woods. It was 7:30 a.m.

The rain had stopped. In this we rejoiced. Still, it was a wet world we passed through. By the end of the second mile, our clothes and boots were soaked. One must dwell on the positive in such a situation, so Jim and I talked more about the ideal hiking weather, which was cool and cloudy, rather than the fact that muscles protested as we built up steam and felt more amphibian than human in our clammy wardrobes.

After nearly eight miles, we reached a lean-to beside well-named Uphill Brook. Here began the day's hardest work. After a short break and study of the map, we marched into the woods, pushing toward the summit.

Moving quickly to avoid getting chilled in our wet clothes, we slogged up, up, and up some more, one cautious step at a time. Steps were cautious because the ground at our feet was concealed by a lush growth of ferns and wildflowers. It would have been easy to plunge an entire leg into a hole between rocks. This had to be avoided. A broken leg or badly sprained ankle miles back in the woods here throws a hiker into an unappealing muddle. Does the healthy partner leave the injured to hike out for help? If so, how would he locate his friend again, a mile or more from the nearest trail in woods so thick you wouldn't see a moose if it were standing twenty feet away? Or would the injured man set the pace on a splinted leg or bandaged ankle, reducing progress to a snail's pace? A night spent in the cold, dark wilds without camping gear would not be fun, even in summer. Still, we could bivouac overnight if circumstances demanded it. We carried extra food as well as raincoats, warm sweaters, and waterproof matches.

We reached Redfield's summit at a quarter past noon. A hiker's register, tucked in a length of pipe lashed to a tree, confirmed that we had in fact climbed the right mountain—no mean feat when you can't see where you're going, and you attempt to follow compass bearings for long distances over rock piles, around thundering waterfalls and ice-cold pools, and through tangles of fallen trees. My journal entry sums up the romance of reaching our goal. "The fog was thick and there were no views," I wrote two days later. "Brisk winds and wet clothes made our time on the summit short."

Down we came, picking our way carefully back to the lean-to. We used arms for support as much as legs, climbing lower and lower through soft, fragrant balsam firs and hard, spiny spruces down into deciduous woods thick with sugar maple, bigtooth aspen, quaking aspen, white birch, yellow birch, and red maple. At the shelter we peeled off boots and treated ourselves to dry socks—oh, happy hour! Then in waning afternoon light we made the final push to the car.

Seven and a half miles later, at quarter past five, we broke out of the trees and into the parking lot. We moderns romanticize the glories of the wild, yet there's nothing like an epic hike through rough country to make the most humble evidence of civilization—in this case, a patch of gravel at the end of a dirt road with three or four dusty cars parked on it—shine in a positive light.

In emphasizing the difficulties on Redfield, I'm guilty of giving the story a heroic slant, one that, it must be admitted, is not altogether honest. This is what we do in the Adirondacks. We tell outsiders about the snows that fall for days and the forty-below-zero nights, and about plagues of biting insects in summer and terrain that punishes the bodies and minds of hikers used to conquering mountains two and three times higher out West. Yet to give the truth, the whole truth, it's only fair that I finish the account with what happened next.

We arrived back at the Alsina compound at 6:30. As we walked into the house, Jim's mother, Margaret, pounced on us, asking for a report of the day's adventures and filling us in on the epic meal she'd been preparing. Cheese and crackers were put before us while Jim's father, Pierre, speaking in the most elegant and musical of French accents, prodded me for a drink order. "A Scotch!" he cried, as if the expression of my desire had provided the supreme delight of his day. Pierre Alsina offered a cheer, clicked glasses with me, and sipped his own amber fluid. Only years later did I learn from Jim that his father didn't drink. Yet hospitality meant everything to him. He'd pass an apple juice off as whiskey in order to put a guest at ease.

Dewars burning pleasantly in the belly, I shuffled off to the camp's outdoor shower. There I stood in a torrent of hot water, listening to the day's last hermit thrush songs, contemplating my blessed good fortune.

Margaret took great delight in pampering her son and his friend, partly because she had a generous spirit, and partly because Jim lived and worked in Africa in those days, and she was squeezing a year's worth of ardent mothering into two Adirondack weeks. The meal and the conversation, all enjoyed in front of a crackling fire, went on and on. Then came dessert, coffee, and an offer of brandy. I can't summon all the details, but the feeling of that extraordinary day, the sheer agony and the ecstasy of it, has never dimmed. Indeed, it was transformative. The man who woke late the next morning, refreshed, with tender legs and sore feet, was not the same man who had set off in the dark and the rain scarcely twenty-four hours before. I was the better for the pain, and the better for the antidote. Such a day points toward the capacity of the Adirondacks, and of Yellowstone and Yosemite and other wild and difficult places, to test and transform us. Perhaps it's why most of us come in the first place.

Debbie and I arrived as gypsies and set about reinventing ourselves as stay-at-homes. True, we did not entirely change our stripes. Two years after plunging into home renovations, we took a holiday for a month and flew to Australia. There we spent half our time soaking up the hospitality of friends and the other half wandering in the bush, as we had during an epic 25,000-mile, nine-month camping trip around the continent six years earlier. This time, though, circumstances were different. We had a base to come home to. Would we stick? Could we change? Time would tell.

BIOLOGICAL SURVEY RECORDS:

Tsuga canadensis   Eastern hemlock
2/26/00: big tree in woods SW of house

Martes americana   American marten
5/10/06: John Timmis [a friend and professional wildlife photographer] briefly saw and videotaped a marten west of the house, near our property line, at 12:35 p.m.

8

Home Economics

I compose this sentence in mid-October. Beside the house, a simple shed, consisting of little more than four six-by-six tamarack posts and a metal roof, stands loaded to the eaves with firewood. I built the shed with help from my wife and my mother. The materials that went into it—galvanized iron roofing, rough-cut structural members, nails, concrete, cardboard sonotubes, post anchors—came to about twelve hundred dollars. That's about forty-three times the $28.12 Thoreau paid for the materials that went into his cabin at Walden Pond.

The split lengths of maple, beech, and birch stacked inside cost us $500 or thereabouts. The wood will heat our house for one winter. After that, the shed will yawn empty and cry for another loading. In this era of expensive fuel oil and propane, $500 is a bargain, especially to heat a home in a place as cold as the Adirondacks. But hold on. There's more to the arrangement than money.

There's time. The wood in the shed no more appears split, stacked, and dried in neat rows than a baby gets dropped off by a stork. A fact of life is that a winter's wood heat remains long in the gestation. Most years, we start by buying logs from a local forester, although the first winter, when we were nearly broke and had no woodshed, and when the small amount of split wood we could afford to purchase ran out before Christmas, I hauled the lion's share out of the woods on snowshoes, one armload at a time. When we bought it, the property abounded in dead, dry, standing black cherry trees. They had been killed by a fungal disease called black knot. The trunks had dried on the stump, and they were of mercifully small diameter. All winter long, I hauled a chainsaw into the forest every chance I got, felled cherry trees, and cut them into stove lengths. Many a subzero winter night, often at midnight or one in the morning,

I stepped outdoors, strapped on snowshoes, and, humming "Good King Wenceslas," slogged into the woods to retrieve a few hours of fuel.

There's an old saying about firewood. It heats you twice: once when you split it and once when you burn it. That's an understatement. You get hot when you fell trees, hot again when you cut their trunks to length, hot again when you haul them out of the woods by sled or wheelbarrow, hot again when you split them, hot again when you stack them, and hot again on a biting day in January when you carry five or six armloads into the house. By my reckoning, burning represents the seventh and final heating. I can stretch it to eight if I count all the times I shovel ash into a bucket, buckle on snowshoes, and pad outside into the arctic air to empty the crematory remains of trees in the garden.

Our heating plan supplies exercise, too. Getting wood out of the woods is grueling work. If you split the logs by hand as I did the first few years, you have no need of a gymnasium.

Gazing at a full woodshed, I feel less a sense of accomplishment than an urgency to get out in the trees and start gathering the next winter's supply. Hardwood destined for burning is best split a year or more in advance. We must stay ahead or risk having to buy wood already split and dried, which is, according to my frugal notions, shockingly expensive. We have a backup heating system, a faux woodstove that burns propane and keeps the house from freezing when we go away, come down with the flu, or can't satisfy the woodstove's hunger. All the same, our income is modest. If we supply our own heat rather than buy it off the back of a truck, we stay ahead.

One advantage I have over Thoreau in making ends meet and keeping proverbial wolves from the door is that I have a hardworking wife. As people are fond of reminding me, Debbie has a real job, a steady one with regular hours and a paycheck that comes every other week. Her steadfast and satisfying work as activities director at a beautiful apartment complex for seniors helps make our life in the woods possible.

I, on the other hand, live a life of perpetual leisure. With no regular job to dictate my comings and goings, I have the pleasure of shoveling nearly all our snow, hauling and splitting nearly every piece of our firewood, sweeping the chimney, carrying out the ash, keeping the plumbing and electrical systems in repair, tilling and cultivating two vegetable gardens, writing books, writing columns and stories for magazines, teaching classes, giving lectures, and running a guiding business. That, and for years I served four out of seven days a week as househusband and caregiver for our kids. Now, as then, I cook dinners, wash dishes, do countless loads of laundry (we have no dryer and hang the washing out to dry on the porch when it's warm and on racks by the woodstove the rest of the time), and once in a blue moon cut the grass. I have so much spare time that some nights I throw the to-do list out the window at one and enjoy five or six hours of sleep.

The typical Adirondack household gets by, and has always gotten by, on several tributary streams of income. Guides were often carpenters and carpenters guides. Women with or without children ran day care centers before the name had been coined. They sold the surplus from their gardens, ovens, and home canneries. My quadruple-great-grandfather Daniel Brownell appears on census records as a farmer, but no doubt he dabbled in a trade or two to help pay the bills. His son Orra, next in the male line, ran a sawmill and founded the family tanning business, but he farmed, too, as census listings attest. Lewis Brownell, next in the succession, took control of the family lumber business and its two tanneries and, perhaps having developed a taste for money, operated a Northville hotel called the Brownell House and a bottling plant. Lewis's son Elmer, my great-grandfather, was a farmer according to the census but also, as we've seen, a teamster. My grandfather worked as a painter, wallpaper hanger, and fur trapper as well as cutter of glove leather and mayor.

The women in the family were every bit as hardworking in their labors as their husbands, or more so, yet little record of their toil survives. The plentitude of children they bore begins the story of their professional lives. To this add cooking, cleaning, gardening, canning, solicitude to domineering husbands at a time when men were encouraged by the culture to be despots at home, and, in the case of my artist great-great-grandmother Elnora, teaching and painting.

The earliest surviving photo of a female in my direct Adirondack line shows my great-grandmother Jenny Lawton. Jenny married Elmer Brownell on the 12th of May, 1890, nearly two years to the day after Elmer's mother, Elnora, died. The Reverend "Geo. K. Fraser" performed the ceremony, with two relatives of Elmer serving as witnesses. Flowers adorn the margins of the wedding certificate, and at the bottom, a woman appears. She's wearing a head scarf, gathering grain.

Elmer and Jenny's union lasted forty-five years. After Elmer's death in 1935, Jennie continued on in the family homestead on Third Street in Northville for five more years. Her 1940 obituary reports that "the bearers were her six sons: Lewis Brownell of Johnstown, Elmer Brownell of Gloversville, Burdett Brownell, Lynn Brownell, Graves Brownell, and Kenneth Brownell of Northville." My grandfather picked up the bill for his mother's funeral and burial. The receipt, dated September 28, 1940, is marked "Received in Full." Itemized expenses included "[o]ne grey emboss Deluxe Casket silvered handles. Satin inliner, embalming, grave, hearse, cemetery chapel, assistances, Professional services and use of entire equipment." That came to $166.00. To this was added $35.00 for "one 1½" pine vault," $8.00 for "one grey dress," and $12.00 for "Opening grave." Even then, death didn't come cheaply.

Grampy paid the expenses, but money was tight in those days. Long gone was the era when Lewis, flush with lumber and tanning income, built a large and gracious house on Bridge Street. A tax bill addressed to Elmer Brownell only months before his death refers to a delinquency of payments and assesses a penalty of seventeen cents. A note signed by assessor Florence L. Delaney at the bottom reads warmly, "You may pay by the week if you would like; the above is the tax amount and the Collector's fees." That said, Delaney concludes with steel. "We will adjust," she adds, "when you finish paying."

Another document among my grandfather's papers shows that on the twenty-eighth day of February, 1928, Elmer and Jennie Brownell paid off the mortgage on their house with a $1500 bank check. Did they enjoy a windfall of some sort? The mortgage had been granted only the previous November.

If the settlement signifies good luck, as it seems to, another item in my grandfather's files suggests the opposite. Two years after his mother's death, during which time he had acquired ownership of the family home, Burdett fell behind in paying the taxes and lost the place in an auction. The tax sale for "Residence of Burdette [sic] Brownell Third Street" is dated March 18, 1942. It shows that a Harry Drake won the property at public auction on May 17 and paid $21.90 for it—this scribbled later in ink on August 6.

Somehow, Grampy regained ownership quickly. Perhaps his well-to-do Aunt Carrie, married to his namesake, Northville banker Burdett Eglin, bailed him out. As far as I can tell, he was never evicted. The house remained his until his death in 1978.

The contretemps over back taxes did not blacken Grampy's reputation, at least in any lasting way. Four years after the tax sale, in 1946, he won election as a village trustee, and in 1953, he was elected mayor. He served in the post on and off (mostly on) for eighteen years. He retired in 1975.

I'm inclined to think my grandfather was a good mayor. He was, after all, generally a good man. Happily, the record supports the theory. A

1969 letter to him after he'd opted to sit out a term came from Village Clerk Helen Angell. It reads, in part:

> On behalf of the Village Board, I wish to take this opportunity to thank you for your many years of service to the village of Northville. Your years first as Trustee, then as Mayor, have seen new innovations and the Village has grown in stature because of your devout interest and determination to keep taxes in line. You will be greatly missed, as you served faithfully and well.

To the typed formal tribute, sanctioned by the Village Board, the clerk added a postscript in ballpoint. It reads: "Burdy: May I add my own personal note of thanks for your many kindnesses to me. Without your patience and understanding I never could have survived the past 15 years at this post. I am indeed proud to have served with you and extend my very best wishes to you and yours. Helen."

Grampy worked hard as mayor. Once, visiting Northville more than twenty years after his death, I hailed an old man with a walking stick, hobbling down a sidewalk. I wondered if he might have known my grandfather. "I'm Bob Van Arnam," he said, shaking my hand. "Born 1913. Yes, I knew Burdett Brownell. Your grandfather was a doer and a shaker, and I mean it. He got things done. He was a good mayor and a good man, and everybody in the village, at least everybody who was fair-minded, thought highly of him."

The same day, I also met a ninety-four-year-old woman who turned out to be a distant relation of mine. She was Charlotte Russell, my grandfather's second cousin. She had snow-white hair, piercing flinty eyes, smooth pink skin, and a girlish smile. "He was a good mayor," Russell said, echoing Van Arnam. "He worked with me in getting a stop sign put up at the base of the hill. Every time I go down that hill, even today, I thank Burdett for that stop sign."

I formed a sense of Grampy as mayor because I had the privilege of watching him in action. On several occasions, I remember being at his house when cries for help came over the phone or a distraught neighbor or village official came knocking at the door, pleading for assistance with a broken water main or some other crisis. Sometimes Mayor Brownell was called away in the middle of a meal and kept busy for hours. He reacted in a fashion typical of him. He refused to be caught up in anyone's frenzy. Instead, he spoke calmly and deliberately, asking questions, trying to get a fix on things. Being mayor was the perfect job for him.

Yet there's another truth about Grampy's mayoralty: he needed the money. His salary would have represented a pittance for most people. Yet for my grandfather, income of any kind meant a great deal.

When Grampy finally stopped serving at seventy-one, it wasn't long before he was back at work. A one-room factory on Main Street in Northville was attempting to revive the old glove-making industry. Three years later, when he died, Burdett was still cutting leather.

What would he make of my own ways of bringing home bacon? He'd be quietly pleased, I think, at my writing. A ravenous and indiscriminate reader of books, he would pick up the nearest volume at hand, whether it be highbrow or low or something in between, and bury himself in. He read Zane Grey and Agatha Christie, James Joyce and D. H. Lawrence.

The books I've written, all published since his death, would occupy my grandfather for a time. Then he'd have questions. He wasn't a talker, as I've said, but he wanted to know things, and he worked hard to get them right.

My work as a licensed Adirondack guide would command Grampy's attention, too. Here his world and mine most closely overlap, and here his great influence on me is felt most. I tend to show up for work in wool plaid shirts, the same kinds he used to wear. "Beware of all enterprises that require new clothes," wrote Thoreau. Agreed. That's part of the reason I enjoy guiding. I show up not in a suit and tie, but in the wool and cotton flannels and twills I wear when my time is my own. My grandfather always looked like he'd walked out of an Adirondack history book. He had. He'd been born on a hardscrabble farm and grew up milking cows and harvesting buckwheat; he came down with the Spanish flu during its murderous 1918–1919 rampage through the mountains and survived it; he left school and home as a teenager to cook at a backwoods lumber camp; he eked out an existence through the Depression by doing odd jobs, picking and selling wild berries, and trapping mink and muskrat; and he worked in the glove industry. Today when I visit the Adirondack Museum in Blue Mountain Lake and poke around exhibits having to do with the lives people lived here, I feel like I'm rummaging in my grandfather's attic.

When guiding, I aim to look like I've walked out of history, too. Once, early in the morning at an expensive and exclusive Adirondack lodge, a man in a Hawaiian shirt who was smoking a big cigar and playing crochet ogled me. "You look like you're from central casting," he said. He looked straight out of central casting, too, and I told him so. We enjoyed a laugh and agreed we were performing in different films.

I'm a naturalist guide. The people I escort through the woods are nearly all wealthy and include politicians, titans of industry, financiers, lawyers, and, once, a famous English rock star whom I failed to recognize and who didn't mind my obliviousness. Like Grampy's glove cutting, the work will always be in demand, yet it comes and goes. I tend to be busy in summer and fall and quiet in winter and spring. The pattern shifts with the ebbs and flows of the economy.

Out in the woods, my chief job is to introduce the flora and fauna and how it relates to the climate and geology, and to do so without making eyelids flutter. I tell family stories, too. My clients want to know how Debbie, the kids, and I get through the long, hard winters, what is the lowest temperature we've seen on our thermometer, and how we manage to ripen tomatoes in the garden in a place where frosts often come in August. Are the schools good? Are we ever bored? People also want to hear the family history. Why did forebears come here? Why did they stay, and what did they do? At first, I hesitated to talk about personal things, reckoning they were of limited interest. But the opposite proves true. When I explain how a Google search led me to details of my great-great-grandmother's love life, every listener wants to know more.

People who walk with me press for news of those whom I've escorted through the woods before them. I'm careful to be discreet. A politician once showed up to hike after a night of hard partying. He had a whopping hangover and roiling stomach. Every few minutes along the trail, he excused himself to disappear into the bushes. He had laid out a considerable sum to stay at an exclusive lodge that keeps its client list secret, and for that reason alone, his privacy is safe with me.

I have spent time in the woods with a prominent religious fundamentalist, a man who has made a career of championing so-called family values. His identity also remains safe with me, but I will say that during outings I made with his family, he ignored his wife and children and instead hiked twice as fast as the rest of us, uninterested in anyone's company and apparently determined to show off his fitness. The missus and the kids were good companions. The only hitch was that Mrs. Fundamentalist hurried to contradict me every time I mentioned evolution or the twelve thousand years that have passed since the Ice Age.

One of the most delightful people I've guided was a governor who later found himself in hot water over his sex life. I don't know about his relations with his missus, but I'm eager to say this. During an afternoon of kayaking, he proved a boon companion, interested, interesting, and good-humored. The governor enjoyed a close and tender rapport with his sons. I remember him taking them aside at the start of our trip and saying, "Boys, we're very lucky to be here in this place with this man. He has much to teach us, so let's be good listeners." They were. So was he.

The most famous of my companions in the woods is the only one I feel comfortable mentioning by name. He was Tony Blair, former prime minister of England. I met him at one of the Adirondacks' big private estates. The closest I came to actually guiding Blair was taking his chief of staff's parents for a walk. Still, I had the pleasure of his conversation three times during the day.

By coincidence, my mother has a first cousin in England who provided key support during and after Blair's rise to power. The modern wilderness guide enjoys this advantage over his predecessors of a century ago: he can conduct Internet searches before an outing and gain advance knowledge of the big shots whose hands he'll be shaking. In Blair's case, I boned up on English politics. I also Googled our cousin. My sister Maggie had recently been a guest on his Yorkshire farm. She alerted me to the fact that he and Blair had had a falling out.

It was over the Iraq War. Blair sided with George W. Bush and signed on as an active partner. Our cousin opposed the conflict, feeling strongly enough to slip a donation to an antiwar candidate of another party. By this time, however, Blair had installed our cousin in the House of Lords. When Blair's Labour Party learned of what the independent-minded Lord had done, it threw him out, or so I understand. This remained the situation when Tony Blair and I crossed paths in the woods.

"Mr. Blair," I said. I decided to handle the matter as Grampy would have: be forthright, seek the good in people, let the chips fall where they may. I'd bring up my relationship to Chris.

"Please, call me Tony."

"Tony, you and I have a friend in common." Blair has animated eyebrows, and they arched. I told him that a particular longtime ally and backer was in fact my mother's cousin Chris.

Blair gulped. It took him a second or two to compose his thoughts, which is a long time for someone whose career is built on thinking on his feet. "Yes, I know him well. That's amazing."

Blair struggled for more to say. Having taken a liking to him after an earlier conversation, I hastened to indicate that I knew the whole story, or at least enough of it. No need to explain. Blair seemed relieved. He and I exchanged a few more words, now forgotten. Soon he was whisked away by his host for a second round of fly-fishing.

That might have been the end of it. Yet just before Blair rushed off to the airport, he spied me and gestured me over for a final word. "I just want to tell you that your cousin is a great guy. We'll be good friends again soon enough."

Because Debbie has chosen work she loves over a job that provides the maximum reward for her labors, and because in my own piecemeal way I've done the same, we live lives unlike those of my clients. We buy food in bulk or on sale as much as we can. We grow vegetables and get out every year to gather wild strawberries, blueberries, and huckleberries. Before parenthood, I used to do nearly all of our car repairs, and now that the kids are in school, I'm picking up where I left off. It's hard to do a brake job or replace a starter while tending a baby and a toddler. The baby demands a diaper or a bottle when your hands are caked with grease. The toddler runs off with the wrench or the new part and won't give it back.

Sometimes I wonder whether I've made the right choices in life—not about the woman I'm married to or the children we dared to invent, but whether I would have been better off sticking with the career path I set forth on in my twenties, becoming a National Park ranger, say, or sticking with the best job I ever had, running a fine small nature museum in a county park, or seizing an offer that came my way, twice, to pursue a PhD at the University of Hawaii at Manoa, with tuition waived and a teaching assistantship thrown into the bargain. My free-spirited ways have caused my parents, sisters, and friends no end of worry.

If I'd pursued a National Park ranger job that was mine for the taking when I was twenty-three, I'd be making a fat salary now (at least by my standards) and nearing retirement. I'd have an exalted status as a high priest in the Muir mold. I'd strut around nature's "cathedrals," as Muir called them, in vestments of gray and green, a World War I–style campaign hat on my head and a touch of well-intentioned sanctimony on my lips as I counseled park visitors not to take or disturb. Instead, I prowl the Adirondacks in plaid flannels and twill, well-scuffed boots on the bottom and a weatherbeaten felt hat on the top, raising kids, gardening, cutting firewood, fishing, hunting, and scratching out bits and pieces of a living, embedded in the place as a humble citizen in the Burroughs mold rather than collecting a salary to be its manager. This way is not the only way, and it's certainly not the easiest. National Parks are wonderful entities, and I'm grateful that we have them. Yet this path I chose makes as much sense as any, and only time will tell where it leads.

Despite the ups and downs that come with the self-invented life, it's hard to see where I've gone wrong. If I hadn't made the decisions I made, I wouldn't be where I am now, wouldn't be married to a bright and beautiful woman who shares my passions, wouldn't be running around in the yard with two gorgeous and endlessly fascinating children, wouldn't be digging into the family past.

One evening when I was feeling low about my professional life, I browsed Thoreau's journals, seeking affirmation. I own the complete fourteen volumes, bound as two in the Dover Books edition. The books hold 2 million words. They're large enough to press plant specimens in, a use I've put them to and which the author would have applauded. In the middle of a lengthy outpouring by Thoreau on August 30, 1856, I struck pay dirt.

> If you would really take a position outside the street and daily life of men, you must have deliberately planned your course, you must have business which is not your neighbor's business, which they cannot understand. For only absorbing employment prevails, succeeds, takes up space, occupies territory, determines the futures of individuals and states. . . . You will spend this afternoon setting up your neighbor's stove, and be paid for it; I will spend it in gathering the few berries of the *Vaccinium Oxycoccus* [sic—a kind of blueberry bush] which Nature produces here, before it is too late, and *be paid for it also* [emphasis Thoreau's] after another fashion.

The passage continues, so apropos of my life that I'd think Thoreau was channeling me.

> How many schools I have thought of which I might go to but did not go to! expecting foolishly that some greater advantage or schooling would come to me! It is these comparatively cheap and private expeditions that substantiate our existence and batten our lives, as, where a vine touches the earth in its undulating course, it puts forth roots and thickens its stock. . . . Many of our days should be spent, not in vain expectations and lying on our oars, but in carrying out deliberately and faithfully the hundred little purposes which every man's genius must have suggested to him. Let not your life be wholly without an object, though it be only to ascertain the flavor of a cranberry, for it

will not be only the quality of an insignificant berry that you will have tasted, but the flavor of your life. . . .

Thoreau concludes: "It is by obeying the suggestions of a higher light within you that you escape from yourself and, in the transit, as it were see with the unworn sides of your eye, travel totally new paths."

And so I carry on. A great many people fail to understand me, fail to grasp what it is I'm doing with my life. At times, I'm one of them. Yet Thoreau and Grampy would have approved.

Still, I sometimes question what I do to make ends meet, especially when it comes to guiding. When I leave my wife and children to drive to a high-end lodge or private estate and take someone else's wife and children into the woods, I wonder if I'm doing the wrong thing. I'm selling my passion, turning the wild things I love into commodities. My wilderness escort service has things in common with other, more notorious forms of the trade.

Once, at a beautiful backwoods resort where I do some guiding, a motor home pulled into the compound. It was a most unusual occurrence. Compact cars were generally not allowed in that spot, let alone recreational vehicles the size of tour buses. Out spilled a succession of sexy young women, followed by a ragtag army of less glamorous folk, most of them dressed in black. I was baffled. Then I remembered. This was a mail order catalogue shoot. Beautiful models were being matched to exquisite forest and classic rustic architecture, all to sell products manufactured by underpaid, ill-fed factory workers in faraway lands. I cringed. I gawked. It all seemed surreal and manipulative, this staging of spontaneity by a big-city production crew. The place had nothing to do with the items being peddled.

Exploitation? It's hard to say. There are other sides to the story. Catalogue and film shoots help many a Great Camp and rustic retreat pay for its upkeep. Without them, roofs might leak and buildings crumble. What harm comes from dressing up attractive women in casual outdoor clothes and photographing them in boathouses, on docks, on the water, and in the woods? Would the Adirondacks gain by sending the business elsewhere?

And about my occasional touch of queasiness about guiding work: people come here to spend their precious free time and money. While in the Adirondacks, isn't it better that they explore the wilds with a naturalist who can introduce them to the flora, the fauna, and the biological, historical, and geological meanings of it all, rather than just gorge on a diet of superb food, fine wine, rushed hikes, postcard-perfect summits, boutiques, and water-skiing?

William Chapman White, a journalist who wrote the 1954 classic *Adirondack Country*, spoke with renowned Saranac Lake guide Les Hathaway (1862–1952) on this score. "The trouble with people today," Hathaway told White, "is they're so busy coverin' ground they ain't got time to notice what's on the ground they're coverin.'" My job, and I've come to see that it's an important one, is to teach people to note "what's on the ground," as Hathaway put it. I help people explore the woods in their sumptuous totality, not by racing to the tops of all forty-six Adirondack high peaks in three days seventeen hours fourteen minutes, as someone recently did, but in the patient, inquisitive, appreciative spirit of Thoreau and Burroughs.

And so, with saw in hand, I head into the woods like a guide of old to free myself from the market economy and heat our house. Admittedly, my German-made *Stihl* runs on a mixture of unleaded gasoline and two-stroke oil, and I do much of my splitting these days with a hydraulic machine powered by a Honda motor. But that's where modernity ends. I haul and stack and haul again by hand. At day's end, when I stagger indoors with snow on my flannel and slide firewood into the mouth of a cast-iron stove, I'm hewing to an economic model as old as our species.

The bonds we put our stock in can't be bought on Wall Street. They're chemical ones. They bind carbon atoms together to form complex carbohydrates called cellulose and lignin. Solar energy forged the bonds through the alchemy of photosynthesis. With the aid of kindling, crumpled newspaper, and a match, we cash them in, unleashing light, heat, and peace of mind.

In the final analysis, it's tranquility that validates our labors, not just the heat itself. People in our climate spend thousands of dollars each winter warming their homes with fuel oil, propane, and electricity. They live in fear of market forces and the latest reports from the Middle East, never sure how much they'll be paying for heat, or whether they'll be able to pay for it at all. We look out at eighteen forested acres and see heat stretching years into the future. Granted, an interruption in the supply of gasoline for the chainsaw and splitter would make things harder. Still, we're ready for it. I keep two old-fashioned crosscut saws in the wings. One was purchased by my father's father during the Great Depression. He used it when the cost of coal for heating climbed beyond reach. The other saw I picked up at a yard sale. If we had to, we could keep warm without burning fossil fuel.

Water might be a problem, but then, maybe not. When we were excavating foundation drains that first epic summer, we installed a water line from the old dug well into the crawl space beneath the house. I've hooked up an old fashioned hand pump to the line and confirmed that if we had no electricity to power the submersible pump in the drilled well, we could push a handle up and down and have all the water we needed. For bathing, we'd heat the water on the woodstove, or in summer, warm it over an outdoor fire. It's comforting to know that if a severe storm or plunge in the economy ever runs off with modern conveniences, we'll be ready. We can revert to the arrangements my Brownell forebears enjoyed in the nineteenth century.

An idyllic existence? Hardly. Keeping up with it all is hard work, grueling at times. There are times when I stay overnight in centrally heated homes and find myself wishing I could twirl a thermostat in our house and warm the interior as if by magic. Sometimes I ponder what things will be like when I grow old, when hauling logs and splitting them into cordwood will lie beyond my capability and care. I dream of developing a geothermal heating system to warm the house to the deep soil temperature of fifty degrees or so, with only a small amount of wood needed to raise the heat above this baseline. The circulators required to make the system run could be powered by solar-electric panels. Such a system wouldn't come cheap. Where will the money come from? I wish I knew. Meanwhile, I work hard, and tonight I'll be cooking Brussels sprouts straight from the garden.

BIOLOGICAL SURVEY RECORDS:

Acer rubrum   Red maple
2/26/00: in thicket s. of house; outside kitchen door near shed [this more than any other warms us in winter]

Dryocopus pileatus   Pileated woodpecker
2/20/02: 3 birds whooping and flying back and forth and drumming across road from mailbox—11:45 a.m. [in the form of chiseled rectangular holes, this bird, in its tireless pursuit of carpenter ants, leaves its mark on the tree trunks we divide and burn]

9

_____

Neighbors

We arrived in the Adirondacks cynical about the state of the average American life. There are those who argue that the central problems in our country in the early twenty-first century are too much selfishness and not enough community spirit. Everyone, according to the theory, is so busy doing his, or her, own thing that nobody finds time to work for the common good.

There's truth to this perspective, but only up to a point. I see the facts in a different light. Yes, there's rampant me-first-ism in the land, and yes, in some quarters (not here) there's a shortage of old-fashioned, roll-up-your-sleeves, help-your-neighbor-build-a-barn spirit. But is excessive individuality the root cause? If everyone does his own thing, but that thing is the same thing (say, watching a particular "reality" television program on Wednesday nights or owning an iPad), then what seems on first analysis to be selfishness is actually a turning away from the self toward a mass mentality. Millions think they're exercising free will, but few are actually acting freely at all.

Concerned on this score, we made our move to the Adirondacks and were immediately encouraged. In this cold, hard, sometimes hostile place, individualism of the best sort flourishes, and at every turn it demonstrates that it is compatible with community spirit.

Nellie Staves provides a good example. At age eighty-three, she walked into my life with rouge on her cheeks and mud on her boots. My initial request to interview her for a story had been declined. "You'd be wasting your time," she said when I telephoned. A nephew of Nellie who was a friend of my publisher intervened. He changed her mind and my life in the process.

When Nellie started talking, she was hard to stop. But why try? Her life had been extraordinary. She was a mother and grandmother, a trapper, hunter, fisherwoman, teacher of outdoor skills, professional cook, campaigner for conservation, and outspoken champion of the rights of sportsmen and sportswomen. Nellie served as president of her county's Federation of Fish and Game Clubs and sat on several boards, among them the New York State Fish and Wildlife Management Board, the state's Open Space Committee, the Upper Saranac Lake Citizens Advisory Board, and the Local Government Review Board. The last group, she said, "keeps an eye" on the Adirondack Park Agency. Tupper Lake, the village where she lived, had once held a Nellie Staves Day. More than 400 people turned out to celebrate her contributions and wish her well.

These accomplishments didn't all belong to the past. At the time of our first meeting, Nellie was past eighty and still going strong—running a trapline when she had time, marching out on snowshoes in the coldest part of winter to haul in mink and muskrats to skin and round out her modest income. "I like to trap muskrat, mink, coon, beaver, coyote, and fox," she told me. "I trap humanely. I'd rather set three small traps to catch an animal than use one big one that will break an animal's leg."

Although she lived most of her life in the Adirondacks, Nellie was born in West Danville, Vermont. At seven, she met fellow Vermonter Calvin Coolidge when he was running for the presidency. He didn't make a strong impression. I asked Nellie to sum up her childhood. "Well," she said. "This is how it was. We hunted, we fished, we trapped. Dad was a very good conservationist. Mother was, too. They allowed us to roam the whole mountain. The only restrictions were from my father, who taught us to be careful and never take more than our fair share." The family of fourteen lived in a cabin with no central heat, electricity, or plumbing.

Nellie Staves came to the Adirondacks in 1949 with her first husband, Bernard Badger. She took a series of jobs as a cook in lumber camps. "I cooked for fifty-seven guys," she said, laughing. "It was hard work, let me tell you. I got up at 3:00 or 4:00 in the morning and often cooked steady to 8:00, 9:00, or 10:00 at night." For one lumberjack, Nellie fried a dozen eggs every morning for breakfast.

"There was no drinking in our logging camp," she said, referring to her first job with the U.S. Bobbin and Shuttle Company near Long Lake. "I never heard a logger say a dirty word. My husband was foreman, you know, so they knew they'd better watch out. But I think they appreciated having a woman cook. I'd pick them berries and make them something really special."

Nellie and I became friends. A thing I loved about her was a lack of interest in making any particular impression on others. She was, in that respect, like my grandfather: free of guile, her own person, a rugged character who worked in the woods in flannel shirts and trousers but could just as easily turn up at a public event looking like a socialite, albeit one with windburn. When you ran into her coming out of a Park Agency meeting with a notebook in her hand or marching out of the woods with a fungus (in later years, she earned fame and a bit of money drawing animals on the white, canvaslike undersides of bracket fungi), she might engage you in conversation about anything. You could be sure it would have nothing to do with a television program a quarter of the nation's population had watched the evening before.

Rugged, one-of-a-kind women like Nellie abound in the Adirondacks. As I began to toy with the idea of becoming a parent, these gals struck me as marvelous role models for a daughter if we had one. Not that I would necessarily want a daughter to grow up to trap, because I have reservations about trapping, but simply because such people show the rest of us that a woman can do as she pleases. While marching to her own drummer, as Thoreau put it, she can at the same time serve her community.

Nellie Staves died at ninety-two, vigorous until the end.

Just as Staves personified the feminine side of Adirondack individuality, Orville Paye stood as the male archetype. Paye ran a business called the Gold Mine. It made its presence known along Route 3, just north of Saranac Lake on the road to Bloomingdale. For all appearances, the Gold Mine might have been a junk shop or the base of operations of a drug dealer. Heaps of broken furniture and appliances sprawled outside. There were old cars, rusting trucks, furniture, and bric-a-brac. Yet the thing that always caught my eye driving by was not the disarray. It was the shiny new Lexus or Mercedes-Benz parked outside and the glamorous woman climbing in or out of it: a woman doctor on her day off, perhaps, or a diamond-studded widow, or some other pillar of the community. The attraction? The women weren't coming to purchase Paye's treasures.

I heard gossip. It was said that while Paye looked poor, he was the richest man in Saranac Lake. He owned thirty houses, I was told. The best tale seemed right out of Dickens. Paye possessed great wealth but gave it away quietly and freely. His favorite form of philanthropy, several said, was sending promising local students from poor families to college—not loaning them money, but giving it outright.

This was too good not to investigate. One day I parked my rusty car outside, hoping it wouldn't be absorbed into one of Paye's piles, and strolled through into the Mine. Inside I found a room heaped high with books, chairs, tables, old tools, and other artifacts that had once filled homes and camps. In the middle stood a table on which boxes of fruit and vegetables yawned. Overripe peaches sweetened the air. Behind a cluttered counter, beside an ornate cash register that looked a hundred years old, a man sat, reading Bertrand Russell. He wore a tweed jacket that had seen long use and eyeglasses too big for his face. Hair, dyed auburn and not very well, lay in wisps across a freckled crown. Instantly Paye reminded me of my Middlebury College history professor, Pardon Tillinghast. Tillinghast was always too busy thinking and hungering after what you were thinking to pay attention to his clothes or the pipe ashes he was spilling.

"Orville Paye, I presume?" We exchanged introductions. Paye was glad to meet me, but the salesman in him quickly got to work. "I bring my produce all the way from Canada," he said. "Take a look at those peaches. You won't find any half as good at twice the price in the chain stores. Have one!" In went my teeth and out came a torrent of juice that ran over my hands and down my chin onto the floor. Paye was delighted.

As it happened, I was in the market for handsaws, a crosscut, and a rip. I saw one of each on a shelf across the room. "Oh, those aren't for sale," Paye said when I inquired. "I just had them sharpened. Well, I suppose if you really need them, you could have them for four dollars apiece." A deal was struck. When I later put the saws to use, they were dull. Paye was the kind of merchant whom with a mixture of disapproval and admiration Grampy called a horse trader.

Paye and I became friends. From time to time I stopped, along with those women in fancy cars, to buy a tin of maple syrup, a couple of acorn squashes, apples, potatoes, or tomatoes. Sometimes I came just for conversation. Shopping at the Gold Mine was a cultural experience from which you always walked away both poorer and richer.

Paye told me that he was born in Saranac Lake on October 11, 1925. His Aunt Louise Stevens, a midwife, delivered him. The plain clapboard house in which his life began still stands on Payeville Road. Orville's father was a prosperous builder, "the most benevolent man I ever knew," he said. "He owned many houses because you could buy one for 500 bucks in those days. During the Depression, when his tenants couldn't pay the rent, he let them live rent free for more than ten years. That's the kind of man he was." Orville's mother, from Chazy, near Plattsburgh, came to Saranac Lake to work as a tutor. She was a college graduate, a botanist, and a loving mother.

At age four, Paye began his schooling in Saranac Lake. He excelled, he said, because of "an excellent memory and a good head for numbers."

He graduated at sixteen and three days later became a student at Clarkson University in Potsdam. There, in a program run by the U.S. Army Signal Corps, he studied radio engineering. "I lived in Saranac Lake," he said, "and drove back and forth to Clarkson every day in a '37 Dodge, and later a Buick. I earned my degree in twenty-eight months."

That was 1944. Paye moved to Rochester to work on a covert military radio project. "No need to put that in your story," he said. Nearly sixty years after his service ended, the loyal veteran still kept the Army's secrets.

In 1948, Paye was running a used car dealership in Saranac Lake when the telephone rang. Eugene Christian, a Buick dealer, was on the line. A seventy-eight-year-old retired attorney named Paul E. DeFere, a customer of Christian's, wanted to hire a bodyguard and driver. Christian recommended Paye, who took the job. Soon he was driving DeFere for ten weeks each year at $1,000 per week plus expenses, "a lot of money back then." Paye took DeFere in his Buick touring car on lavish sightseeing trips, with stops at fine hotels and restaurants. "He loved Canada," said Orville, with a dreamy look in his eye. "So that's where we spent most of our time. He was a wonderful man. He was about five-foot-four and very distinguished looking. Those were good days."

Paye meanwhile set himself up in various businesses. In addition to hawking used cars, he ran a scrap metal yard and served as a silent partner in a taxi business. "I was a landlord, too, and still am," he said. "Some people say I'm the richest man around. It's not true. But I once owned twenty-nine houses. I own nine now, including the one I live in. My tenants are all good people. I'm going to give them the houses when I die. It's in my will." His eyes twinkled. "The only problem is that I plan to live 150 years."

Paye opened the Gold Mine in 1961. He sold mostly antiques at first, although in time the business gravitated more toward flowers, fruit, and vegetables. He bought his stock at a farmer's market in Canada and trucked it across the border twice a week in an old Chevy van. Once I spent part of a day riding around with him. The image that sticks with me years later is Paye pulling his shabby-looking vehicle up in front of the fanciest antique store in Lake Placid and the owner rushing out to greet him like a dignitary. The man asked Paye to appraise the value of a table. Clearly he considered Paye an expert. Paye rattled off the selling points, pointed out subtleties of style and condition, named an age and a price, and we were back on the road.

I asked Paye about his philanthropy and the stories I'd heard. He changed the subject. I persisted. "I've been successful in business, that's all," he said. "I make money, and there's nothing wrong with that. Have you heard people say, 'Money is the root of all evil?' Well, they haven't got it right. The saying really is, 'Love of money is the root of all evil.' Money can help people, especially young people who are trying to do good for themselves. I like kids, and I like to help them when I can."

Still, was it really true that Paye, as I'd been told, had recently put a local student through four years at Georgetown? Paye refused to comment. To get the lowdown, I drove to a shop called Oxford Ventures. It's gone now, but at the time it was open for business and the last vestige of the once grand Oxford Market, founded in 1923, that sold groceries and dry goods on Saranac Lake's Broadway. Ruth Effenbach, the elderly owner, would know anything that was worth knowing about Paye.

"Orville's as good-hearted as they come," said Effenbach, smiling behind wire-rimmed glasses. "He's helped a lot of people around town, especially a lot of young people. He had no children of his own, you know. He's put several young people through college and probably more."

Effenbach died a few months after we had that conversation. A few years later, Orville Paye was gone, too. He didn't make 150.

These were the kinds of people Debbie and I were getting to know during the months leading up to the epochal decision to roll our genetic dice. Importantly, there were others like them, others who led equally authentic lives, unique in their unorthodoxy, others who would provide any children we might have with wide-ranging visions of what their futures might hold. There was David Vana, a friend who owns an old farm up the road. He trained for the United States luge team and might have competed in the 1980 Winter Olympic Games in Lake Placid if a crash in Germany hadn't mangled one of his ankles. Today, David travels the country buying, dismantling, restoring, selling, and erecting old fire towers. And there was David's quirky, often difficult, lovable wife, Lorraine Wilson, a poet and artist and tribal drumming enthusiast who founded and ran the first organic subscription farm in our neck of the woods. Lorraine developed cancerous anal tumors and died at about age fifty. Yet she lived long enough to welcome our children into the world. One of her last notes to a member of our household was addressed to our daughter, Tassie, months after Lorraine's frightening diagnosis and near the time of Tassie's second birthday. It reads: "Hey Tas, Let's get our beach toys & go to [Lake] Colby this summer! Hula Hula, birthday girl. Lorraine."

We come. We go. Life is so fleeting that we do well to pick our fellow pilgrims with the level of care Chaucer demonstrated. Debbie and I found people to love and admire in all of the places we'd lived, but here such people seemed to exist in unusually high proportion. Maybe it's the fact that this place, with its long winters and blink-or-you-miss-them summers and scarcity of conventional jobs, is a hard place to live. As a result, people who are born here and who remain when half their relations move to Florida and Arizona stay because they choose to. And people who come to start over and who stick, rather than fleeing after a first hard winter, live here by choice, too. All could move away, but they don't. Whether they run around with a deer rifle and a snowmobile or with a butterfly net and set of binoculars, they stay because they love life in this Burroughs-model park, love the lakes and the rivers, the mountains and the valleys, the tight-knit communities. Not a month goes by that we don't see fliers go up advertising a spaghetti dinner or fish fry for someone in need of surgery, or for a family that lost a house to a fire, or for someone who needs to make trips to Fletcher-Allen Hospital in Vermont for chemotherapy. We look after each other.

You can buy insurance policies to inoculate you against some of life's ills, but you can't buy friendship and the tender support of neighbors. These flow from the free and easy sharing of what Shakespeare called "the milk of human kindness." You ski to a solitary neighbor's house and bring him a pot of stew when he's down hard with the flu. Four years later, the neighbor loans you a fruit mill so you can extract the pulp from chokecherries and turn it into jam. Another neighbor, the owner of the camp across the road, lives an hour away in Plattsburgh and can't get down to check his place after storms. So you check on it for him. Once, you find that a fir tree has snapped off and hurtled down and punched a hole in his roof. Heavy rains are predicted. So you put aside your own duties, haul out a ladder, and with aluminum flashing and roofing tar patch the roof. The neighbor, an avid hunter and fisherman, starts bringing you gifts of venison and trout. These are true stories. I had the pleasure of playing a part in each of them.

BIOLOGICAL SURVEY RECORDS:

Storeria occipitomaculata   Redbelly snake
8/15/10: Ned found a beautiful redbelly snake, about 10" long, at the base of our Bali cherry tree. He had been hunting for snakes to show Russell Galen, a visiting literary agent from New York City and New Jersey, who came for lunch.

Gaultheria procumbens   Creeping snowberry
8/16/07: common in boggy woods in SE part of our property; how have we missed out on this plant for so long? I'm eager to try the leaves for tea per the recommendation of H. D. Thoreau.

10

Summer Journal

Note: this and the three chapters that follow bring together journal entries penned over more than a decade. Please bear with any apparent accelerations or reversals in the growth of children. These chapters represent a composite journal, not the record of a single year. Also, in enduring long winters, extreme cold, and hordes of biting insects, we pay a price to live where we do. Compensation comes from far and wide and for us especially from the throats of birds. Songbirds delight our ears from spring into autumn and sometimes even in winter. We love to listen and to distinguish the singers. It's a preoccupation bordering on obsession, as these pages will show.

June 22. I'm sipping coffee on our porch bed, enjoying a rare, leisurely morning. [This was before children.] The day has already included reading, pasting together a photocopied map for a hike to a remote mountaintop, pitching yeast into a batch of home-brewed beer, and chatting with the woman of the house. It's good to be here.

Yesterday at dusk, Debbie and I walked down the road about a half mile into the McKenzie Mountain Wilderness. Just before we turned back, the erratic, staccato song of a Canada warbler burst from the balsam woods. With it floated the swirling, rising voice of a Swainson's thrush. Both birds are scarce hereabouts, more typical of Canadian forests to the north than these woods south of Montreal and the St. Lawrence. The warbler catches the eye with a dark necklace across a bright yellow breast. The thrush wears camouflage. I rarely see a Swainson's thrush, but I'm always thrilled to hear its voice: disembodied, mysterious, extravagant, a signature sound of the great North Woods.

Yesterday, I was replacing the rear half of our car's exhaust system and feeding blackflies and mosquitoes in the process when I noticed a bird singing in the woods across the road. It sounded like a hoarse robin. Good heavens, a scarlet tanager! We hear this bird in sugar maples down the road, but not here in our boreal blend of spruce, fir, aspen, and red maple. The bird flew to a hidden perch just south of the clothesline and resumed caroling. When Debbie went hunting for it, the tanager closed its bill. We haven't heard one here since.

June 28. Sitting up in bed on the porch, feeling dark in the head despite the radiance of the morning, I experience a glimmer of pleasure at hearing *Quick—three beers!* An olive-sided flycatcher is advertising for a mate in a treetop across the road. I also hear, in this order: wind rustling the leaves of trees; a winter wren that sounds like it's playing riffs on a xylophone; a red-breasted nuthatch honking; a blue-headed vireo seeming to ask and answer rhetorical questions; a yellow-bellied sapsucker bleating; a mourning dove cooing; a tree swallow chattering; a rose-breasted grosbeak warbling; a parula warbler buzzing; a blue jay crying; a red-eyed vireo posing and responding to rhetorical questions at a faster pace and higher pitch than the blue-headed; an American goldfinch chipping and chupping; an American crow cawing; a black-and-white warbler squeaking like a hamster running on a wheel; and a veery flooding the air with weird circus music. Are we the keepers of these birds, their stewards, their saviors, their protectors? I think not. They got on well without us for eons.

Ah, for a cheery morning, one where, sunshine or no, the spirit awakes and sings like the birds. Instead I rise in a pool of dread, drenched by shame for things I could have done but didn't, money I should have earned but let slip away, the person I want to be but am not. It's a strange beast, this psyche of mine, far from tame, unpredictable, at times gentle, at times—especially in the mornings—fierce, sinking teeth in their owner. Life in these mountains has a way of rooting out one's weaknesses and hauling them into the open for examination. Self-directed lives like mine are often the envy of others. But living them, especially here, where the climate is relentlessly trying and paying work can be hard to come by, is rarely easy. Time to start over somewhere else? It's a dangerous thought.

The bugs have been vicious lately, inside and out. The wet spring and high heat of recent days (well up in the nineties) produce a cruel and piercing convergence. All four of our most notorious biting insects flourish at once: mosquitoes, blackflies, no-see-ums, and deerflies. Of these, I despise the mosquito the most. Indoors it is the chief attacker, day and night, assaulting not only unprotected skin but also jabbing through clothing. I feel like a pincushion—or a goatskin of red wine.

These are the stinking-hot days one forgets when romanticizing summer in winter. The weather has been Amazonian—temperature at ninety-four or so at midday, with stinging sunshine, a haze of ozone, the humidity thick as axle grease. A malaise grows on us, a sort of psychic mildew. We're grouchy. Pessimism creeps into all subjects. The weather is partly to blame. It's also the bugs.

Spring seems over and summer firmly planted. I was greatly pleased today to hear a bluebird singing. We had males visit us earlier this year, but all lacked paramours. Today's vocalist was more fortunate. He had a plain Jane on hand. When I went for a walk just before dinner, the male was warbling quietly from a perch on a utility wire, just above a birdhouse in the field across the road. I followed the wire with my binoculars, figuring the pale female must be near, and quickly spied her. We'd love to have bluebirds nest here. Their colors and songs would bring cheer.

Gray tree frogs and green frogs call loudly at night. Occasionally we still hear a trilling toad, and leopard frogs have commenced their peculiar habit of summer singing in our tall grass, far from their breeding territories and well after mating is done. What are they up to? Defending summer feeding territories? Having a second breeding? Rehearsing for next year?

Fireflies abound. Tonight, for the first time this year, I noticed the kind that switches on its yellow-green lamp and traces the letter *J* in the air.

Watching the pageant of nature play out at our place, a grand show with tens of thousands of actors crowding the stage, it's clear that appointing ourselves stewards of "our" eighteen acres would be ludicrous. The web of interconnections, an "Internet" if ever there was one, is impossibly complex, so much so that it would be impossible for anyone to comprehend it, let alone manage the system intelligently. All we can do is try to be on our best behavior, live modestly, take care of our needs, and hope for the best outcomes.

June 30. Summer is here. The western sky still glowed at 10:00 p.m. tonight, the air crisp and cool. A crescent moon sent bolts of spectral light through the woods. Rain and thunder came on and off all day. But all is not gloom. Last weekend brought two days of sunshine, and late this afternoon wind blew the clouds away, leaving behind gifts: a vivid blue sky, slanting rays of golden sun, and crisp air washed of all dust and dampness.

July 2. Glorious weather—sunny, breezy, the day's high temp. in the seventies, summer at its best. In the afternoon Ned and I took a quick walk down to the bridge and beyond. A warbler has been singing a squeaky song there day after day—fast like a yellow warbler's, yet not quite that fast, with a drop rather than a drop-and-rise at the end. The song also reminds me of the chestnut-sided warbler's, and there's one of those keeping busy in the same area. Still, the performance is different. It's not as varied in cadence and pitch, and it lacks the typical concluding flourish that makes the chestnut-sided's such a pleasure to hear. I saw a redstart in the area earlier in the spring, and redstarts often fool me.

So I spished. To spish, as birdwatchers often do, is to attract birds, or try to, by imitating a songbird alarm call. Soon Ned and I stood face to face with the prettiest orange-and-black American redstart I've ever seen. The redstart is a songbird, petite yet powerful and prone to pirouettes. It's of the wood warbler tribe. What a treat! Ned was impressed, too. I feel almost dizzy with love at such moments—love for Ned, love for the redstart, love for the world and its beauties and marvels. My dark thoughts of recent days evaporate. Why would I ever want to leave? How can one be sad amid such bounty?

July 9. Excitement last night. Deb woke me up at 3:00 a.m. We were sleeping on the porch, and she'd heard a sound. It was a low moan, rising and falling, almost human. We guessed it was coming from a bear, although neither of us had ever heard a bear, or any other animal, produce such a noise. Another sound reached us, too. This was a banging of metal. We investigated. Peering out the mudroom door, we saw the bird feeder hanging askew. Apparently we'd scared a bear off early in the game. Their usual modus operandi is to pull a feeder to the ground and demolish it. Two hummingbird feeders were nowhere to be seen. Cautiously, we opened the door. Moaning filled the air. If we believed in ghosts we'd have been terrified. With the moans came more banging. The sounds came from the direction of a neighbor's camp.

Curious to know what game was afoot yet hesitant to blunder out in pajamas, we decided to slip in the car and drive. I pulled the Subaru wagon up to the mudroom door so Debbie could jump in. Straight ahead, the headlights illuminated the lower reaches of a white pine just outside our bedroom. A black, hairy shape moved gorilla-like down the trunk, swiftly. It was a bear—a small one. We drove on, seeking the source of the moaning, which came from farther off. Creeping down the driveway, along the road toward the bridge, and up the neighbor's driveway, we found no sign of anything. We drove across the bridge, then back. Nothing. By the time we rolled up our own driveway and climbed out, it was a silent night. Were the moans a mother bear's way of keeping in contact with her cub?

The following morning, I found a big pile of bear feces in the driveway and another smaller heap beside the clothesline. The white pine the cub had climbed had impressive claw marks on it. Down by the river, in mud near our neighbor's camp, I found several fresh bear tracks, probably from the little bear we'd seen on the pine. I made plaster casts. It's fun having bears around—and just a little scary.

July 17. A good week, the kids thriving and rambunctious, all of us healthy, the weather still wet but sunnier than in recent weeks. The day got off to an interesting start with a damselfly emerging from its nymphal skin on the side of a washbasin left outside the kitchen door. In it the kids and I had put tiny pond creatures we'd collected in Moose Pond.

The remarkable happening of the day, aside from the hourly astonishments provided by the kids, was a towhee appearing in a dead spruce in front of the house. A towhee, more a southern bird than a northern, is unusual enough around here, but this one opened its bill and proceeded to speak the language of blue jays. *Jay-jay-jay*, it said, imitating with remarkable fidelity to pitch, tone, and cadence. The towhee also produced the jay call that begins with a guttural clunk and ends with a high-pitched squeak. Once or twice, I heard the bird say *chewink*, as conventional towhees do. Never, though, did it sing its own song, usually rendered *drink your tea,* the last syllable a drawn-out trill. Twice the bird flapped off in haste, joining a band of blue jays gathered in an aspen. The jays paid no apparent attention and departed. The towhee then returned to its singing post and starting speaking jay again.

A white-throated sparrow turned up in Central Park a decade ago, singing the song of the black-throated green warbler. This is the kind of exceptional behavior birdwatchers go nuts for. The sparrow attracted crowds, was recorded by my friend Brad Klein, and made its debut on National Public Radio. The towhee was providing my own first encounter with such behavior. I was puzzled and fascinated. What was inspiring the towhee to cry like a jay? Had it been raised by jays? Was some short-circuit in the bird's brain inclining it to speak a language other than its own?

Our friend Greg Budney, curator of the Macaulay Library of Natural Sounds at Cornell's Laboratory of Ornithology, heard my report and shipped recording gear by overnight courier. With Greg's parabolic microphone in hand and a digital recorder draped from my shoulder, I caught the towhee in the act. Somewhere in the Macaulay Library's archives, the bird's performance lives on.

July 18. The towhee disappeared instantly after I recorded it. Hot, muggy weather continues. This has been a steamy and quite un-Adirondack-like summer. One dare not complain. Winter and profound cold will be here soon enough.

Last Thursday or thereabouts, I walked back from the mailbox via our former lawn, now a miniature tall-grass prairie. On an Adanac apple tree we planted five years ago, a tree that has grown only a little in that span, something remarkable caught my eye. An apple! The sight of an apple on an apple tree would not be worthy of remark in another context. Yet here, where fruit trees seem to rise vertically more slowly than glaciers creep horizontally, this was a great event. I searched among the leaves on each branch and eventually counted twenty-two pomes. Hooray! I felt a rush of paternal pride.

July 21. It's a sultry summer morning. We've been camped out on our porch bed for hours, sipping hazelnut coffee, eating breakfast, and reading. [This was pre-children.] Thunderstorms are coming. A gusting wind stirs the trees, shaking a branch here, a crown there. Birds sing—a scarlet tanager, a robin, a red-eyed vireo.

July 22. A cuckoo has been making weird gulping sounds on and off the last few days. It's a first for us. Yesterday morning the bird appeared in the red spruce we see from the porch. It was a black-billed cuckoo.

Plants are green and lush. Virgin's bower, a leafy vine, drapes extravagantly over the viburnums and alders across the river. Flowers cover the vines like soap suds and give off a strong, musky scent. Along the river, spires of purple loosestrife have provided color the last couple of weeks. They tell me it's midsummer. We can look forward and backward and say that this is the heart of the season.

Bird song is much diminished. Now that I've made that statement, I sit on the porch and hear the voices of five species: white-throated sparrow, song sparrow, swamp sparrow, American robin, and magnolia warbler. Still, that's all. I also hear a multitude of chips and twitters, some of which I can't put my finger on. Wait! I hear a red-eyed vireo warble, and a chickadee repeats its name. Winters are so long here and summers so short we don't want to rush autumn. The growing silence of birds in midsummer comes as a dark omen.

Common St. John's wort bears its tattered, yellow flowers now. Red-osier dogwoods hold ripening fruits, green tending toward white. Highbush cranberry drupes catch the eye and at this unripe stage are colored a lime green. They'll turn a brilliant red. I'm not half the botanist I'd like to be, but I love being immersed in plants even when I'm not sure what some of them are. Mosses, for example, confound me. I relish their presence all the same.

July 23. When I stepped outside this cool, golden morning, bound for the garbage transfer station and post office, I heard the downward-slurred scream of a red-tailed hawk. This is a common bird in most North American places but unusual here. Apparently in response, songbirds were making a ruckus.

If I listen closely this morning, I hear the high, sibilant musical performance of an insect—whether cricket, katydid, or grasshopper I'm not sure. About a week ago, the first insect spoke up, a night singer. Its *rat-tat-tat* made me suspect it was a katydid of some sort. A changing of the guard is under way. The songs of birds usher in the summer. The songs of insects escort it out. It's a poignant time, the middle age of the year. The great drama of life in this intensely seasonal climate passes the halfway point. The slow, inexorable process of withering and dying begins.

Last night, I stepped out on the porch before shuffling off to bed. It was midnight. I paused for a few minutes to listen. At first I heard only the *knock-knock* and *knock-knock-knock* of mink frogs, calling in a stranded oxbow swamp down by the river. Mink frogs are amphibians of the Far

North. If you get near one and sniff, you'll find it smells faintly like a mink—which is to say, pretty awful, a bit like stale urine. Disturb a mink frog, and it cranks out the stench in earnest.

July 29. A clear, cool, quiet morning. I'm refreshed by a shower. Tassie naps in the bedroom and a breeze rustles the leaves of the trees.

Yesterday I realized I hadn't heard an alder flycatcher broadcasting its buzzy *free beer!* for a week or more. Today, down by the river, somewhere deep in thickets of alder and holly, the flycatchers are singing again. A waning half moon floats high in a radiantly blue southern sky. I took Ned out to see it. "Moon!" he cried, spying his favorite celestial object, his smile reflecting bliss. A catbird babbles. No yellow warbler has sung in days. I suspect they've left us. Insect voices float on the air. I hear the soft *tick-tick-ticking* of sword-bearing conehead grasshopper. Earlier, I heard the distinctive *zah-zip* of an oblong-winged katydid.

I have a sense of the preciousness of days that have never come before and will never come again. Even though it's still July, we teeter on the brink of autumn—not just any autumn, but this one, unique in the endless expanse of time.

Dark, nearly black wood nymph butterflies turn up everywhere, especially on patches of spreading dogbane, a plant that is in full flower behind the house. We've also begun seeing Milbert's tortoiseshell butterflies. They're a flying dessert for the eye, their wings dark and chocolate-colored toward the middle, ringed by a creamy orange sherbet border with edges dappled in black licorice. A dot of white frosts each forewing. It's the final master-stroke, the feature that makes the Milbert's tortoiseshell the most striking of Adirondack butterflies.

August 12. Not a single bird voice graced the air as I sat listening on the porch this morning—at least, that was the case at first. A cricket or cricket-like creature fills the air with a continuous trill, and a katydid chimes in with an occasional *zah-zip*. Eventually, as I continued to sit, birds chimed in one by one. A goldfinch uttered staccato chirps. A robin chuckled. A catbird mewed. Waxwings, here to steal our blueberries, jingled. A nuthatch honked. A chickadee announced its identity, *chick-a-dee-dee-dee*.

August 21. A bird peeps in the darkness. Who is it?

A jet roars high in the night sky, making for somewhere, people strapped in seats reading magazines and watching movies, oblivious to the bears, beavers, and people sporting around in the blackness beneath them.

Insects are so loud and pervasive on this late summer night that in their ubiquity I could almost fail to notice. They're simply there, like the air. The chorus consists mostly of snowy tree crickets, which trill in enormous number. Here and there among them I pick out the rhythmic *cha-cha-cha* of katydids. These are not the loud, frank common katydids of my youth downstate, but a higher, thinner, no less insistent species, with the same sort of three-syllable delivery.

The end of summer and the onset of autumn stir thoughts of beginnings—of new teachers and classrooms, of new schools, of going off to college, of that peculiar fall of 1978 when, at twenty-one years of age, for the first time since I was four years old, I had no school to go to. Instead, I flew off to Europe with my lifelong friend James Junker to roam the cities and breweries of Europe. We ended the trip in the Bavarian Alps with a week of hang-gliding lessons. Seven finished out of our class of ten. Three pulled out because of injury. Learning to fly through the air was dangerous but glorious, the closest I've ever come to being a bird.

August 22. The calendar tell us that autumn arrives on September 21. Here in the northern Adirondacks, the season has been under way for a week and more, and Labor Day still looms a week in the future. Nights are cool. Days are brisk, with temperatures no higher than the sixties. Birds are on the move. Flocks of warblers turn up in the bushes between the shed and the woodshed every day or so.

Last Thursday, I walked to my writing studio on a blazing starry night and looked skyward. The shift of my ears from horizontal to vertical brought the faint twitter of songbird voices uttered high, high overhead. Our small, insect-eating migrants travel mostly at night, when falcons aren't out looking for them, and on starry nights in particular. This was a humdinger. The Milky Way all but dripped from the sky.

August 24. This morning a red-eyed vireo caroled in the trees as I loaded Ned [then a baby and only child] into the car. I hadn't heard one in a week. Will this be the last I hear? Operas aren't over until the fat lady sings. Adirondack summers don't end until the red-eyed vireo, a little green and white bird with a gray cap, gives its final performance. Then, quietly, it wings off to spend our winter (another summer for the bird) in the Amazon.

Around the hummingbird feeder, activity is frenetic and has been so for days. We go through a half-gallon of sugar water in forty-eight hours. Every year I'm amazed. One day, hummers fog the air in numbers that would frazzle an air traffic controller's nerves. The next, all is silent. It's as if the birds are all booked on the same flight to Cancún.

I also heard a black-billed cuckoo *coo-coo-cooing*. A pair of the birds surely nested here. We've heard them on and off all summer. Cuckoos aside, the woods are generally silent of birds. All the racket is provided by crickets, katydids, and grasshoppers. The songbirds that remain have more important business than singing. Music is for territorial defense and courtship, but what's the need? The driving impulse has changed. The need is to eat, eat, and eat some more, building body fat. Fat insulates, and it stokes the metabolic fires that keep birds warm in cool weather. If the birds are migrants, fat is aviation fuel, propelling them south to their wintering grounds.

August 26. Summer arrived, and summer departs. Red maples catch fire. So does the shrub called hobble-bush, and so does the groundcover plant, a miniature dogwood called bunchberry. Birds exercise their right to remain silent, except for the occasional red-eyed vireo that can't resist making one more parting remark. Hummingbirds still patrol in force, although yesterday their insatiable consumption of sugar water slacked off. Today their numbers and appetites rebound. Migrants?

Eastern bluebirds nested here this summer. They raised a single brood of four or five scrawny hatchlings in a ratty birdhouse I knocked together from wood scraps. I love these birds. Honestly, I'm not sure why. Maybe it's their passionate, conspicuous, highly vocal courtships. Maybe it's their pretty rust-and-blue colors. They also endear themselves by plucking bugs out of the vegetable garden. Bluebirds appear in spring around the time the snow begins to melt and the sap starts running in maple trees. It's a time of year I love and dream of all winter.

Last week brought two light frosts. The garden, which Debbie planted in tomatoes, sugar snap peas, cabbage, beets, Brussels sprouts, broccoli, and zucchini, felt the chill, even though we tarped the whole patch.

This summer brought sadness. We learned of the death of our friend and stalwart advisor Joe Gilbert at a nearby lumberyard. Without Joe's expert advice and encouragement, we and our marriage might never have survived the first years here. Children? They might not have happened. Joe deserves credit, direct and indirect, for all sorts of good things. We will miss him.

You know you've lived in a place a while when people whom you at first didn't know, but then got to know, die. Years pass, and you carry on. Part of me loves this place and wants to stay here until my own time is up. Another part of me, with only slight provocation, could pull up stakes and flee. Stay in a place for a long time and you gain a sobering awareness of life's brevity. You realize you're on a conveyor belt that picks you up at birth and drops you off at death, and the belt is constantly moving, and it's one-way.

Our writer friend Alex Shoumatoff, his sons, Oliver and Zack, and his nephew Edgar were here for a visit last week. The boys are reptile and amphibian enthusiasts. Every time they come, we set off into the woods to turn logs and rocks and root around in wet spots and see what we can find. On this occasion we found only one herp—a red-spotted newt that I plucked from a brilliant bed of moss. In a dense stand of balsam fir, Alex's keen eye spied Labrador tea, a shrub we'd never before recorded here. Nearby, I found creeping snowberry, another new record. The white pea-sized fruits of this delicate prostrate vine hide beneath tiny leaves. If you hunt for the fruits and get lucky, you enjoy the privilege of popping in your mouth the most exquisite delicacy the forest has to offer. The fruits are soft inside and wintergreen-flavored. After frosts, they're sweet, dreamy, and custard-like.

September 10. Only a few straggling hummingbirds. Robins and flickers present in great number. Flickers are big, multicolored, ground-feeding woodpeckers that somewhere in their evolutionary path decided that chiseling wood in search of grubs was for the birds. So now they probe anthills for their sustenance. Mind you, flickers haven't given up wood-pecking entirely. They mortise nesting chambers in tree trunks, but that seems to be the beginning and end of it. We see astonishing numbers of flickers in September and October. Then the ground freezes hard. Ants die or retreat into the soil, and the birds move on. A near frost last night. Touches of color in the trees. Still, it's a green world. I relish autumn once I'm resigned to it, but I hate to see summer end.

September 18. A cold, clear, starry night. Frost is predicted. We've had a few, but we haven't had a really hard, death-dispensing one yet. Tonight the weather feels too mild for it to happen. I stacked firewood in the woodshed until past eleven. A silent night—no road noise, no owls hooting, no yipping and wailing and howling of coyotes, no insects. Quiet grows ever more rare in the modern world, yet we swim in it.

Today several eastern phoebes hunted the yard for flying insects. No idea whether these birds, a kind of flycatcher, were ones that summered here and nested, or whether they're just passing through. We experience a phoebe-less month or so after nestlings fledge in early summer. Then early September brings them back, and late September whisks them away.

We had a single hummingbird yesterday, and red-eyed vireos were singing.

The forest remains overwhelmingly green. Even so, touches of red and orange multiply, and roadside swamps burst into flame as red maples turn scarlet and crimson. A soft, warm rain fell this morning. It highlighted the poignant beauty of this pivotal point on the calendar when summer lingers but slowly yields the upper hand to fall.

September 20. At last I find heart to look back nine days and report. Monday, the 10th, we worked all day organizing the house, then crawled off to sleep on the porch. Crickets trilled. Katydids rasped in the grass. The night was calm and dark, the moon down.

In the morning, the telephone rang. It was my mother. "Turn the television on," she said. This was odd. Mom rarely watches television, and never before evening. My sister Nora had called, she said. An airplane had struck the World Trade Center.

About the time an image of a smoking tower materialized on our TV, a second jet plunged into the building's other tower. We watched, dumbfounded. By now everyone realized that a terrorist attack was under way. A third jet had crashed into the Pentagon in Washington, said newsman Tom Brokaw, visibly rattled. A fourth, he said, perhaps commandeered with the idea of striking another target, had gone down in Pennsylvania.

We kept the TV on in horror and sympathy and, I confess, out of morbid curiosity. Soon we saw something I'll never forget, something no one seemed to anticipate. One of the World Trade Center's two great towers began collapsing in on itself, straight down into its foundations. The sight was unspeakably awful. People inside were trying to get out, and others were rushing in to help or milling around on the street. The tower's fall looked like films I've seen of rockets that misfired and slumped backward into their launching pads. I shouted as it happened, and I'm not prone to shouting. "Deb, Deb! Look! Oh, no! Oh, that's sickening! I can't believe it!" None of us could.

A few minutes later, the second tower went the way of the first, killing more people and inflicting another wave of horror on those millions of us looking. Meanwhile, a gorgeous Adirondack day proceeded to unfold, minute by placid minute.

The word "evil" crosses many lips these days. Some of John Burroughs's thoughts, expressed in his book *Accepting The Universe* (1921), come to mind:

> There is no problem of evil until we have made or imagined an unnatural and impossible world. When we have enthroned in the universe a powerful man-made God who is the embodiment of all we call good and the contemner of all we call evil, then we have our insoluble problem. To help ourselves out we invent another being who is the embodiment of all we call evil and enthrone him in regions below. Upon him we saddle the evil, and thus we try to run the universe with these two antagonistic principles yoked together, and no end of confusion in our religious ideas results.

Were the terrorists evil? No more so, and no less, than the fanatical Christians, slaughterers of innocents, who brought us the Crusades, the Inquisition, and the Salem witch trials. Burroughs calls for us to abandon old creeds. Some fear the world would fall into chaos if we did. Is the fear justified? I think not. During a 25,000-mile trip around Australia, Debbie and I found freethinkers (I recoil from the negative connotations of "atheist") in an overwhelming majority. Yet of all the places I've traveled, Australia seems the most kind, generous, and civilized. Complete strangers from the other side of the world, we were invited again and again into homes, fed, given shelter, and accepted for who we were. All this with no Bible thumping or fanatical devotion to the Koran or any other so-called sacred text. Do we need deities to threaten us with punishment, or tempt us with virgins, to behave well? I think not. We simply need to make good decisions, as kids are taught to do these days in school.

Nine days later, the shock remains profound, but it has lost its edge. A gruesome feeling lingers in the gut. The surreal quality of the events that transpired on September 11 only heightens as we resume old routines, gaze up at the mountain in the nearby wilderness, and move on. Meanwhile, uneasiness grows. What next? What will the terrorists do? What will we do? I feel a deepening of my commitment to this peaceful place where we live. Perhaps we're in the right spot after all, embedded in nature rather than removed.

BIOLOGICAL SURVEY RECORDS:

Polites mystic   Long dash skipper
6/28/03: caught and, after hard work and much scrutiny, identified this butterfly; abundant in the yard this warm (80s F) sunny day

Chelone glabra   Turtlehead
8/6/01: six or more plants flowering just east of s. end of bridge; along bank of river [this species disappeared from our property by the end of the decade]

11

Fall Journal

September 24. Yesterday Larry Master, friend, former chief zoologist for The Nature Conservancy, and expert on small mammals arrived with his wife, Nancy, for a cookout. Before dinner, Larry broke out a container of rolled oats and several dozen aluminum box traps. The traps were so tiny they looked more likely to be swallowed by animals than to catch them. Ned and I tromped around the property with Larry and Nancy, baiting and setting. Mainly, we put traps in two places—in wet, mossy woods on land we own across the road and along the river beside the bridge and a sandbar.

The following frosty morning, Larry reappeared in the driveway. Ned, Tassie, and I made the rounds with him. Debbie joined us for a few minutes, then zoomed off to work. Here's what we caught: a half-dozen or so deer mice; a red-backed vole, a gorgeous creature that would attract crowds in zoos if it was one hundred times larger; a tiny gray poker-faced beast that Larry identified as a smoky shrew; and a second tiny shrew, this one brown, which Larry at first thought might be a pygmy but then decided was a masked, or cinereus, shrew. He said our place also likely supports southern bog lemmings, the two eastern species of jumping mice (meadow and woodland), and water shrews. We'll soon be on their trails.

Why the fuss over little furry things? Our passion could be seen as a sort of worship, I suppose. Instead of dressing on Saturday or Sunday and going to temple or church, we venture outdoors in the clothes we're comfortable in, often in the company of like-minded friends, and celebrate life in all its richness, mystery, and diversity.

October 1. Freezing nights, clear cold mornings, and fall color are here, yet summer refuses to give up. I found a black-and-yellow argiope spider yesterday. It tends a web among hydrangea blooms along the driveway. Given the frenetic insect activity on the hydrangeas at flowering time, the spider chose its place of business well. Still, how long can the game go on? The days grow shorter and colder. The spider offers a model for us to emulate. Rather than focusing on the annihilation looming, it exists moment by moment, flourishing on love and food.

Yesterday I heard a ruby-crowned kinglet singing where I often find them caroling in springtime—just west of the north end of the driveway. Why now? Perhaps it's a matter of day length. This day in fall, and a corresponding day in March, have identical hours of sunshine and darkness. Perhaps the birds are calendrically confused. Then again, maybe not. If the kinglet thinks it's spring, it'll fly northward, not southward. I bet it doesn't make that mistake. Deep in the woods, a robin caroled and a grouse drummed. Every bird that sings now might well be the last of the year.

Ned and I walked to the river. In a neighbor's driveway, we startled two ruffed grouse, one clamped to a birch limb, the other strutting on the ground. The bird in the tree eyed us warily, but it did not flee. On the ground, the strutting bird stalked slowly toward the woods, its ruff thrust out like an Elizabethan collar, tail fanned like a turkey's, crest raised in a state of high excitement. Ned took in the show. So did I, but with adult sensibilities I felt the embarrassed chagrin one feels in disturbing lovers. What were the birds up to? It seemed too late in the year for genuine courtship. Were these juveniles playing at romance, an adolescent Romeo and Juliet, he on the ground, she in the balcony? Then again, grouse may court throughout the year, and perhaps the passion I sensed was real. Do ruffed grouse form permanent pair-bonds? I think not. Males thump the air with their wings to attract females, and they're not fussy about which, or how many, hens they mate with. After copulation, parenthood is the female's job.

Handsome Ned and his beautiful little sister thrive. Debbie and I grow exhausted keeping up with them, the dishes, the cooking, the washing, the nursing, the diapers, the dishes, the cooking, the washing, the nursing, the diapers. . . . All the same, life is good. Life is poignant. We watch our kids grow bigger, stronger, brighter, and more coordinated by the day while, as middle-aged parents, we're acutely aware that our own senescences have begun. The knowing of what lies ahead feels at times like a curse. Yet I remind myself that it's also a gift. Without it we might not savor the here and now.

October 2. A fire hisses softly in the woodstove. Tonight the air outside feels as crisp as a fresh-picked apple. A half moon waxes in the western sky. Maples glow red, orange, and gold. We haven't seen a hummingbird in weeks. The last one turned up the day after I'd pronounced them gone. It zoomed over our heads and jerked to a halt on a spruce twig— a delicious juxtaposition of the tropical and the boreal, the bird bound for a balmy winter in Central America, the tree steeling itself for nights at forty below zero.

Tonight Ned and I walked down to the river and looked for hollies. I was writing a story about the plants and wanted a fresh look. Close by the road, we found a spot where winterberry and mountain holly grow side by side. Both were still in leaf. These are deciduous hollies, not like the better-known English and American hollies, with their thick, waxy, prickly evergreen foliage. The leaves of these shrubs remained green. Hundreds of fat red berries supplied glamour to the winterberry, while the mountain holly, its fruits far more appealing to birds, had no berries on it at all. Either it was a male holly, which produce no fruit, or it was a female that had surrendered all of its berries. Deer had been browsing both plants. The mountain holly was hit hard. The winterberry appeared untouched.

While we walked across the bridge, a flock of songbirds rocketed in from the direction of the setting sun and landed on the summit of a big white pine. Waxwings? They seemed too large. Binoculars told the story. They were robins. When the angle was right, their breasts flashed orange in the rose-colored sunshine.

Ned and I climbed through an alder thicket to a sandbar. There we tromped through tall cane grass to the far end and back, Ned delighting in the adventure of thrashing through stems that towered over him, as if he were an ant crossing a lawn. Judging by his smile, Ned had a ball. So did I.

October 18. A cold, hard, brittle day with blue skies and a bright but icy sun. Yesterday's inch of snow melted by noon, the water pouring off the roof in rivulets, the trees dripping, the roads glistening. I cut the first rafter for a woodshed today. As accomplishments go, slicing a single board sounds small. Still, those four bites out of a two-by-six taken with a circular saw represent the culmination of a couple of weeks of thinking, reading, and playing on paper with dimensions. I have a lot to learn as a carpenter.

October 20. A coyote chorus shook the night air a few minutes ago. We listened to the yips and wails, muffled by the bedroom walls but still thrilling. We haven't heard coyotes in ages. It would be easy to demonize these animals, as many do, claiming they're bloodthirsty deer killers. It's equally easy to romanticize them, to listen to their wild, improvisatory choruses on a dark night and think exciting thoughts about the beauty and adventure to be found in places like the Adirondacks. In the middle lies the truth. The coyotes whose music I savor wrap up a performance, trot off into the night, and seek victims to hound, terrify, run down, hamstring, rip apart, and devour, sometimes while the victim remains alive. Like humans, coyotes are what they are—neither saints nor demons, just creatures that act in their own self-interest. Coyotes are wild cousins of the wolf, the fox, and the Rottweiler. We expect a certain amount of ferocity in them. Humans, for all our pretensions otherwise, are also wild animals. Perhaps we should expect a certain amount of ferocity in ourselves, too, even as we attempt to walk gently upon the Earth.

October 23. A light snow on the ground this sunny morning. We saw a few flakes during the week, but this is the first snow to stick.

October 29. Yesterday was my birthday. Hard to believe. My life seems short and long at the same time—short in the way time speeds by, and long in all the things I've done and all the people I've known along the way. Many of those people, including some of the finest, are dead. It's sobering. One day I'll join them, ready or not.

What to do in the meantime? There are times when I find myself envying the lives of others around me, others who have strictly defined jobs to go to, paychecks that arrive on schedule, retirement pensions waiting, and insurance programs to see that they're cared for when they get sick. I, on the other hand, invent myself anew day by day, never quite sure where I'm heading. At times I feel I'm out on a limb—the wrong limb.

A passage from Ralph Waldo Emerson's essay "The American Scholar" consoles me. I consult it from time to time in the same way one might take a dose of cough syrup. Emerson writes:

The office of the scholar is to cheer, to raise, and to guide men by showing them facts amid appearances. He plies the slow, unhonored, and unpaid task of observation . . . in his private observatory, cataloguing obscure and nebulous stars of the human mind, which as yet no man has thought of as such,—watching days and months sometimes for a few facts; correcting still his old records,—must relinquish display and immediate fame. In the long period of his preparation he must betray often an ignorance and shiftlessness in popular arts, incurring the disdain of the able who shoulder him aside. Long he must stammer in his speech; often forego the living for the dead. Worse yet, he must accept—how often!—poverty and solitude. For the ease and pleasure of treading the old road, accepting the fashions, the education, the religion of society, he takes the cross of making his own, and, of course, the self-accusation, the faint heart, the frequent uncertainty and loss of time, which are the nettles and tangling vines in the way of the self-directed.

Thank heaven for Emerson. He goes on, delivering more cheer:

"Let him not quit his belief. . . . In silence, in steadiness, in severe abstraction, let him hold by himself; add observation to observation, patient of neglect, patient of reproach, and bide his own time,—happy enough if he can satisfy himself alone that this day he has seen something truly. Success treads on every right step. For the instinct is sure, that prompts him to tell his brother what he thinks."

That said, here's one thing I think. Everyone seems to agree that society today abounds in moral, ethical, philosophical, economic, and environmental ills. Surely there's truth in the view, although one can argue that the world of men, women, and children has always existed in such a state, and it always will. "Same shit, different day," say the cynics. Who is to blame?

Right and left, fundamentalist and freethinker, tend to agree on one thing. Runaway individualism is the culprit. We have created, goes the widely expressed notion, a society of supreme selfishness. Everyone does his own thing. No one gives a rat's derriere about anyone else.

I don't buy it. If everyone is doing his or her own thing, then why is that thing the same for nearly everyone? Why does everyone have to own an iPhone, drive nearly identical automobiles, watch *American Idol* on TV, and spend precious free time on social networking Web sites? Runaway individualism is largely an illusion. We, the heirs of Aristotle and Shakespeare, Madame Curie and Toni Morrison, are becoming a great multinational, multicultural herd, stampeding this way in reaction to the prodding of cowboys.

When I connect to the Internet, my server tells me "What's Hot," as if I could give a hoot what most people are doing or searching for. Why would I care? We need not less individualism to make the world a happier, more nurturing place. We need more. We need to think for ourselves, not let religious leaders, political leaders, advertising agencies, and our friends and neighbors do our thinking for us. We need to be real, even when that means years of struggle and soul-searching to determine the nature of one's authenticity.

"To thine own self be true," wrote Shakespeare. That's what I tell our kids. Being true to oneself is easier said than done. Getting to know oneself deeply, and making peace with the angels and demons each of us carries around in our heads, takes time and patience. The process demands those rarest of modern resources, solitude and silence: quiet, private time when we step out of the raging river of stimuli thundering toward us every moment of every day; quiet, private time when we switch off electronic communication devices that would drown us in information and conversation; quiet, private time when we open our ears to the faint voices that speak within us. And only the sound of wind in the trees and our own heartbeats.

Tamaracks, our only conifers to shed their needles in fall and sprout an entirely new set in spring, stand in full color. Other deciduous leaves are down, save for a few dry bits of quaking aspen foliage rattling in the crowns. Tamarack color is distinctive and not easy to describe. It's a sort of mustard, not quite yellow, not quite orange, closer to orange than to yellow. The leaves of shrubs called viburnums stink where they molder. This time of year, a blind man or woman could find them with ease.

I am not yet resigned to winter—still hope for another run of warm. Winters are long. It's been said, with not as much exaggeration as you might think, that there are two seasons in the Adirondacks: winter and the Fourth of July. When the cold gets under way in earnest, there's often no break until March or April, and late in May, we're still making fires in the woodstove.

Tonight, here I am: home in a warm, snug house, home with Debbie, Ned, and Tassie, all of us healthy, home as a husband, home as a father of two. Given all the hurdles and hazards the world throws at us, and has thrown at me in particular, it's remarkable and marvelous to be alive and well in the wild and beautiful Adirondack Mountains, here on this blue and green orb, spinning through the cold, star-spangled vastness of space.

November 11. We lounge on the porch, sitting up in bed, sipping coffee, writing in journals, basking in warmth. It is sixty-five degrees in mid-November! Friday, Saturday, and Sunday were balmy, too. Each afternoon the mercury squeezed a little higher. Global climate change? Likely it's a factor, a worrisome one. All the same, the hot streak—it feels hot, coming at this time of year, even though sixty-five would feel cool in July—follows weeks of cold. One day the temperature never climbed out of the twenties. One night we plunged into the single digits.

A warm wind gusts through the trees. The current blast of air sounds like a waterfall. The one before it sounded like rush hour in a big city, except that here there is no rush, only hours.

Today, for the second day in a row, Debbie and I will climb back on top of the house and work at restoring the roofing where it butts up to the chimney. A mason we hired to repoint the mortar did a sloppy job of ripping out shingles after we insisted he honor a promise to replace flashing. He drove away leaving an open wound in the roof. We were hoping for a dry day to do the work, but the sky looks iffy. Still, what's the choice?

November 15. Another spectral duck on the river this morning—dark, solitary, floating downstream off the sandbar, dipping into the water, grappling with something long, ribbon-like, and flaccid. The morsel was probably an aquatic plant called *Vallisneria*, or water celery. The duck had the general profile of a mallard or black duck. Curious, I grabbed a jacket and walked—still in pajamas—down to the water's edge. I scanned the river and scanned the banks. The ghost had vanished into the mist.

Cold and gray this morning with a mix of sleet, snow, and rain. The drops fell straight as a plumb bob from a dirty gray sky.

A glittering, brilliant night tonight. Deep, powdery snow everywhere, including all over the trees. A moon just past full illuminates everything. The river is particularly fetching—a narrow channel of glossy black, as perfect and inarguable as death, pouring between snow-covered flats of ice. Bits of ice and slush sift downstream, brushing the narrowed banks and breaking the silence with a soft rasping.

December 13. A cold, clear, bracing day. After a leisurely morning, I spent the afternoon carrying split lengths of firewood out of the woods, sharpening chainsaw chains, and sawing up a dead, dry aspen that toppled behind the woodshed. It was glorious to be out in the fresh air and sunshine.

I was carrying a splitting maul toward a stash of black cherry I'd cut when I heard sharp, distinct pecking to my right. A woodpecker, certainly. No, two. What kind? Something seemed different about the pecking. It was sharper and more aggressive than the desultory tapping of hairy woodpeckers, which are common, yet it was nowhere near as loud and human-like as the raps made by crow-sized pileated woodpeckers. I left the trail to investigate. One of the peckerwoods (as old folks in the Deep South call them) flapped off. The other stayed. The view was poor, but the bird looked awfully dark. So I abandoned my own wood pecking and ran for binoculars. They confirmed what I'd guessed. This was a black-backed woodpecker, a female, rapping here and there on a balsam trunk. A handsome creature she was—a soft, charcoal-black on the back, on the front finely etched with black and white bars. The discovery gave me a glow. How lucky we are to occupy a piece of land where such sightings are possible! Birdwatchers drive hundreds of miles to the northern Adirondacks to search for black-backed woodpeckers. I'd found one without leaving the yard.

December 14. Twenty-five below zero last night, and twelve below tonight when I clumped into the house at 11:00 p.m. after writing a newspaper column in my studio. Before heading to the house, I tromped through calf-deep snow down to the bridge. A bright, nearly full moon bathed all in a ghostly glow, making the scene feel timeless and universal. I might have been trudging through drifts on Pleistocene tundra in 15,000 BC, or slogging through a spruce forest near Hudson Bay yesterday. The sounds of grinding and scraping filled the biting air. Their source? I could see it. Rafts of ice were bobbing down the river, scuffing the ice shelves that extend from each bank and halve the width of open water.

Tassie is up with us. She's a gorgeous, bright, engaging little girl, full of life, smiles, joie de vivre. She may be small but she's a powerhouse. People see her and say she's tiny. That's true. Yet she looms large in our household, delighting her brother and her parents with her sheer Tassie-ness. Thank the forces of the universe and our own good sense (better late than never) that we had these wonderful kids. They drain us, utterly. Yet we love them, utterly.

December 20. This morning at 11:00 a.m. I finished cutting up the last of the trees we bought from our forester friend, Tom Bartiss. Two enormous truckloads of cherry, beech, and maple trunks are now reduced to stove length and ready to split. Hooray! Plenty of hard labor lies ahead, yet the noisy, dangerous, monotonous chainsaw work is done.

Today it's snowing lightly. I'm hard at work on a story for *Adirondack Life* magazine. Appropriately, it's on snow. If, back in 1967, the conservationist Laurance Rockefeller, chairman of the New York State Council of Parks and brother of then–New York governor Nelson Rockefeller, had had his way, an Adirondack National Park would have been created, combining just over a million acres in the central part of the range with 600,000 acres of private land. The result would have been another of Muir's wilderness cathedrals, presided over by priest-like rangers supervising the rest of us in exercising limited visitation rights and in making obeisances. Bloomingdale would have been left out. But the scheme was scuttled. New Yorkers of right, left, and center rose up in outrage and in unlikely unison against it. So here I am, inside a giant state park, on a private inholding, celebrating and honoring this wild place and its heritage—snow included—in my own way.

BIOLOGICAL SURVEY RECORDS:

Plectrophenax nivalis   Snow bunting
11/5/10: two perching on guardrail, 4:00 p.m., and flying up and down road in front of house

Fomitopsis pinicola   Red-banded polypore
10/4/05: several fine specimens on dead balsams, just south of w. end of a [neighbor] Rich's driveway

<hr />

12

Winter Journal

January 6. Temperature in the low fifties, rainy, with winds gusting violently in the afternoon. Almost all the little snow that lay on the ground has melted, save for a shrinking clump here and there. April is in the air!

Something peculiar in me longs for winter, then craves its departure as soon as it arrives. Perhaps this sort of chronic dissatisfaction is part of the human condition, a built-in downside of the big brains we're so proud of. I wonder. If having a supercomputer in one's nervous system is such a great thing, then why have so few living things evolved to have them? In the high-stakes game of survival on planet Earth, a keen intelligence may prove less a help than a hindrance. Tunicates, primitive marine organisms that possess what are essentially spinal chords without spinal columns to house them, will outlast us, I suspect. They preceded us by 500 million years, and as a result, we tend to view them as primitive. But maybe they're not throwbacks at all, but superbly adapted survivors.

January 9. Half an hour past midnight last night, trudging out to cut a board on a miter saw in the studio cellar, I thrilled to the sound of coyotes. They were yipping and howling somewhere off to the southeast. Snowshoe hares were scarce the last couple of years, but last winter and this, the tracks have multiplied. Are the coyotes back in force because hare numbers are rising? The ups and downs of prey populations tend to dictate the numbers of predators, rather than the other way around.

January 13. Black-capped chickadees were singing their spring song yesterday. They're broadcasting it again today, serving up cheer amid the white and gray.

January 14. A mild night compared to last—fifteen below zero rather than thirty below. The highest I ever saw our thermometer climb this afternoon was fifteen below zero, and it's stayed there ever since. A bright, cheery sun lit up the white world, casting a gorgeous mix of golden light and sharply defined shadow. Global climate change may yet turn our climate into that of present-day Savannah, Georgia, but in the meantime, the old regime still knows how to provide a Big Chill.

We've had a run of frigid weather the last couple of weeks, with a brief warming over the weekend. Last week we had several subzero days in a row. One night the temperature dropped to thirty-four below zero. The next morning, neither of our cars would start. This morning, I tried firing the engines again. Same result. A battery charger eventually got the Subaru running at 9:30, in time to get Deb to work not quite an hour late.

January 15. Thirty-four below zero this stunningly clear and sunny morning. To my astonishment, both cars rumbled to life. Even more to my astonishment, I heard black-capped chickadees caroling in two directions. This morning's abysmal temperature suggests it's the strengthening sun that inspires them, not warmth.

January 20. I stepped out on the porch tonight around midnight. Heading for the recycle bin, I was stopped in my tracks by sounds—loud, crunching noises of a sort an enormous animal might make when breaking through ice, accompanied by a high-pitched hissing. The clamor was coming from the direction of the river. It's half frozen, with shelves of ice advancing out from each bank. The shelves grow wider as fractured bits of ice drift down from upstream, adhering here and there. In some places the new shelves lie smooth and glossy; these probably formed on the spot. But in places where the Saranac flows most powerfully, the new ice forms as a collage. Where do the fragments come from? I suspect they crystallize in quiet pockets and eddies. Then, as the ice reaches out into faster water, pieces break off and float down to our place.

January 28. A sunny day—hooray! We've seen the sun in only a few scattered hours since early November, so it's a treat to wake up and find bright light streaming in the windows. The days are noticeably longer now than they were a month ago. In December, daylight was snuffed out by 4:30. Now it lingers well past 5:00.

Evening grosbeaks, male and female, robust of bill and body, yellow and black and white, swarm around our feeders this morning. Gray jays, blue jays, black-capped chickadees, red-breasted nuthatches, pine siskins, a downy woodpecker, and a hairy woodpecker bustle out there, too.

We're about to head off on skis to watch for signs of breeding activity among white-winged crossbills and pine siskins. Both birds are present in great number, lured here by a combination of poor cone crops in other places and a banner year for cones in the northern Adirondacks. Crossbill males make long, circular nuptial flights, trilling and chirping to females in the nearby trees. The birds breed in winter when the pines, spruces, firs, hemlocks, tamaracks, and white cedars bear cones that provide food for their young.

February 8. Cold, dark, and still. It's one of those winter nights of discontent when I'm my own worst critic, when I wonder if I've tossed my chances of a sensible life away in a mad, impractical pursuit of what's wild, beautiful, and true. Shouldn't I, like most of my college classmates, be going to work in a suit and tie? Shouldn't I have a giant nest egg tucked away to take care of me and mine when the going gets tough, as it inevitably does for all? Most of my contemporaries, or at least those of similar backgrounds and education, are nearing a day when they'll slip into comfortable retirement. I, on the other hand, look ahead to continuing toil and struggle, stretching as far as I can see into the future. Should I be ashamed or proud? How can I know? Where to go from here? Such questions try my soul this dark night.

February 11. Have I mentioned the northern shrike that visits a turkey carcass we put out? Or the two gray jays that appear on the same carcass nearly every day? Or the weasel, brilliantly white of fur except for black eyes, a black nose, and black tail tip, that leaves tracks near the feeder, and that we've seen three times? Based on tiny footprints and the modest leaps between them, I'm pretty sure the weasel is an ermine, or short-tailed. Sometimes I feel I have more in common with the wild animals that surround me than with friends and neighbors. Their spirits are free. They seize life as it comes. Weasels burst with devil-may-care gusto, and I salute them.

February 12. It's nineteen below zero outside, the sky clear, the stars bright. You can tell it's bitterly cold because the snow crunches underfoot, as it does only at extreme low temperatures. Today I spent five hours shoveling the porch roof. The rafters that hold it up are old and dry and not very substantial, and the outer wall on which they bear isn't much of a wall at all, broken up down its length by windows. I scooped and slid snow by the ton, letting it fall to the ground with great thumps.

Looking up to the roof, the snow looked only moderately deep and fluffy. But once I climbed a ladder and dug in, I realized the stuff represented several feet of powder, compressed under its own weight and well on its way to becoming glacial ice. A vein of ice ran through the snow a few inches above the bottom. Hour after hour I chopped through it, carving the packed powder into movable blocks. I could have made an igloo. The highlight of my first session of roof shoveling of the season was having Ned [then three] with me. The temperature dropped toward zero, and a stiff wind lashed at exposed skin. Yet our boy relished the adventure and the pleasure—I hope it was that—of working with his father. Ned is a sun as well as a son, radiant, warm, a boundless fount of energy.

Tuesday night through Thursday morning we're due for a big snow. A foot? More? At the moment, I'm enjoying the winter even though I've had little chance to play in it. Global warming concerns me deeply, and the non-winter we had for so long seemed dire. Then early January brought a cold, snowy regime that still rules. I don't think we've made it out of the teens in a month.

February 13. A few minutes ago I stepped out on crackling floorboards. Walking down one side of the porch and around the corner, I pumped icy air into my lungs and felt a dull ache. The thin artery of mercury substitute in the porch thermometer said twenty-four below zero.

The air was Sahara dry. I stood listening for a minute or two. I wanted to know if the cold was shattering tree trunks. It was! Every few seconds a sharp crack rang out in the night. Some were as loud as rifle shots. Others were mere snaps. The whole business astounded me—living trees shattering like chunks of wood split by an ax.

A goshawk visited this afternoon. What a thrill! I had stepped into the mudroom for a bracing dose of cold before returning to the warm house to work. Through the storm door I saw a big raptor swoop silently and gracefully into a tree. I slipped inside for binoculars. They showed that the hawk had red eyes, a bold white stripe over each, a slate-gray back, and a white breast finely etched with crosshatching. Never before had I seen a goshawk close enough to admire its eyes.

I watched for ten minutes. The bird changed perch three times, always staying within a hundred feet or so of our bird feeders. To my surprise, there was little fuss. Blue jays, black-capped chickadees, and a red-breasted nuthatch continued to come for seed. The jays made half-hearted cries of alarm, but that was all. I saw no mobbing. The closest thing was a single chickadee that hopped through branches toward the goshawk, scolding it. Brave or foolish bird! This lasted only a few seconds. I wondered why the others made so little complaint. Was it the cold? The day's high temperature was five below zero. Perhaps the birds were running too tight an energy budget to sacrifice calories harassing an enemy.

There's inspiration to be gleaned from the lives of wild birds. At every turn predators, hostile weather, and starvation loom over their shoulders, yet they do not despair, or if they do, they never surrender to it. The black-capped chickadee seems a perfect, pugnacious little Churchill. It spits danger in the eye. "The only thing we have to fear is fear itself," said Churchill's friend Roosevelt. The chickadee knows this intuitively. Day after day, season after season, it soldiers on in the face of great hazards.

February 14. I drove into town today to take in the Winter Carnival parade. The temperature was mild—in the twenties. Snow showered down, and a biting wind shrieked up Broadway. A cold front arrives tonight. The temperature will plunge. We may see twenty below zero by morning. Tomorrow's high may be five below zero.

February 16. Deb and I bundled Ned [at age five months] in clothing and blankets today, propped him in an old wooden sled, and pulled him down the road and back. At first he protested, loudly. Then he grew philosophical. Then he slept. Then he woke up in good spirits. For most of the second half of the journey our little boy remained awake, cheeks red, eyes teary from the cold, busy taking in the world around him. Deb and I wore snowshoes. We walked from 3:00 to 4:15 or so. The temperature was twelve degrees when we started. Upon our return the thermometer read twelve below zero.

Today a bright sun brought cheer. We slept late, then eased into the day with the serenity of the well rested. Two gray jays were picking at a chicken carcass we'd put out.

February 20. A mild, snowy night, soft, velvety, the temperature in the twenties, the air still. The world was utterly silent when I stepped out for firewood around nine. In the sky a planet gleamed brightly in a sky otherwise blotted of stars.

A small window into the cold black waters of the Saranac opened just upstream of the bridge on Sunday, February 15. I haven't checked today, but a return of cold weather may have closed it. Still, the river will open soon.

Other happy portends of change: a red squirrel on the feeder today was looking very red. The animal's pelage is generally gray in winter. Spring coat coming in? Bright sunshine simply showing the fur to great advantage? Perhaps both. Two nights this past week, we had a big, fat raccoon on the bird-feeding platform. It looked incredibly woolly and was the first we've seen this year. A flicker appeared on the back side of the tube feeder. It was quite a surprise seeing the dagger-sharp tail pointing down, catching a glimpse of black spots on yellow, and then having the bird stick its head around the side and look me in the eye. Larry Master, who runs the local Audubon Christmas Bird Count, tells us the flicker is the first ever recorded here this time of year. Our neighbor Sandy Hayes spied it first. In February the bird belongs in Dixie. It's a mystery why it's with us.

February 19. A mild night, near thirty. I finished splitting stove lengths I cut out of a five-trunked maple a few days ago. The tree was dead. So nearly was I when I crashed through the last chunk. This is exercise!

Today brought another of the kind of day that has outnumbered all others this winter, a day through which the sun almost shines but doesn't, and snow falls diffidently throughout the illuminated hours, never adding up to much in any given hour, yet deepening an inch or two over the course of the day.

February 21. A cold night! The thermometer on the porch reads eight below zero. Driving home from an artists' gathering in Saranac Lake, the defroster made little headway melting ice that glazed the inside of the windshield.

The sky is blue-black and full of stars. I cut up a dozen small, dead cherry trees today and carried armloads of the wood back to the house. With temperatures like these, we need good dry hardwood to keep warm.

February 24. Cut and carried firewood, swept the chimney, cleaned out the woodstove, and made a brief outing to see snow buntings on a nearby ridge. It was a brilliant sunny day, cold but cheery. Tomorrow morning we expect snow, then rain, then sleet, then more snow. Right now it's eight degrees outside and I'm crawling under the covers.

February 25. Today the river opened in earnest. Yesterday, after several days during which the temperature at midday edged above freezing, a few potholes appeared in the Saranac's smooth hard surface. Now the potholes are coalescing into great patches of open water. Spring is coming! Spring is here!

February 28. Debbie and I celebrate our wedding anniversary today. We took the leap on Leap Day—February 29—but choose to honor the event more than once every four years. We eloped in a Vermont cornfield. Our only witnesses were a justice of the peace (she owned the corn field) and a flock of noisy crows.

Spring is coming! A clerk at the local general store reported two chipmunks at her bird feeder this morning. A neighbor, she said, reported a chipmunk a day earlier. This is what Adirondack people talk about this time of year.

Another cold day—high in the teens. Temperature now, just before midnight, is about four degrees on the porch. The low tonight may dip to five below. Spring is here! I heard a woodpecker drum at midday—a steady vigorous drum roll on a hollow trunk.

A gorgeous morning, bright and mild. Spring is in the air! Winter is like a well-intentioned dictator. There are things about its reign I enjoy, but still it's a dictator. When I see signs like the open river and hear sounds like the woodpecker's percussion, they tell me a populist revolt stands poised to topple the regime. I smile.

March 3. Tonight a barred owl and I enjoyed the same dinner. I had just settled Ned in his seat at the table and Tassie in her bouncy seat when Ned requested a drink. Standing at the kitchen sink rinsing his cup, I happened to look up and be startled. A big owl was staring at me through a pane of glass.

The rotund bird—a barred owl, with horizontal bars across its throat—looked indignant that I'd caught it thieving. It was picking at a chicken carcass we'd put out to feed songbirds. At first I couldn't see the oven-roasted prey, so big was the owl, and so thoroughly did its bulk cloak the prize. Then the bird stood erect. Now I could see black talons clutching the well-picked bones. Of course, the owl wasn't really indignant. It was alarmed.

I ran for Ned, hauled him out of his seat, and hustled back to the window. At this point, Tassie was too young for bird-watching. Ned gaped. The owl gaped. I could see the bird shifting nervously, weighing its options. To encourage it to stay, I switched off the indoor lights to make us invisible. Too late. The owl turned, spread its wings, and flapped off into the dark snowy woods, the chicken dangling from its landing gear.

March 6. The ice broke up on the river today. For the first time in months, we see black water flowing between white banks, pouring past our house, draining in leisurely, winding fashion down the bedrock's gently inclined plane toward Plattsburgh and Lake Champlain.

Today I expected to see ducks. I didn't. We will spy some any day. This year, all through January and February, a vein of open water, a foot wide or so, split the otherwise frozen Saranac in two. Then a string of frigid March days came along. Later than ever, the river closed. It's ironic that an entire winter was required to put a roof over the river, and as soon as the covering was in place, spring came along to destroy it.

On the hillside opposite the house we note a cast of pink. Buds on the twigs of red maples are fixing to burst. Birds are quiet. On a snowshoe hike today I saw one stoic chickadee and heard a pileated woodpecker chuckle twice. That's it. A week ago, Debbie saw a flock of red-winged blackbirds. I hunger to see blackbirds but haven't.

A magical night—just below freezing, the moist tang of spring in the air, a gusting wind, a light snow falling. Now that winter is dying, I feel nostalgic and a little sorry to see it go. How did Daniel and Hannah

Brownell feel on exquisite nights like this? Lewis and Elnora? Elmer and Jenny? My grandparents? I wish I could ask them. Some might think it possible. But alas, since my first glimmerings of reason, I've been convinced in my heart that I have no more claim to an afterlife than an amoeba or a grasshopper. We have the here, and we have the now. That's all, folks. On nights like this, that's enough. "One world at a time," said the dying Thoreau when asked if he'd made peace with God.

March 7. A storm was predicted to dump heavily on the coast, with little accumulation in the interior, so we made an overnight expedition to Vermont. Monday, people in Burlington asked why we weren't rushing to get home. We'd missed a change in the forecast. We were oblivious to the fact that the storm had changed course and was headed straight for us. At last informed, we started back. A skid on Grand Isle nearly sent us careening into another car. I was doubly cautious driving after that. The roads were slick. Few cars were moving, the snow piled up steadily, and we chugged up the long, steep hills with no crazy drivers to dodge. Greatly relieved, we reached home at nightfall. Twenty-two inches fell.

March 9. About thirty-two below zero this morning. Then the sun came out, a front slipped through, and the thermometer shot up, recording fifteen above zero by noon. It feels like Florida. No kidding.

Thursday morning—or was it Wednesday—Debbie looked out around 6:30 a.m. and found the porch thermometer at thirty-seven below zero. This kind of cold is expected in January or February. In March, it surprises us.

Hard to say how much packed snow and ice lie on the ground—perhaps four or five feet. Whatever the depth, it's enough to require snowshoes for every trip to the compost pile. I grumble about the chore, but when I'm out under the glittering stars, even if it's thirty below zero and my cargo stinks (historic broccoli commits the worst olfactory offense), I relish the journey. I am careful. Temperatures like these present no great challenge until you hurt yourself and can't get up. If I broke a leg at thirty-five below, I might not be able to crawl the 250 feet back to the house. Drunks homebound from bars hereabouts fall in snowbanks, sometimes only a few feet from warmth and safety. The next morning, somebody makes a ghastly discovery. There lies poor Jane or John, frozen hard as a board.

Driving home from town this morning with the kids, I spied an adult bald eagle standing on the river ice, just downstream of the Pine Street bridge. The bird was hunched over, apparently eating something. A duck? Probably. Hooded mergansers have been hanging around the spot all winter. Rapids near the bridge keep the water open, creating opportunities for ducks and for eagles.

March 13. Winter and spring overlapped at the bird feeder today. A northern shrike has been hanging around, a dead-of-winter bird that is usually gone by this date on the calendar. As it came to pick at the remains of a roast chicken we'd put out, a flock of eight or nine red-winged blackbird males swooped in to rummage for sunflower seeds. I popped out to check the temperature. It's five degrees on the porch. We can't have many cold nights left.

March 14. A snowy night with a steady wind roaring through the trees. Snow is hard to take seriously this time of year. That's true except when it comes in massive accumulations. Still, you know it won't last.

March 17. Red-winged blackbirds provide cheer as I grapple with a gastrointestinal bug. In spring these birds are part of our everyday lives. By midsummer they're gone, at least in terms of sightings. Migrants sometimes turn up in fall and sometimes not. Then comes March. We get cackling hordes. Hooray for blackbirds! I salute their ability to skim the cream off the year, arriving as one winter ends and leaving before the next begins. As much as I love this place, part of me feels like going with them.

BIOLOGICAL SURVEY RECORDS:

Pinicola enucleator   Pine grosbeak
12/6/04: three in the driveway at 9:15 a.m.; flew across the road and landed in a tamarack; fed on the cones; two beautiful red males and one possible female (the "female" might have been a russet-colored male)

Fagus grandifolia   American beech
2/26/00: behind house in woods; sprouts; no big trees (victims of recent lumbering?)

13

Spring Journal

March 22. We've had a week of warm, rainy weather. Yesterday the ice broke up on the river. We're in that entertaining stage now when great crystalline rafts come speeding by, smashing into each other like bumper cars. They batter the remaining shelf ice along the banks, too. Altogether the collisions make quite a racket, day and night.

This afternoon in Bloomingdale village we saw a mixed flock of red-winged blackbirds and common grackles. Later we stood on the bridge near the house, watching a gathering of beavers. There was one—two—three—four—five—at least six! Very fine beavers they were, too, plump, glossy, bright of eye, swimming, diving, slapping tails, hauling out on the banks, grooming each other, and gnawing on things with the tools of their trade, big marmalade-colored front teeth. We were glad. Wild animals surround us, but aside from birds and red squirrels, it's rare that we see them.

March 24. Spring's coming! We've had nearly three feet of snow during the last week, so it doesn't look like spring. But birds are returning. Do they have the right idea, summering here and wintering someplace warm? I'm not sure it's "wintering" when you spend the northern winter in another place's summer.

John Burroughs once complained to his journal that the freedom to live in a place of one's choosing is a curse because one is left forever after to wonder if the choice he made was wise. Today, Burroughs is praised for his devotion to his native Catskill Mountains and to the Hudson Valley where he lived much of his life. Yet he was never completely sure he belonged there. I grapple with similar angst. Given my roots in the Adirondacks and my longing to anchor in a wild landscape, it would seem I have come to rest in what is for me the best possible place. Yet my feet still twitch.

Yesterday, March 23, we saw our first song sparrow of the season. It joined the mob of evening grosbeaks, black-capped chickadees, blue jays, red-breasted nuthatches, hairy woodpeckers, and downy woodpeckers that bustled around our feeders all winter. We've also seen dark-eyed juncos.

Monday, Tuesday, and Wednesday the sun broke out. The weather turned warm and joyously springlike. Great heaps of snow on the roof melted into lesser heaps. In the nook between the north wall of the living room and the west wall of our bedroom, snow fleas appeared. There were countless thousands of them. In the aggregate snow, fleas look like soot. If you focus on one, it soon catapults itself from view. Snow fleas were long considered insects, but biologists now assign them and other species in the order Collembola in an arthropod class all their own.

March 27. Warm, gray, and muddy. The river surges toward its banks. The mire at the base of the driveway is so gooey our cars can't make it up to the house with groceries.

I've been admiring a grackle all week. When you see these birds every day, it's easy to overlook their beauty. But the sight of a lone male, hanging around the feeder day after day, nearly takes my breath away—the bold yellow eye, the glossy black plumage with a hologram of iridescent blue and purple hovering just above it, the sleek, elegantly proportioned torso and long tail, all testaments to nature's capacity for invention.

April Fools' Day. First amphibians of the year tonight! Debbie moved two wood frogs off the rain-drenched surface of River Road. I saw one wood frog in the same stretch, and also an American toad whose hind-quarters had been crushed by a passing car. I considered stepping on the toad and ending its misery but didn't have the stomach for it. With luck a weasel, raccoon, fox, or coyote will come along quickly and end the poor creature's suffering.

A fox sparrow here this morning—first of the year!

April 4. Spring has sprung but now the temperature sinks. Snow fogs the air. It's Sunday night. Snow is predicted to keep falling, lightly, until Tuesday morning.

I'm reading *Don Quixote* slowly and relishing every twist. The language in the Edith Grossman translation isn't always easy, and progress comes slowly. Still, the tale, with all its embellishments and digressions, and with Cervantes's wickedly delicious senses of humor and human hubris, make the hours invested in the book some of the finest in my life. In laughing at the lovably feeble-minded knight and his squire, we laugh at ourselves. Through the character of Don Quixote, Cervantes reminds us that there's wisdom in viewing human endeavor through a lens of the absurd.

April 5. A brilliant starry night borrowed from Van Gogh. I savored a taste of the glory in the heavens shortly before midnight when I shuffled out to the woods for firewood. Four inches of fresh snow lie on the ground. They represent last night's contribution by the north wind.

A phoebe and a tree sparrow put in appearances around the bird feeder this morning. I felt sorry for the phoebe. It's a flycatcher. A cold north wind has been keeping the temperature in the twenties, and flying insects are nowhere to be seen. What drives it and other essentially tropical birds to fly here at great hazard for a brief fling of child rearing? Scientists can't be certain. Relative day length may be a key. Near the equator, bug-eating day-active birds have to squeeze all their hunting into twelve hours of sunshine. Yet as the ancestors of today's migrants edged incrementally northward, away from the equator, they found summer days growing longer. No phoebe Marco Polo or Christopher Columbus set off mindfully on a long journey of exploration, then wrote home, "Plenty of bugs up here. Come as soon as you can." Something lured them northward one small step at a time. Perhaps it was the light.

Spent much of the afternoon getting our car unstuck at the bottom of the driveway. Coming home last night, I tried to drive up to the house, hoping that the soft spot had frozen. It hadn't frozen at all. The chassis bogged down, the wheels spun, and we hauled Ned and all his gear up to the house in the dark.

Today I tried driving the car out. It didn't work. Then I tried jacking each front wheel. This required digging and knocking frozen clods of earth that had welded themselves to the undercarriage. I put about one hundred pounds of sand under the drive wheels and tried backing out. The car dug itself deeper. A man driving by in a pickup truck offered to extract me. I asked if he had a tow chain or rope. He didn't. I told him I was all right—I'd have the car out shortly. That was before I tried the sand.

In the end I drove our 4WD Subaru wagon down the north driveway, rigged a rope, and, with Debbie at the stuck car's wheel, tugged it out. All this was done with the temperature in the low twenties and a north wind stinging my face and fingertips. Nothing like a little suffering to produce an afterglow of triumph.

April 9. A placid day of electric blue sky and golden shine. Temperature today around fifty degrees Fahrenheit—neither cool nor warm but hovering in a delicate suspension between the two. We wait so long for spring to come that when it does come, it's hard to trust it, to believe, to accept its arrival as a genuine change in paradigm. At any time, another cold snap, another snowstorm, can send us spinning back to January.

April 12. A perfect spring day—warm, sunny, an orchestra of birds singing and cackling and drumming, a lively breeze kicking up in gusts, and in the middle of it all the Saranac River clear and rising. It's glorious. I feel I could stay here forever, or as close to forever as fortune allows.

April 14. Spring is here! Really! At least, I think it is. The temperature's in the upper forties. A strong sun punctuates a bright blue sky, and a fickle wind gusts cold one moment, warm the next. The Saranac swells by the hour. This morning the river began to spill across the road in two places. We ate breakfast—pancakes, raspberries, and maple syrup—on the porch for the first time this year. As we did, a bald eagle drifted in from the west, several hundred feet up, wheeling and advancing on massive wings.

Snow banks melt like glaciers, their blunt snouts withdrawing up the slopes, their surfaces unkempt and gritty like old men who have forgotten to shave. Still, if you walk off a beaten path, your legs break through the crust, and you plunge in up to your groin. How deep the snow is I can't say in a general way, but in shady places, four feet or more still cover the ground.

The return of the birds amazes me. One day we have no song sparrows, and the next they're everywhere. As I write these words, one sings tirelessly in the thicket south of the house. Winter wrens started up a few days ago, and now we take their long, tinkling arias for granted. Debbie reported tree swallows overhead in town yesterday and a pied-billed grebe in the village of Saranac Lake, on Lake Flower. Brown creepers broadcast everywhere you aim your ears. Walking along our road, I skirt one creeper territory after another, and rushing cascades of staccato notes, so high-pitched they're at the threshold of hearing, come glittering out of the woods. I noted today that the first note of the creeper's song is generally longer than those that follow. It suggests an inhalation. Then comes a jumble of descending notes, suggesting an exhalation of spirit as well as of air.

April 17. Tonight, grilling pork chops outside at dusk, I heard strange, melodious fragments of a piccolo solo coming from the woods. The music beatified the air for minutes, then tailed off. When did I hear that performance last? August? Every time I hear the hermit thrush's wild, magical song I'm left a little more amazed at the majesty and mystery of life.

April 18. At exactly 5:00 this morning, as I lay in deep slumber on the couch, and as Deb and Ned snored in the bedroom, I was wrenched to consciousness by a mousetrap. I'd set it beside the kitchen stove. A mouse rattled inside and gnawed at the trap's aluminum walls. With great reluctance, I unzipped the sleeping bag I'd crawled into in the middle of the night and creaked to my feet. First light had seeped over the horizon. A blue glow trickled in the window. I found boots and slipped them over bare feet, pulled on a hunting jacket, grabbed the mousetrap, and stepped out the back door.

All was still. No bird yet sang, no woodpecker or grouse drummed in the woods. Half asleep, working methodically, I dumped the contents of the trap into a small plastic bag filled with fluorescent yellow powder. I shook the bag, put it on the ground, and opened it. Out darted a yellow mouse. It blinked powder out of its eyes, twitched yellow whiskers, and shot through a gap in the foundation, a gap that immediately became yellow, too. Its point of entry has been revealed.

Back in my sleeping bag, I was just falling asleep when I heard the *thump-thump-thump* of a ruffed grouse. Amazing how that sound travels through the woods and sails right through siding, insulation, and wallboard. A songbird's warble doesn't cover a tenth the distance or penetrate half as well. Low frequencies have great carrying power, as great horned owls and the makers of foghorns know. It must have been 5:10 when I slipped back to my dreams, the grouse still drumming.

April 19. A woodcock's nasal *peent* sounded an early reveille as we slept on the porch this morning. We'd gotten to bed at 2:00 a.m. after a long drive. I would have cursed the woodcock except that last year we had none. The wake-up call brought glad news.

A short walk tonight turned up a spotted salamander, three wood frogs (two of these flattened by cars), and two spring peepers. The rain had stopped, and the sky held a few faint stars. A gusting wind made conditions dangerous for amphibians. The skin of those I moved off the road felt as dry as the surface of this paper.

Saw a yellow-bellied sapsucker behind the shed this morning—first of the year. Outside, the wind roars. You'd think we lived near an airport.

Ned and I set off on a walk this radiant spring morning and, while soaking up sunshine like poikilotherms, made two herpetological discoveries.

We heard frogs chattering faintly in a discarded oxbow of the Saranac just upstream of the bridge. Eager to investigate and share the fun, I picked Ned up and bushwhacked to the edge of the water. At a distance I thought I was hearing wood frogs, perhaps the same ones we heard clucking last night. But no—these amphibians were snoring. Leopard frogs! We also heard rhythmic grunting, two, three, or four syllables sounding like fingers rubbing a balloon. A check in a field guide suggests these are alternate leopard frog calls.

Scanning the edge of the pond with binoculars, I spied heaps of stones, wet and glistening. A close look showed that the smooth surface of each stone was patterned in polygons. Painted turtles, first of the year! I counted fifteen.

April 28. We're out on the porch. Rain spatters over the gutters after a brief, torrential downpour. Wood frogs and spring peepers fill the moist air with their singing. It's deliciously warm, the temperature around sixty. I love a night like this. The nose fills with rich, earthy scents unimaginable a few weeks ago. Life is rich.

April 29. A cool, blustery day, the river high and within inches of coming back over its banks. Uncommon here, the field sparrow that sang in the thicket near the house yesterday was doing it again today. The bird's full, round, accelerating notes joyfully evoke my days living and working in a Westchester County park called the Ward Pound Ridge Reservation. Pound Ridge is a 4,700-acre island of wildness amid New York City's civilized suburbs. I lived and ran a nature museum there for a little more than four years, 1984 to 1989. It used to be fun boasting that more open land surrounded my house than stretched around the mansions of my better-known Westchester neighbors, the Rockefellers.

No new birds today. The last before the field sparrow was a blue-headed vireo. I heard it, then tracked it down for a look, in the woods west of my writing studio. When I came upon the vireo, the typically sedate vocalist was babbling like a happy child.

The black-backed woodpeckers I've had my eye on are still carving out a nest cavity in a dead balsam fir just over our property line. The tree is thirty or forty feet from a neighbor's camp. Dogs run around, men sit a few feet away at a picnic table jabbering and cleaning fish, and the birds don't mind. In the last few days, though, the woodpeckers have been more secretive. They fly at any approach, so I keep my distance.

Wednesday night, I drove the river road in our old Toyota. It had rained all day, on and off, so conditions were promising for amphibians. I was disappointed to set off at 9:20 p.m. and discover that the rain had stopped. A light fog may have helped, though, because I found seven live spotted salamanders, three road-killed spotteds, and one gorgeous gravid female Jefferson's complex salamander just off our property line. I've seen two Jefferson's complex animals this year, the first in three years. Battleship gray flecked with sky blue, they seem to exist here in modest number, unlike the rest of our spring amphibians, which burst out in hordes.

Herpetologists call them "Jefferson's complex" because without biochemical analysis one can only place the salamanders in a knotty tangle of four closely related and recently diverged species, one known as Jefferson's salamander. All salamanders are living relics of an age that long preceded the dinosaurs. Small and soft to the touch, they're frail and delicate. At the same time, they must be monumentally hardy and resilient, having endured down through the ages and still looking like the illustrations of their ancestors in a paleontology text.

One afternoon this week, I slipped out during Ned's nap and set myself up in a photographic blind. The camera port looked out on a rotting log—not just any rotting log, of which there are hundreds within a stroll of the kitchen door, but one that serves as the drumming post of a ruffed grouse.

Earlier the same day, I'd risen at 5:00 and sat in the blind with a camera from 5:30 to 7:10. Once I was ready to shoot, the bird failed to appear. I had spied it briefly as I approached the blind, but alas, it spied me, too. Instantly the grouse exploded from the ground and rocketed away. Then another appeared—at least, I suspect it was another—and watched me slip inside. No luck with that bird, either. The morning turned out an uncomfortable, bone-chilling failure.

The afternoon began without promise and without a grouse. I sat in the blind for an hour reading a book on child psychology. A baby monitor broadcasting sounds from Ned's room [he was not quite seven months old at the time] brought the soft sounds of his breathing. The bird failed to turn up. Just as I was closing the book and preparing to head home, a grouse drummed. I didn't expect it to be *my* grouse, but I looked up. It was! I shot a roll and a half of film. The best part was just being there, sitting in secret, watching the bird's earnest, heartfelt performance. Amazing to think how many grouse there are here in the woods. Stand outside on a day when they're drumming, and in different directions you hear two or three. How many must there be between here and Moose Mountain? Why do I care?

All my life I've been drawn to life of all sorts. I love my own species, despite its maddening flaws, yet if confined with my own kind alone, I'm miserable. For my psychic survival I need to be immersed in things that creep, crawl, run, slither, fly, beat their wings, sprout blossoms, unfurl leaves, and dust the world with their spores.

May 4. Spring is thoroughly sprung. Red trillium bloomed today. Trout lily has been open for a week. Blue-headed vireos sound as if they sing and answer incessant rhetorical queries, sapsuckers beat tattoos on dead dry limbs, winter wrens chime, robins carol, tree swallows burble, and myrtle warblers warble soft, erratic trademark trills. At night, spring peepers sing loudly. Wood frogs grow quiet. Toads speak up occasionally, as do leopard and green frogs. Spring is launched, to be sure. Well, maybe it is. Tonight's temperature is thirty-four degrees Fahrenheit. The morning arrived with snowflakes.

May 6. Went fishing with Ned [a burbling, babbling, fast-growing baby at the time] and Joe Hackett [a renowned fishing guide] on Moose Pond today. We left here around 10:00 and were back around 2:30. It was a busman's holiday for Joe and a gorgeous outing—bright blue sky, warm sun, sharp breeze, bald eagle wheeling overhead, osprey peeping loudly near the inlet stream, northern waterthrush [a kind of warbler] *chip-chap-churping* on the shore near the outlet. The year's first black-and-white warbler sang as we loaded the boat. It was still singing when we pulled out. We caught no fish, despite three hours of trolling along the pond's western shore. There the bottom drops to seventy feet. Joe's fish finder showed several big fish, lake trout or landlocked salmon, at fifty-two feet, a cloud of smelt just above them, and scattered rainbow trout at twelve feet. None showed interest in self-sacrifice. It pleased me to think of the trout and salmon deep in their green, dappled universe, and us above them in ours bathed by sun, each mysterious to the other, each full of satisfactions, fear, and wonder.

May 7. In the forty minutes I've been reading in bed on the porch this evening, I've heard the voices of spring peepers, American toads, a barred owl (they've been hooting a great deal again after a long silence), and, for the first time in ages, a yipping, wailing, howling chorus of coyotes.

Tonight I find myself thinking of the future that lies beyond our lifetimes. What will our children inherit? Unless our ship comes in, not much in the way of liquid assets, except our stretch of the Saranac River and a few acres of goldenrod and soggy *sphagnum*. Still, Ned and Tassie stand to receive other things perhaps more valuable—this blessed place with its fruit trees grown tall and bearing apples, its sugar maples that I planted with the notion that someone will tap them for sugar and syrup decades hence, roses and daffodils put in the ground by Debbie, the woods, the mountains, the warblers that come in spring. Perhaps, too, the kids will inherit a devotion to kindness and fair play, and curiosity, too, and love of people, and love of all things living. My head swims with poignant imaginings. What will be the state of things here in fifty years? A hundred? A thousand? A million? One can go mad thinking this way. The present and past are our only rightful homes.

May 9. A hot day—the second or third in a row, above eighty degrees Fahrenheit at midday and still equatorially warm at night. A peeper chorale fills the air. Toads pipe in with trills, and leopard frogs snore as persistently as my grandfather used to. Wood frogs have gone silent. We won't hear them again until next year. Tonight we heard what sounded like a young and uncertain bullfrog clearing its throat after a winter of silence.

Migrants pour in. This morning we heard our first brown thrasher ever. Yesterday rose-breasted grosbeaks and a mockingbird, the mocker a rare bird in the Adirondacks and also a first for us, showed their faces and exercised their operatic voices. Black-throated green warblers and parula warblers are singing, too. We pay so much attention to the sounds made by birds, frogs, and insects partly because it's hard to spy wild animals in our deep, dark forests, and we all hear far more than we see. Without my ears, I might think there were hardly any animals here at all.

Tonight in Saranac Lake I saw a gorgeous yellow warbler, as bright as an egg yolk.

Today, for just a millisecond, I saw the year's first hummingbird. It blasted by like a rocket, nearly striking my face as it shot in to check out the red in my plaid flannel shirt. I also saw blackflies, trout lilies, red trilliums, greening grass, and rain, rain, rain. We had a big booming thunderstorm today with pounding rain and pea-sized hailstones.

Yesterday I saw a crow perched in a distant pine. Something drew my eye to it—the posture, perhaps, seemed a bit too upright. Binoculars showed the bird not to be a crow at all. It was a merlin, a kind of falcon. The raptor added a touch of glamour to the staid old tree. A few minutes later, feeling jazzed after picking out the merlin, I scrutinized the swallows resting on the utility wires near the bridge. One after another proved to be a tree swallow. The last had rust on its breast and a deeply forked tail. A barn swallow, first of the year.

Last week's great flood of the Saranac ebbs. We still can't drive to the house, and mail and newspaper delivery seem like dim memories. School buses and the United Parcel Service and FedEx still won't brave our submerged road, yet at last the tide has turned in our favor. Since last week's peak, the river has dropped thirty-two inches. I measured the change with a yardstick. I also checked the depth of the water over our road. At the deepest, it flows nine to ten inches deep.

May 16. We enjoyed a week of mostly sunny, dry weather, and the river eased back within its banks. For three or four days, the road dried out and we could come and go as we pleased. Doing wonders for morale, there were gifts from the flooding: heightened camaraderie among our neighbors, two-lined salamanders that turned up on the road one dark wet night (the two-lined is a typical streamside amphibian that had eluded us in eleven years of searching), and a tiny seashore bird called the least sandpiper. The sandpiper was one we might have never recorded, but the flooding and subsequent ebbing created flats of silt and mud with a thin film of water flowing over them. It's in such places that the least sandpiper plies its trade.

Then came a shocking weather forecast. Seven days of rain were predicted. The first two would bring downpours expected to total three or four inches. Would the river, just inches below the road at long last, rise again, and how far? It did. Greatly. Today icy water flows ten inches deep at the deepest, and our cars once again wait on the far side. Neighbors with pickup trucks are again ferrying us to and from school and outside work.

May 17. Northern bush-honeysuckle in full bloom behind the house. Yesterday its yellow flowers began unfurling petals. Today a handsome male rose-breasted grosbeak appeared near the studio. Rather than singing, which seems the chief pastime of male grosbeaks this time of year, the bird hopped from one low branch to another and onto the ground occasionally. What was it up to? Perhaps hunting for bugs.

The whole family watched a spotted sandpiper working its way upstream along the riverbank today. While we watched it, we heard the year's first yellowthroat, a kind of warbler that tends to skulk around in heavy cover, singing *witchety-witchety-witch*.

The black-backed woodpeckers nesting across the road are done with excavating and seem to be engaged in egg laying or incubation. When I come for a peek, I find the female inside the hole, poking her head out now and again and often withdrawing entirely within. Today I found the male in the hole, leaning his head out and resting his chinless chin on the windowsill. The golden crown that distinguishes him from her shone brightly.

May 21. Planted more trees today, including nine sugar maples—three along the driveway and six along the road. It's sobering to think how long-lived these trees are and how, if I live a long life and they keep on growing taller and adding a ring of wood every year, I'll be an old man when the trees are only beginning to mature. Among mammals, humans live lives of extraordinary length. The average opossum, by contrast, develops cataracts and arthritis and dies of old age at two or three. The longest lived mammal known to science was a bowhead whale, determined to be more than 200 when it was pierced by a harpoon. Trees? The sugar maples I've planted might live to 400, the hemlock in the woods behind the house to 1,000. Yet that's nothing compared to a bristlecone pine alive in the mountains of California today. Scientists took a core from its trunk, counted the growth rings, and found the tree's age to be a whopping 4,800 years. That means it was alive when ancient Egyptians carved the Sphinx and built the celebrated Gizeh pyramids.

I transplanted maples that were just a few years old, growing on a neighbor's property down the road. Joe Strobel invited me to take as many as I pleased. It stirred me to dig up the trees, which had little chance of surviving in the deep shade where they'd sprouted, drive them to our place, and plant them in sunshine.

I love sugar maples. A gorgeous one stood, and still stands, in front of the house I grew up in. In our tumultuous household, full of conflict and unresolved grief, I could always look out the east window of the living room and gaze on that tree and find comfort in its serenity. I come from a physically undemonstrative family not prone to hugging, but at times of strain—when family pets died, and around the time of my fourteenth birthday when my mother's mother, chronically ill and full of bitterness for the hard turns her life had taken, killed herself with sleeping pills—I can remember putting my arms around the big maple and hugging for all I was worth. The tree was as calm and solid as bedrock, yet, like me, alive and breathing, proof that sanity amid insanity was possible and good. Our Adirondack place feels more like a home to me now that we've planted sugar maples. Will the trees clinch my attachment to the spot? Will I cast aside lingering qualms and sink my psychic roots among them? Visiting National Parks is a fine thing, yet, in sheer richness of experience, even a pilgrimage to the bottom of the Grand Canyon falls short of the involvement we're having here with our land and it's having with us.

May 22. Rain gushes out of the sky. It sounds as if we're living in the middle of a waterfall. An eventful week has just come to a close. On Wednesday I had my first guiding job of the year at [a high-end lodge], taking a group of well-heeled Californians and a Thai couple for a nature walk. It was a great group and a gorgeous day. From the moment we hopped in the lodge's plush SUV to the time of our return a few hours later, I was barraged by good, thoughtful questions that made the day a delight. Curiosity about wild things has a wonderful way of bringing people together. Shakespeare was right: "A touch of nature makes the whole world kin."

A roar outside. The downpour intensifies. I feel certain the river will rise but not enough to reorganize our lives.

May 30. The kids get along beautifully except when they're getting along miserably. Alas, miserable times come often these days. Ned can be kind and loving to Tassie one moment, an ill-tempered bully to her the next. He's just human, I guess. As for Tassie, she saves most of her own disagreeable behavior for abusing the house and its contents, and by throwing food and spilling drinks. She can be a real Tasmanian devil and Ned a brutish wombat. Of course, this is the nature of childhood. Both our marvels grow more bright and beautiful by the day, and our love for them, already vast and deep, expands accordingly.

Spring rules the landscape, and a gorgeous spring it is. Tree leaves are nearly all open and at the stage where every species radiates a slightly different shade of green. The variations are ones of nuance, yet they make the hillsides sing. I look across the river to a far slope and see a patchwork: pale green and kelly, reddish green and yellow-green, deep dark green and olive.

In counterpoint, the biting insects are absolutely awful. Morning, evening, and night, mosquitoes fog the air in despair-inducing number. A good many make it somehow into the house. There they torment us as we eat and read and brush our teeth and attempt to sleep. As I sit here on the porch, writing, mosquitoes gather on the far side of the window screens, licking their chops.

When the sun shines, and even when it does not, blackflies swarm. You step out the door and think, with willful optimism, "Oh, they're not that bad." Then within seconds you're the focal point of a swarm. The nasty little bastards are all over the back of your neck and stampeding under your hair and clothing, biting, biting, biting. Poor Ned. Like his mother, he swells in response to assaults. One blackfly bit him on the eyelid, and for the next several days the lid drooped half-shut, as if he'd been in a brawl.

At the moment, indoors, my skin is free of assault. Still, I twitch, scratch, and swat. All-out aggression by the insect class on the mammalian brings on a sort of madness. At midday, as Tassie and I set off in the car to retrieve Ned from town, we saw a full-grown red fox sitting at the side of the road. It had brought its rear feet to bear on its head and was scratching frenetically. Slanting sunlight illuminated a great cloud of blackflies with the fox in the center, harried and exhausted. On those occasions when Debbie and I can bear looking in a mirror, we look harried and exhausted, too. This is life in a wild place. Whether it be the high Sierra or the Rockies or the great swampy lowlands of the Southeast or the frigid beautiful Adirondacks, suffering mingles with joy.

Now 8:44 p.m., still light, sixty-eight degrees Fahrenheit. I hear sounds: a motorcycle passing along the road by the river; green frogs saying *thung, thung*; a swamp sparrow's series of chips, not quite forming a trill; a chorus of spring peepers, sounding at this distance like sleighbells; a veery, its notes swirling around and around as if pouring down a drainpipe; *Old Sam Peabody-Peabody-Peabody*, the voice of the white-throated sparrow; the bleating of gray tree frogs; a chipping sparrow's metallic trill; a chestnut-sided warbler's emphatic *Pleased to meetcha!*; a song sparrow's snippet of Beethoven; the splashing of a large animal (a beaver?) in the river.

June 1. On the way home after I picked up Debbie at work, we stopped at a hardware store and bought mosquito netting. It cost twenty bucks, but that'll be a bargain if it keeps the vampires off Ned [then a baby in a crib]. There are more in our bedroom some nights than in an Anne Rice novel. They pock his sweet face every night and also drill for his oil when he naps. When I squash a mosquito and red stuff squishes out, I feel more sorry for my son than I do for the insect. That's my dear boy's blood they're stealing! Tonight Ned sleeps in peace, under the netting.

June 9. Blackflies have been tearing into us in Hitchcockian numbers for about a week. We wear hats with veils when stepping out for more than a minute. In the woods, clouds surround our heads when we stand still. Blackflies ignore a hand until you raise it. Then, as if you've cried "Bon appetit!," they dig in with gusto.

Goldthread, a delicate creeping wildflower named for its yellow, twining roots, blooms in the mossy woods behind the house. With it appear red trillium (also called, because of the malodorous scent of the flowers, "wet dog" and "stinking Benjamin"), painted trillium, a graceful but uncelebrated northern lily known as rose twisted-stalk, marsh marigold, and foamflower. These are plants I've known all my adult life and used to go to nature sanctuaries to see. Here they are neighbors.

We expect a frost. Last night we had one and it damaged tomato and squash plants. This can be a vexing place to live! The Fourth of July is only three weeks away, and still it sometimes feels like winter. June? So says the calendar.

June 10. Violent thunderstorms boomed, flashed, shook, and strafed their way across our patch of the planet tonight. They brought pounding rain, sideways downpours, and wind gusts that bent trees in half. We lost power several hours ago. Now, at 10 p.m., I sit on the porch, serenaded by hundreds of bleating gray tree frogs and a background chorus of spring peepers. The tree frogs are sometimes called tree toads because, like so-called true toads, they're squat and have rough skin. They sing in greater-than-usual number this year. A gauzy half-moon hangs low in the western sky.

Full darkness descended in the last quarter hour. The night is black. So is our house, its silence not even disturbed by the groans and complaints of our cranky, historic refrigerator.

Last Friday brought the birthday of our beloved, sweet, spunky, bright, articulate, impish daughter, Tassie.

June 12. Awake—sort of—after a night passed in a torture chamber thick with vampires. Debbie and I tossed, turned, swatted, switched lights on, switched lights off, and ran around with flyswatters. Eventually we slept, but not for long. The excruciating whine of mosquito wings roused us around five, and we spent the next couple of hours doing battle. At seven, we struggled to get back to sleep. At seven-thirty, unsuccessful, resigned, exhausted, and dispirited, we staggered to our feet.

Big thunderstorms are predicted for the middle of the day, storms that will bring powerful winds up to seventy mph. The sun oozes through a greasy wet sky, dark in the east and bright overhead.

This is an insect-ridden place. Last night Debbie plucked Ned out of bed, and without waking him set him up in our bed near the porch. She came back a minute or two later and found him twitching and waving his arms, although still asleep. What was amiss? She looked closely and saw that his face was covered with tiny, aggressive biters called no-see-ums, or punkies. Near the bed a French door, lights shining through it from the living room, swarmed with hundreds. No-see-ums are aptly named. Each is so tiny as to be all but invisible, yet the bite—a fierce gnaw—hurts more than the delicate jab or anesthetic-numbed rasp of a mosquito or blackfly.

We are under siege! Mosquitoes pour into the room where we sleep. No-see-ums flood onto the porch, sailing blithely through window screens. Outdoors, blackflies join them, the triumvirate ruling the yard in a reign not of terror but of dread. Last night I cut grass behind the house. Mosquitoes, blackflies, and no-see-ums seized the opportunity to join me. It was as if they'd heard the mower and cried, in three-part harmony, "A picnic dinner!" I itch everywhere.

At night, if we open the house's two French doors to let in cool air and to hear the evening frog concert, no-see-ums throng inside and render our living space uninhabitable. What to do? I'm heading to the crawl space. My plan is to explore in the dark, looking for spots where light—and biting insects and cold winter air—slip through gaps in the floorboards.

On the porch this morning, I heard the following birds: song sparrow, great crested flycatcher (first of the year), tree swallow, alder flycatcher, chestnut-sided warbler, magnolia warbler, parula warbler, blue-headed vireo, American goldfinch, white-throated sparrow. We have our own private orchestra. Granted, the taste for this kind of music must be acquired. Yet it's acquired easily, and afterward there's no turning back from the pleasure.

June 13. Ravens made a ruckus in the woods west of the house this morning. There were four of them, and possibly more. *Quork, quork,* some of them called, while others simply screamed. Some of the voices sounded thin compared to the others. Young birds? When I walked into the area, two ravens circled overhead, calling loudly. The parents? Meanwhile the others *quorked* in the trees. Had I blundered on young in a nest? Was it fledging day? Questions abound. I love having ravens around. They confront life with verve.

Finished writing a story on hermit thrushes for *Bird Watcher's Digest* today. Threatened rain all day but none fell. A wet weekend predicted.

In faint gray light, I scribble notes while sitting on the porch. What do I hear? Dozens of green frogs, their loud deep voices sounding like fingers rubbed across the taut skins of balloons. A catbird delivers a loud, rambling soliloquy in the alder thicket across the river. An accomplished imitator, it gives snatches of rose-breasted grosbeak and scarlet tanager, connected by slurred warbles and chips. Among the green frogs, I hear an occasional, *Knock, knock.* These are the interjections of mink frogs.

Other, more high-pitched voices blend and are not readily differentiated. If I concentrate, I pick out the trills of chipping sparrows; the Beethoven riffs of song sparrows; the rolling warble of a robin; the dreamy, lazy, cascading notes of a veery; the hurried song of a magnolia warbler; the burry *free beer, free beer* of an alder flycatcher; the nagging *fee BEE, fee Bee* of an eastern phoebe; the dry, dull, relentless, unceasing *cheBEK, cheBEK* of a least flycatcher; the whistle triplets of a white-throated sparrow; the cooing of a mourning dove; the territorial chortle of a robin; the insistent *pleased pleased to MEETcha* of a chestnut-sided warbler; and the hasty warbles and whistles of a purple finch.

All the birds I hear are biological tourists. They come to enjoy the Adirondacks' long, warm summer days and produce offspring, and then they flap off to Florida, Haiti, or Brazil—anything to avoid the winters we year-rounders have to endure.

A fawn appears amid the uncut lawn. It seemed to materialize by spontaneous generation straight out of the grass, and in a way, that's exactly what happened. This creature of flesh and bone is made almost entirely of plants, and of mother's milk derived from plants, although a scientist friend recently told me of a deer nosing into a rusty blackbird nest and eating the babies—the whole thing captured on video. The fawn's legs are long and slender, its ears splayed and alert. It tiptoes in stylized jerks, reminding me of modern dance. A doe appears, and she's nervous. I don't think the mother has seen me, but she's caught my scent. Again and again she dips her muzzle for a mouthful of leaves and stems, then snaps up. Occasionally she belts out an explosive snort.

A woodpecker drums very, very slowly. A downy?

Three minutes before five in the afternoon. The chorus has faded considerably, the individual voices less distinct. Still, the catbird keeps up a game effort, burbling, babbling, doing less rose-breasted grosbeak and more original work from its own stuttering repertoire. A yellowthroat sings *witchety-witchety-witch*. I missed it earlier. Somewhere out there I'm also hearing the *nah nah* of a red-breasted nuthatch.

Mosquitoes gather on the far side of the screen, poking their stiletto tongues at me, their desire for blood inflamed by my incessant ooze of carbon dioxide. Life with Adirondack bugs demands a thick psychological hide. Inside the house, mosquitoes, blackflies, and no-see-ums stalk us. Outside, they are joined by deerflies that circle and circle until they dive and sink sharp blades into your scalp. To them, that spot on the top of the human head from which hairs radiate is filet mignon, served rare. Oh, joy!

A crow caws, its volume a multiple of any other singer's.

I look out on a lush scene—green leafy trees, tall grass on the far side of the river, highbush cranberry bushes dotted with clusters of white blossoms. I hear the buzzing of a passing hummingbird. The whole picture appears eternal, beyond time, yet it's as ephemeral as my life or yours—no, more so, because the earth's shifting position in relation to the sun will soon shatter the image.

June 19. A lush, still, magical night, erotic in its fecund wetness and in the sexually charged voices of frogs—green frogs, mainly, hundreds of them, with the occasional mink frog adding its two cents. The amphibians call lustily as the river surges between its banks. Moisture is their aphrodisiac. We've had weeks of rain. The Saranac is at flood stage again, as if the clock has been turned back to April and May, when melting snow poured down from the mountainsides. I stepped out just now and a barred owl called. Its voice rang out loud and full, as stirring as any opera singer's.

Mosquitoes! Seven of the miserable things harassed me while I brushed my teeth, and seven died. Their bodies now adorn our blue-green bathroom walls, inspiring an idea. How about Adirondack products that should exist, but don't? My first entrepreneurial idea would be to manufacture wallpaper decorated with faux squished mosquitoes and imitation bloodstains. That way, when you flattened new ones, the carcasses and smears would simply contribute to the pattern.

Yellow-bellied sapsuckers feed young in a quaking aspen behind the house. The nestlings scream incessantly for food all day long, but the eager parents don't seem in a hurry to oblige. I know the feeling.

Bluebirds seem poised to raise young here. A female sits on a nest in a house I built. Nearby, the male serenades her. Is it love exercised with free will, or simply hormones? Can any of us say?

Our first sunny day in recent memory. It produced horrifying numbers of blackflies and was enough to make one plead for rain. An insect cloud formed around me each time I stepped out the door. I noticed chipmunks scratching and twitching along with me. No-see-ums are fierce as I sit up reading in bed on the porch tonight. I'll shut off the light soon, and the Draculas will fade and leave me alone. Then I'll only have to contend with mosquitoes. Blast them!

Ah, country life! I feel defiant. The bugs will not drive us away, nor will the cold and the snow and the hurdles that must be surmounted to carve out livings here. We will stay if we want to stay. For me, as for Debbie, the wanting grows with time. Still, sometimes it scares the hell out of the nomad in me. Yet where else would we go? In the Adirondacks we eat our cake and have it, too. We live in a wild place on the scale of a giant Alaskan national park, yet we mingle here with the flora and fauna not as high priests or acolytes, nor as policemen or custodians, but as full-fledged neighbors responsible, as neighbors are, for the well-being of the place we inhabit together.

BIOLOGICAL SURVEY RECORDS:

Rana septentrionalis   Mink frog
4/23/05: small (2½") mink frog found on road just n. of bridge; we've been pretty sure we've heard this species in the past, but this is the first sighting; very mottled; not much of a dorsolateral ridge

Tiarella cordifolia   Foamflower
6/2/00: blooming behind house
6/2/06: same day, same place; has been in bloom for several days; at the height of bloom now

14

Into the Future

I wasn't sure I could find it. Debbie had indulged me, agreeing to a detour down an obscure road in the central Adirondacks. What I hoped to discover was a camp formerly owned by my grandfather's friend Wayne Hammer. If I identified the place, I would root around in the woods. The aim was to find the place where my grandparents had parked their travel trailer. It had stayed there for years, a second home on wheels. My grandfather had wired an electric hookup, dug a well, and built a wooden platform to serve as the floor for the screened tent he and Grandma used as a dining room. Nothing unique in all this—my grandparents were like millions of others with gray hair, time on their hands, and scant money in their pockets, enjoying a taste of rustic life, not as the Vanderbilts and Rockefellers did it, but on a shoestring, improvising at every step. There was something archetypal about them that made me love them all the more.

My grandfather's lionheart had convulsed here in its final beat. It was a July morning in 1978, time for his annual fishing trip to the Oswegatchie. For the first time in a dozen years, no grandchildren would join him. There would be no staying home and crying in his milk. Grampy and Wayne Hammer, also a widower, were lighting out for the territory, just like Huck Finn and Tom Sawyer, just like old times. Grampy had a screwdriver in his hand and was fiddling with the electrical connections on a well pump. He had the kind of death many would wish for themselves, alive and able and full of purpose one moment, stone dead the next. The doctor's conclusion on the death certificate was that he'd had a heart attack. I was fresh out of college. When the news reached me at a backwoods summer camp where I was working in Maine, I felt numb and lost. Grampy had been my North Star, my guiding light in a confusing universe. Now he'd vanished into the night.

I decided to locate the exact spot. The search provided a sobering lesson in the changes wrought—or, as they seemed to me, *overwrought*—by time. The dirt road I remembered from childhood had been widened and paved. Patch after patch of woods had been cleared. Houses—not camps, but proper year-round structures with central heating and flower boxes—stood in woods where wildflowers had grown and bears searching for insects had demolished rotting logs. We overshot the Hammer driveway. I was thinking that a run-down–looking place on the right couldn't possibly be Sweet's Retreat, a pretty little camp that was knocked together when I was eight or thereabouts, but then, the size and shape were right. It had to be.

I climbed out of the car. Certain things were wrong. Everything was too small. The camp by the road that had caught my eye was a miniature of the place I remembered. The driveway I was seeking was too narrow and too short, and the buildings by the lake, which loomed large in childhood, looked puny and unimportant. I remembered a long walk down to the water. The distance had been halved. A wooden outhouse sided with asphalt shingles, a structure whose stink and spiders remain fresh in memory, had stood beside the driveway. There wasn't a trace of it. Yet the more I poked around, the more certain I became that this was the spot.

Tears came as I pondered the fact that my grandparents, once so vividly alive and now so vividly dead, had passed many of their happiest days here. They knew this place intimately and over a long period of time.

I arrived not quite sure what I was seeking, yet soon an agenda took shape. I wanted to see if anything remained of a dock Grampy had built. To it he had tied up his boat, the one in which he took me bullheading. I wanted to see if a utility shed he had made, a structure about the size and shape of the phone booths of the era, remained. It stood a few feet behind his trailer and was painted yellow.

Most of all, I wanted to visit the well I remembered watching my grandfather dig with a shovel, back when I was a little boy. My father shot an 8-mm film of Grampy doing the work. My motivation? It wasn't clear, more an impulse than a thought-out thing. I suppose I wanted to connect with the spot where the arc of my grandfather's rich life had gone to ground. Perhaps I felt compelled to go back in the same way that grieving families of car crash victims flock to bends of the road where loved ones last looked out upon the world. I wouldn't erect a cross and make anniversary pilgrimages. Nor did I fancy Grampy watching me. I am a skeptic in all things metaphysical, and he was, too. Yet, yet—the electrical currents that had flickered through his one-of-a-kind brain for nearly seventy-four years had switched off here. Where had they gone? Might faint echoes linger? If they did, I wanted to savor a few moments in their presence.

Wayne Hammer had been dead a decade. The camp had new owners. I knocked on the door to ask permission to snoop. No answer. I decided to go ahead anyhow. It felt surreal to walk down to the lakeshore, as I had done a hundred times as a child but not in thirty years. Just like everything else, Adirondack Lake had become a miniature of its old self. I felt like Gulliver in Lilliput. The dock? I was flabbergasted. It jutted out over the water exactly as I remembered it, the weathered wood and cloth bumper around the edge no different than when Grampy tied up his boat there in the 1960s. A time warp? Alas, no. Glancing at my hands, I saw not the taut, flawless skin of a boy, but the loose, sun-spotted skin of a middle-aged man who has spent the better part of his life outdoors. My hands looked, it occurred to me, like Grampy's. The thought pleased me.

How to explain the dock, frozen in time? Either Grampy had built it wonderfully well, and it had somehow deflected the assaults of ultra-violet radiation and fungi, or, more likely, someone had taken his original, sensible plan and rebuilt the thing as it had been.

Back up the driveway, I took a breath and plunged into the woods. In the old days, the landscape was open and airy here. You could look down from the driveway, which was higher than the low ground I was about to explore, and through scattered birches and balsams see straight to the shed and trailer. No more. The forest had grown up. A tangle of trunks, limbs, and leaves blotted out everything.

I plowed through saplings and leaves. Ten or fifteen paces in, right where I remembered it, I found the shed. Like the dock, it had survived in good condition. Unlike the dock, it appeared to be completely forgotten. The wooden building was engulfed by plants, a sort of Mayan ruin in the forest. The siding, of a type called "novelty" still popular in the Adirondacks, retained most of the paint Grampy had brushed on it. His tools and fishing tackle were gone, and the electric cable that had brought power had been taken away. But the circuit breaker box was still there. It served as a home for insects and spiders.

The flat ground where Grampy had parked the trailer, and the area beside it where Grandma, working cheerfully under the dining fly, had fried many a bullhead and scrambled egg, were lost in a thicket. I estimated where the well had been. Grampy had lined it with fifty-five-gallon drums from which he'd cut out the ends. Maybe I could find them. On my knees, I probed the leaf litter. Soon a ring of rusting metal turned up. I traced its shape with my fingers.

In my journal that night I described what I found and how I felt. "I touched it. The last warmth in my beloved grandfather's body had warmed this patch of earth, so I put my hand there and warmed it, too. I could see a wire jutting out of the ground . . . [which] ran to the power box in Grampy's tool shed. I fled, happy that I'd found it after all these years and shaken up by all the changes—changes in me as well as the place."

Would I, if I could, turn back the clock? Would I breathe life back into my grandparents, make my parents young again, make my sisters and me children once more? What then of Debbie, our kids, the friends I know today, the hard lessons I've learned, the adventures I've had? It is for the best, hard and tragic as the arrangement may seem, that time moves only forward. The dead stay dead. Every day comes once, then is gone forever. Stark terms—yet without them, nothing would hold value. Scarcity makes us treasure what we've got. Every joy, were it to persist unendingly, would grow stale and cease to be joyful.

Once, in an experiment conducted on impulse, I took a pillow filled with the fragrant needles of the balsam fir, a classic Adirondack souvenir, and held it to my nostrils. On any other occasion, I would have taken a sniff, relished the evocative scent, and put the pillow down. This time, I kept it in place. After a minute, the scent had lost its ability to enthrall. After two minutes, the balsam needles smelled like nothing more than what they literally were: dead, dry leaves. Yet nothing had changed. The shifting variable in the equation was my perception. The next morning, I picked up the pillow, sniffed it, and smiled. The fragrance and the happy response were back.

All things end. It's a principle as fundamental as gravity. But oh, if only there were another way, one where each of us didn't have to grow old and feeble and die, or die young by tragedy! I remember grappling with these feelings when I was four or five. A mutt named Sam was our dog then, and the fact of his death had brought on a painful revolution in my consciousness. My grandparents would die. My parents would die. I would die. Our home and our family would someday be no more. Yet on a particular summer afternoon I remember vividly, about 1961, I sat with Sam on our neighbors' lawn—the neighbors being a kindly, white-haired couple who died a few years later in a car wreck—and hugged him and kissed him, telling him how much I loved him. It had dawned on me that I would likely outlive Sam by decades. Yet here we were, exquisitely alive. I cried and cried. I remember singing what I knew of "Beautiful Dreamer" to him until my tears ran dry.

Fifty years later, I cannot sing the song without sobbing. Tears fill my eyes now. Beautiful, faithful Sam! I promised him that day that if I ever married, I would tell my wife I could never love her as much as I loved him. Sam developed cancer of the liver a few years later. He died while we were away on Cape Cod.

At times I wish my emotions didn't run so strong, that I could forget the losses of the past. But I cannot. Nor do I want to. I revisit them again and again, stirring up feelings both painful and beautiful. The Adirondack Mountains are full of life and joy for me, but they are also a 6-million-acre cemetery. Everywhere I go, I drive roads Grampy drove with me, and I picture him at the wheel, gazing ahead, ever thoughtful and mostly silent. For years now and again, I used to break out Bond Street, his favorite brand of pipe tobacco, fill a bowl, and light it. Smoking has never given me pleasure. This was a ceremonial act. The aroma brought bring back fishing trips and long, happy rides in the car, rides steeped in an imperfect hero's secondhand smoke.

After our kids came, I put away the pipe. Still, I open a pouch of old tobacco and sniff the stuff now and again, and I pick up an old pipe of Grampy's and hold it.

Whenever I travel Adirondack roads, I think, too, of Elmer Brownell, sitting in the front of a massive wooden sledge, squinting into the face of a snowstorm on a rapidly darkening winter afternoon, hoping his team can haul him and his cargo as far as Long Lake or some other isolated village before night overtakes him. He's on his own, except for the company of the horses. He's hungry. He's thirsty. Perhaps he hears the howling of wolves or, occasionally, the caterwaul of a mountain lion. He longs to reach a warm hotel where he can stable his animals and hoist glasses with old acquaintances. Yet Elmer has "miles to go before he sleeps," as Frost put it. All he can see is snow.

I think of Elmer's mother, Elnora, the Methodist minister's daughter who in 1868 gave up a civilized life in Penfield, near Rochester, to take her chances in the wild, wild East. Would she have come to the mountains if she had known what lay in store—not only a husband, a grand house, and healthy, happy children, but also three infant sons who died and, at forty-one, her own untimely demise? It was a mercy that she never had to know the epilogue to her death: that four months after she was buried, her twin baby girls, Nora Fulton and Gail Hamilton, were lowered into the soil beside her.

I think of Lewis, Elnora's husband and Grampy's grandfather. Imagine him in 1888, at the peak of his worldly accomplishments, losing his still youthful wife and then, one by one within days of each other, suffering the deaths of twin girls. Elnora wasn't the only wife Lewis lost. His first, Mary, died at twenty-six. Twenty-one years after Elnora's death, Lewis perished. It was the twelfth of May, 1909. Grampy was four and a half. Lewis had been the star of the family, at least in terms of his curriculum vitae: state assemblyman, county judge, owner of a hotel and bottling plant, and owner and overseer of two tanneries and a sawmill. Surely there was a grand funeral. Despite it all, it's sobering and instructive that a man so accomplished could be so completely forgotten in the space of a hundred years. In Northville, Lewis rose to exalted status in his lifetime, yet today, he is remembered there by no one. Only a headstone in a cemetery rarely visited marks his passing.

Of Orra Brownell, Lewis's father, I know little, save that he founded a sawmill at Hope Falls and was a devout Baptist. I can hold his crumbling family Bible in my hands. Inside, his handsome signature remains legible. Of Orra's first wife, Nancy Harris, my thrice-great-grandmother, I know little except that she came from Scotland. What was she like? It's a pity not to know.

Daniel and Hannah, Orra's parents, the Adirondack pioneers in the family, remain ciphers, too. No portraits of them survive, although Daniel lived into the photographic age. (Nor, that I know of, do any survive of Orra and Nancy, or of Lewis and Elnora.) Except for the names and dates on their headstones, the two have been erased from the Earth. Soon even those testaments will be gone if sulfuric acid keeps raining and snowing from the sky.

Documents outlast us, or at least a smattering of them do. Of all the bits and pieces that have sifted down to me from Adirondack ancestors, perhaps the most poignant a century and more later is an autograph book. It belonged to Elnora Graves, later "Nora Brownell," as she was known. The entries begin in 1864, the year Nora turned seventeen. She was a student at a seminary in Lima, New York. The last inscriptions date to 1882 and 1883, well after Nora had moved to Northville and married. The sentiments tend to be flowery, as was typical of the time, and religious, as is to be expected of seminarians. Still, the expressions of minds long extinguished touch the heart. One page begins:

> Dear Nora, The time is near when we must part, each to go to
> our loved homes. But when you are there surrounded by many
> dear friends, will you think of one whose prayer shall ever be
> that God may give to thee his choicest blessings. The hours
> that I have spent with you in Lima will ever be remembered

by me, for they have been hours of joy. May Heaven reward you for your noble example and kind words. If we never meet again in this world, may we meet in Eternity.

The writer signs her name Libbie C. Hoig. Her home is "Wellsboro, Penn.," and she dates her words "Nov. 10th, 1864." Lincoln had won reelection two days earlier, defeating George McClellan. The bloodbath we call the Civil War, which took the life of many an Adirondack soldier, still had a few months to go. "Eternity" was much on the nation's consciousness. Nora, though, was likely in good cheer. In a letter dated November 6, her friend Cora Benton reports that Cora's brother, Howard Beach, is home on leave and "going to see his lady love [Nora] in Lima."

Another page, penned by a woman friend from Tehama, California, dated June 15, 1864, reads: "Dearie, In the pleasant last fall term I met you, love you now, and in the coming time, whether shady or lightsome, 'Nora' shall be one of my precious heart-treasures. Then at the end I will look for you among the angels. And if in the roll-call of death I shall come first, I will meet you just inside the pearly gates. 'Dinna forget me.' Lovingly yours, Celia F. Wilcoe."

To modern sensitivities, the young women and men who autographed Nora's book are morbidly obsessed. Nearly all dwell on the prospect of death. Yet these were perilous times. The Civil War raged, with no end in sight. Fatal and crippling diseases threatened the life of every child, and in an age before antibiotics, adulthood was no guarantee that tuberculosis, typhus, or some other scourge might not come along and extinguish you within a matter of weeks or days. When I think of the precarious nature of life at the time, I think of Henry Thoreau's beloved brother, John. The elder Thoreau boy nicked a finger while shaving, contracted lockjaw, and died eleven days later.

Biology can be cruel, but it also manifests a generous side. The dead live on because every one of us is a walking sack of chromosomes. These gnarly bits of genetic code inherited from forebears hang around for eons, or at least until the next killer comet, asteroid, or plague comes along to drain and scrub the gene pool. I carry my Adirondack ancestors with me everywhere I go. Sometimes I feel I can sense their presence, as when I show a little flair with a pencil or watercolor brush and suspect a little guidance from Elnora. I never knew her, never even knew her children. Even Grampy, her grandson, came sixteen years too late to hear the sound of her voice. Still, she's with us, and with young children in the house, she's not going away anytime soon. Maybe that's partly what

William Faulkner had in mind when he wrote, "The past is not dead. It is not even past."

Of all the apples on the family tree, the one I keep most faithfully in my pocket, traveling with me wherever I go, even to the far side of the globe, is Grampy. His genetic contributions to me are great, providing a quarter of my cellular operating instructions. My mother always said my gait was exactly like his, although I never had luck getting her to explain. My hands require extra-extra-large men's gloves. That's probably a contribution from him, too, just as my father's genes demand I wear extra-extra-large hats.

Double helixes of nucleic acids aside, time spent with Grampy left the greatest marks. I hope that through contact with my kids and the miracle of cultural evolution, I'll pass these along, too. The very fact of our lives here in the mountains, and my lifelong passion for all things outdoors, are part of his legacy to us.

Sometimes we carry the flame purposefully. Once, for example, on the thirtieth anniversary of Grampy's death, Debbie and I took Ned and Tassie fishing at his favorite fishing hole. The place was Eel Weir State Park, a quiet campground on the cold, tannin-stained Oswegatchie River, just outside the Adirondack Park's northern border. Grampy and Grandma spent a week or two camping there every year, beginning around the Fourth of July. Grandma used to talk rapturously about the place. When I was invited to join them in my tenth or eleventh year, I could hardly believe my luck.

Just downstream from the camping area, just past where Grampy had once hooked and lost a big muskellunge, the outlet of Black Lake pours in from the right. Grampy's favorite fishing spots were in the outlet, on the lily pad–fringed right-hand side. There, with his help, I once used a live frog as bait and caught a big northern pike. There Debbie and I paddled the kids in a canoe.

I had fished here dozens of times, yet not in thirty years. Being back felt surreal. Nothing much had changed. The campground, the riverfront, the Oswegatchie, even the little grocery store where Grandma went for milk and eggs, were just as my grandparents had left them decades earlier. I felt like a time traveler as I helped Ned and Tassie bait hooks, just as Grampy and Grandma used to do.

Soon poles were bending, and the kids were squealing. Ned caught a bluegill, broad and shiny with a ruddy breast. Tassie caught a pumpkinseed, a rainbow-colored cousin of the bluegill named for its oval, flattened shape. Debbie and I persuaded the kids to return the fish to the water. While most things remained the same, Grandma was not back at the campsite, ready to roll tender flesh in milk and flour and fry the fish in a skillet.

Returning to Eel Weir brought satisfactions, but grief came, too, and it was strong. I still feel the pain of losing my grandparents thirty years and more after their deaths. This is how it goes in life: for every gain, a loss. By taking me fishing and camping with them in a place that they loved, Grampy and Grandma made me feel like the luckiest kid in the world. But grandparents don't last forever, and neither does luck. In middle age, I realize the value of what I had, and I feel the enormity of what I've lost. Thirty-five years after his death, I still think about my grandfather every hour of every day. I miss him, and oddly, the missing only grows stronger with the passage of time.

Grandma's younger sister, Ina, told her daughter, Sandy, that she felt at sea after Grampy, whom she called by his first name, Burdett, died. Ina had always found quiet comfort in Burdett's presence. Somehow, by being neither an optimist nor a pessimist, and by simply accepting the inevitable progress of things, he had a calming effect on those around him. I remember being at Claude Lipe's funeral home in Northville, with my grandfather lying in a box before us, cold, inert, his face daubed with makeup. One moment I felt accepting of the situation, happy, even, that Grampy had died in his beloved woods. At seventy-three, he had still been strong and vital. He was spared the indignities of old age. Suddenly, though, a logjam of feelings broke, and I sobbed inconsolably. Here we were in Grampy's hometown, chatting with his closest friends, pausing to listen as the Northville Fire Department staged a tribute to him. Now, when we needed him most, all he could do was lie inert, stone-faced, big hands clasped, giving those who came near a whiff of embalming fluid. He was marvelous at funerals, except his own. I shuddered with grief. Without my grandfather, the world would be a radically different place. I wasn't sure I wanted any part of it.

Sandy told me that one night at her mother's home in Johnstown, near Northville, shortly after Grampy's death, Ina was feeling frightened and unsettled when an extraordinary thing happened. A big owl flew in, landed on the roof of the garage, and hooted. Nothing like this had ever happened before. Ina was convinced that Burdett had found a way to come back and assure her things would be all right.

Not one for metaphysics, I see and hear owls at our house and sense only the presence of birds. Yet I like Ina's thought: that Burdett, or Grampy, is still out there, on the wing, and Grandma, too, and Elmer

Brownell and Jenny Lawton, and Elnora and Lewis, and all the others, still active presences in the Adirondack landscape.

American Indians, Australian Aborigines, and other peoples with long associations with landscapes have developed deep spiritual connections with their respective geographies. Despite good intentions, these connections are destroyed when we create parks in the usual mold, ones where we depopulate the places we aspire to preserve. I'm grateful the Adirondack Park is different. For me, the land here looms large in the present, yet it's also a reservoir of past joys and sorrows, of people I knew and wish I'd known, of former lives, of dreams that floated and of others that sank. It's also the future, whatever that will turn out to be, years, centuries, millennia, and epochs hence. We go fishing here, my family and I, and the waters run deep. I won't be going elsewhere for long anytime soon.

BIOLOGICAL SURVEY RECORDS:

Bubo virginianus   Great-horned owl
7/26/02: A great surprise! We were sleeping on the porch at 1:30 a.m. I awoke in increments. Slowly it dawned on me that I was hearing the voices of old friends—two great horned owls hooting in the woods across the road and east of the house. I woke Debbie so she could hear them, too. These are the first we've heard here.

Mentha arvensis   Wild mint
8/27/00: flowering along river, near northern end of bridge, e. of road
8/31/09: found on sandbar by Ned, Tassie, Debbie, and me; made a delicious tea!

Acknowledgments

Like all big projects, this one benefited from the generous assistance of friends, colleagues, and family members.

In my research into family history, I am grateful for the assistance of the following: Jim Alsina, longtime friend and skilled genealogist, for tracking down Brownell family history; Don Amell, historian for the town of St. Armand, for information about the old Bloomingdale train station; Jan Couture, historian for the town of Saranac, for information on Shepard Bowen; the late Micky O'Brien, Frank Tuthill, and Sandy Hayes for educating me about the recent history of our property; Dick Beamish, Rachel Rice, Tom Woodman, Betsy Dirnberger, Phil Brown, Sue Bibeau, and the rest of the crew at *The Adirondack Explorer*, whose research and writing assignments contributed to this book at many turns; Peter Betz, Fulton County historian; Dan Haughey, Bruce Brownell, Brad Brownell, and Sylvia Brownell Elwood for help untangling Brownell genealogy; the late Burdett Eglin Brownell Jr. (my mother's brother, whom I called "Uncle Bud"); Gail Cramer, Northville historian, who hunted down obituaries in her archives; Sandy Tichy Douglass; Betsy Folwell, Annie Stoltie, Mary Thill, and others at *Adirondack Life* magazine who by commissioning stories helped subsidize the work; Phil Gallos, author of a first-rate book about Saranac Lake's days as a TB cure center; my cousin Joan Gordon, my Aunt Dolly's daughter, for critical facts about her parents' lives; Jim Groff, Northville's mayor when I enjoyed an interview with him in 2000; historian Mary Hotaling of Saranac Lake, for patiently answering questions whenever I called; Joyce Brownell Kanze, my mother, for years of help and encouragement and for curating an important collection of documents; Edward J. Kanze Jr., my father, for his own longtime help and encouragement, for curating his sister's letters, and for photos; Peter Kanze, for important research help at critical junctures; Jack Leadley, renowned man of the woods from Speculator, who identified the mystery man in a hundred-year-old family photograph, and Floyd W. Abrams, whose identification of the same man as his grandfather closed the case; Sadie McVicker, Catherine McVicker, Art and Joanne Higgins, Charles and Peg Hebson, Anne Hebson, Catherine Hebson, and Walter and Caroline Stutz, for lunch and an instructive tour of the former site of Stony Wold Sanatorium; the late Charlotte Russell of Northville, for her reminiscences of my grandfather; Jane Schneider and Mary Hodge, who sleuthed for me at the New York State Library; Bill Thompson, Elsa Thompson, Jim Cirigliano, and all the fine crew at *Bird Watcher's Digest*, for underwriting research that informed these chapters; Michelle Tucker, curator of the Adirondack Room at the Saranac Lake Free Library; and the late Bob Van Arnam of Northville, for a memorable conversation on the street.

For biological survey help, an incomplete list of supporters must include Greg Budney; Carl Clark; Daun Dahlen; Charlotte Demers; Lang Elliott; Celia Evans; Wayne Gall; Carol Gracie; Jackie and the late Bob Hagar; Sunita Halasz and family; Ed Hecklau; Bernd Heinrich; Susan Hopkins; Taro Ietaka; Ed Ketchledge; Robin Kimmerer; Jason Klein; Michael Klemens; Larry Master; Janet and Tim Mihuc; Scott Mori; Luke Myers; Bill and Nina Schoch; Mark and Mary Rooks; the Shoumatoff gang, Alex, Zachary, Oliver, and Edgar; and Ken Soltesz.

Without the kindness of the following people, we would not have a roof over our heads, or if we did, the roof would leak: Jim and Cecilia Alsina, John and Anne Alsina, Steve Amstutz, Nancy Bernstein, Peter Dupree, the late Joe Gilbert, Sandy Hayes, the late James Junker, John Junker, Joyce and Ed Kanze, Em and Hank Koester, Brian Ladue, Tom LeBaron, Walt and Vannesa Linck, Nora and Paul Manuele, Maggie and Andy Silton, David Vana, the late Lorraine Wilson, Elaine and Frank Zika, and the forty-two people, more or less, who showed up here one rainy Sunday morning and helped us erect a timber frame, the frame that supports the writing studio in which this book was conceived, gestated, and birthed.

Finally, I am eager to thank my excellent editor, Amanda Lanne, and all her colleagues at SUNY Press, as well as the members of my family who aided me along the way, most notably, in addition to those mentioned above, my wife, Debbie; our children, Ned and Tasman; my "big" sister, Maggie Kanze Silton, and her husband, Andy; my "little" sister, Nora Kanze Manuele, for her tireless efforts over many years on behalf of our parents and without which this book would not have been possible, and her husband, Paul; and my Aunt Nina, for her tender concern for my parents, especially during the years in which this book came into existence.

33837942R00150

Made in the USA
Lexington, KY
11 July 2014